AF291973

MARK
ARMANI
JEANS
blished in 1981
S

THE FASHION ICONS

GIORGIO ARMANI

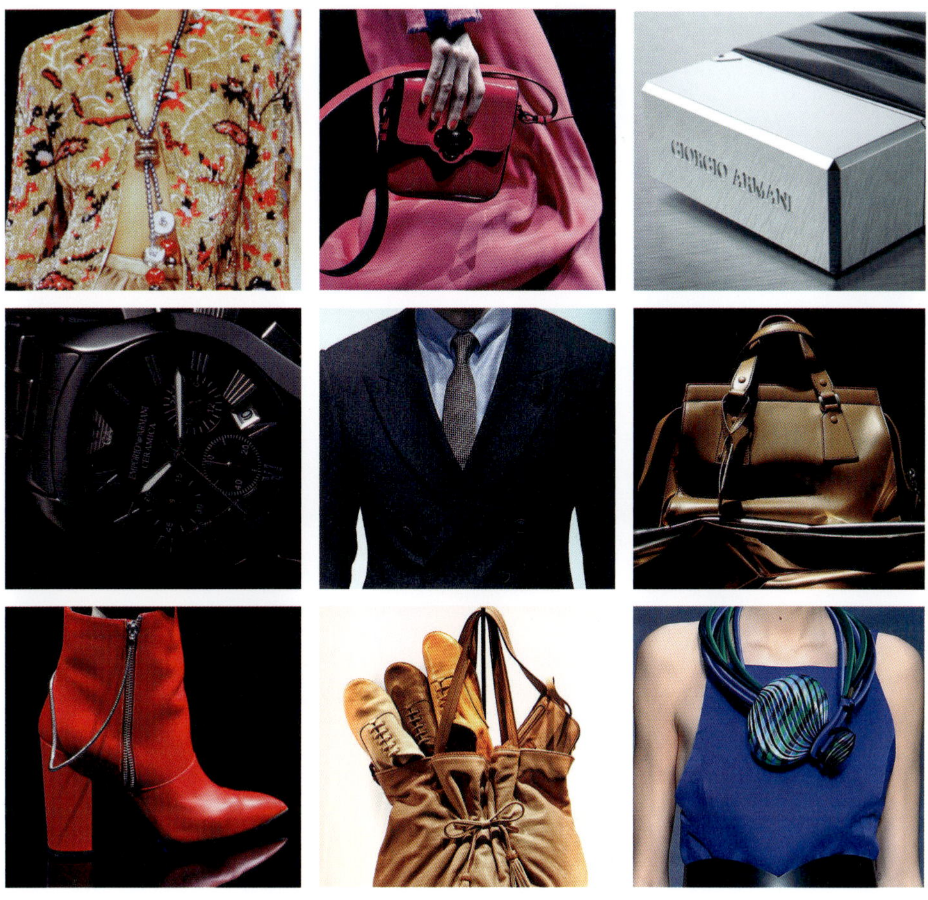

Alison James

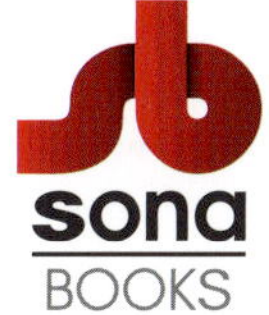

sona
BOOKS

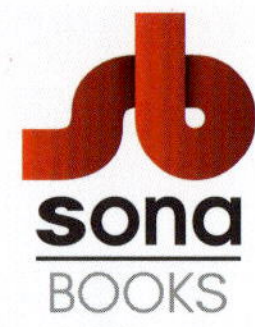

sona
BOOKS

CONTENTS

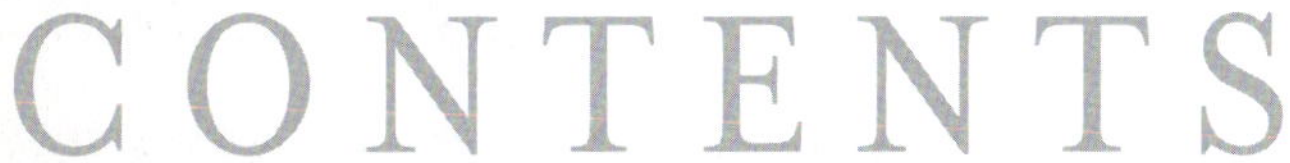

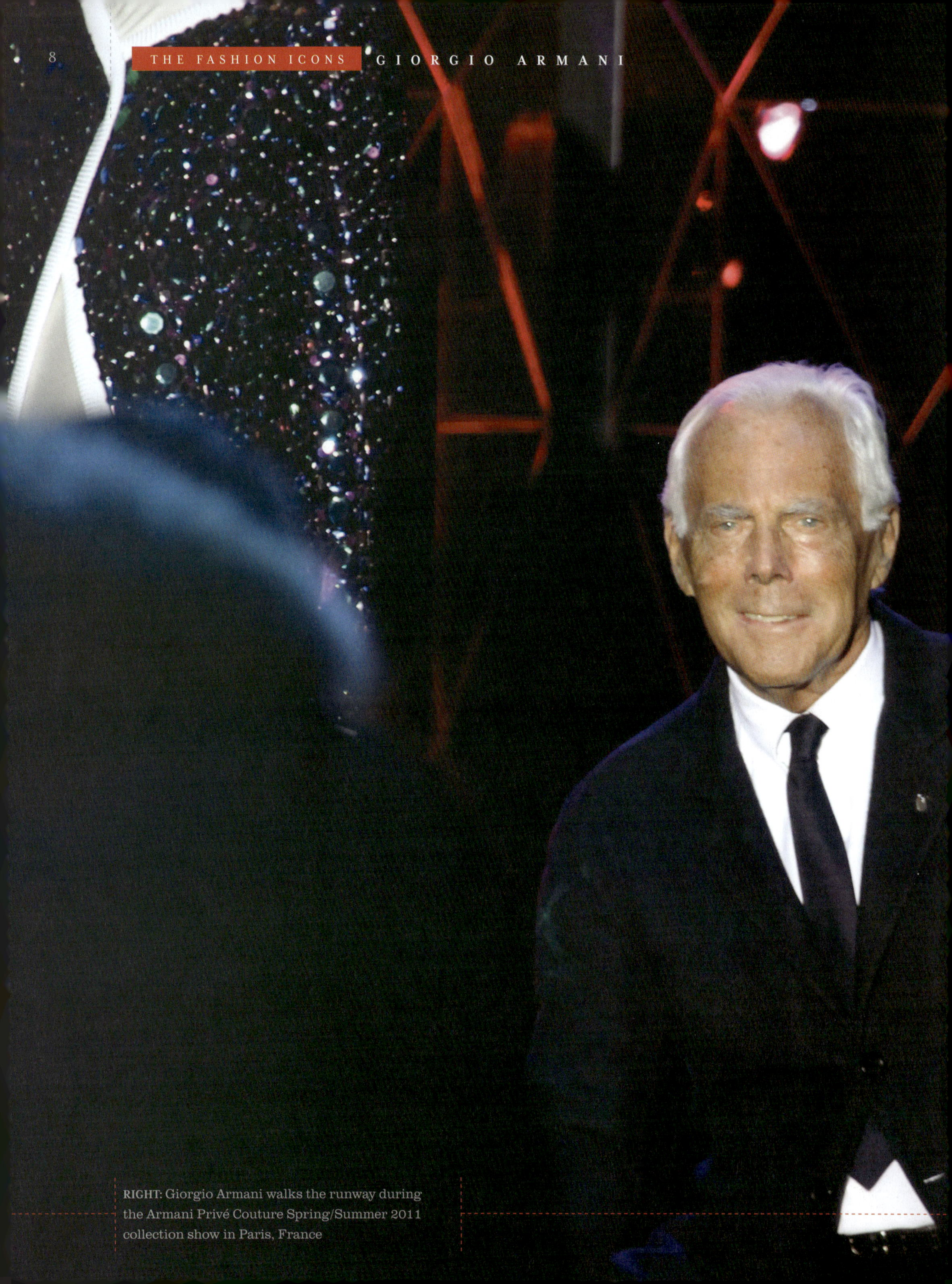

RIGHT: Giorgio Armani walks the runway during the Armani Privé Couture Spring/Summer 2011 collection show in Paris, France

INTRODUCTION: ELEGANCE AND INNOVATION

"Mr. Armani can walk into a room and turn everything upside down in this very quiet, authoritative way"

Jodie Foster

Few names in fashion evoke an aura of timeless sophistication quite like the House of Armani. Since its inception in 1975, the brand has become a global symbol of understated luxury, reshaping the landscape of contemporary style with its signature blend of relaxed tailoring, refined minimalism and impeccable craftsmanship.

This beautifully illustrated book is a celebration of Armani's enduring influence, tracing its evolution from Giorgio Armani's unconventional entry into the world of high fashion, journeying through his revolutionary approach to menswear and exploring the vast empire that now spans Armani haute couture, ready-to-wear, accessories and even interior design. With exclusive imagery, archival sketches and behind-the-scenes glimpses, this volume captures the very essence of the Armani aesthetic which champions grace over excess, power in simplicity and a commitment to innovation.

From the iconic draped silhouettes that redefined the modern suit to the exquisite red-carpet gowns that have been worn by Hollywood's most illustrious stars, Armani's legacy is one of quiet confidence, undeniable impact and incomparable style. In the Armani universe, fashion transcends trends and is a way of life. Welcome to the house of Armani—where elegance is eternal.

ARMANI THE BEGINNING

"Never in my wildest dreams did I entertain the idea that I would become a fashion designer"
Giorgio Armani

On July 11 1934 in Piacenza, Italy, a small industrial town south of Milan, Giorgio Armani was born to Ugo, a shipping manager, and his wife Maria. Giorgio was their second child, following his elder brother Sergio. Younger sister Rosanna was born a few years later. Life was simple and happy but not without hardship. Italy was heavily affected by the second world war and there were food shortages and bombings which included the destruction of young Giorgio's hometown. However, these early struggles gave the boy a strong sense of discipline, resilience and staying power.

Armani showed no early ambitions to work in fashion or indeed to become a designer. He had a passion for anatomy, and initially aspired to become a doctor—going so far as to enrol at the University of

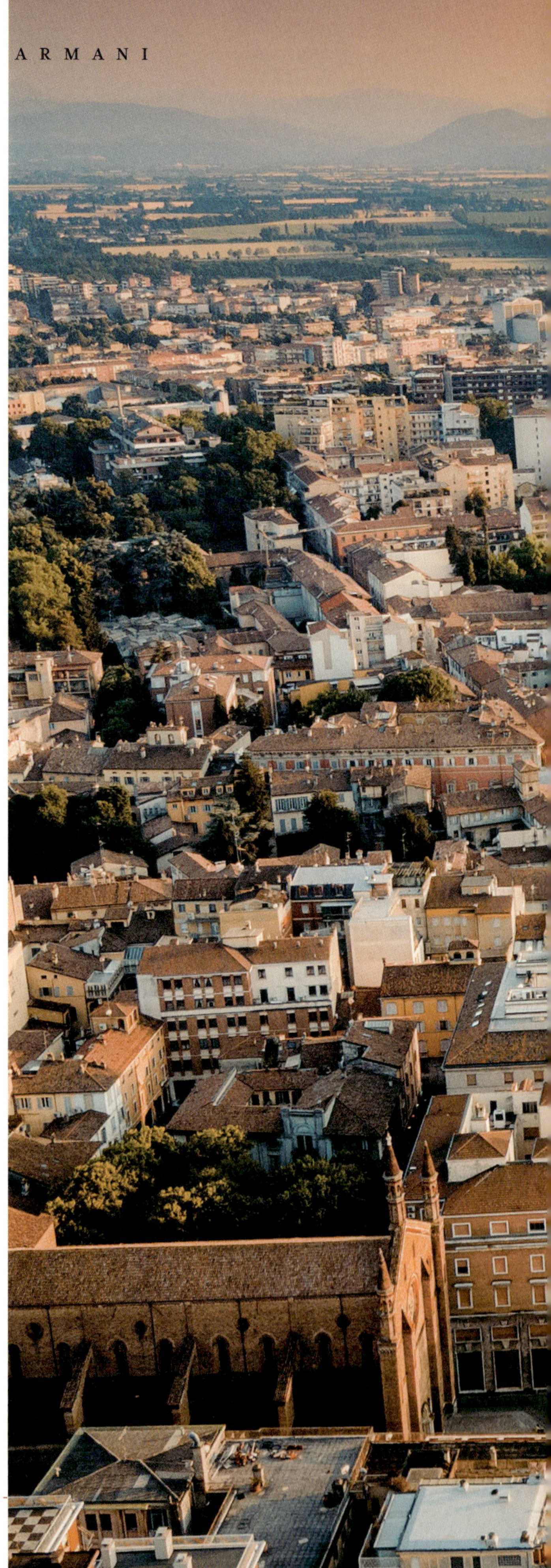

RIGHT: Aerial view of Piacenza, Italy

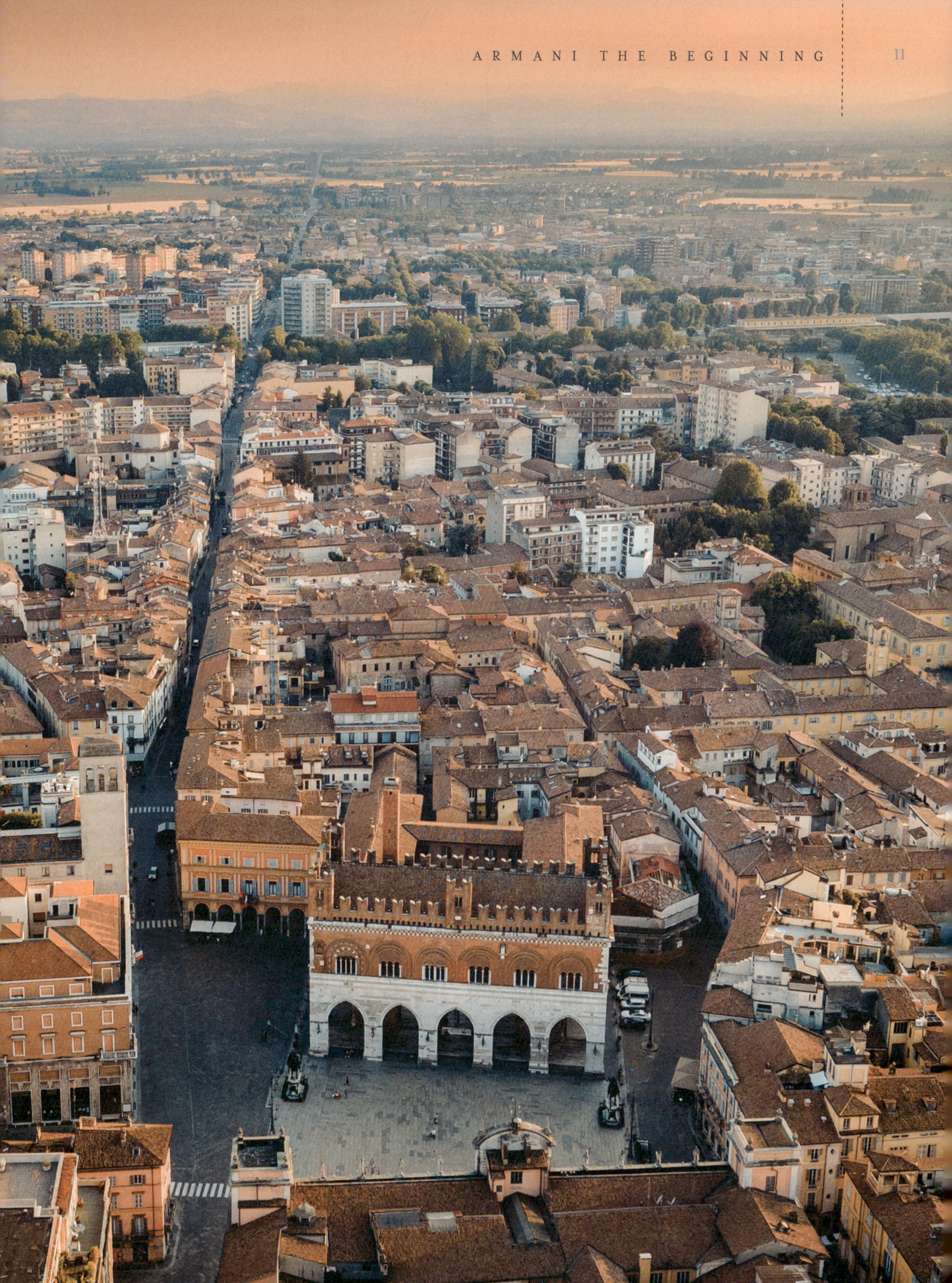

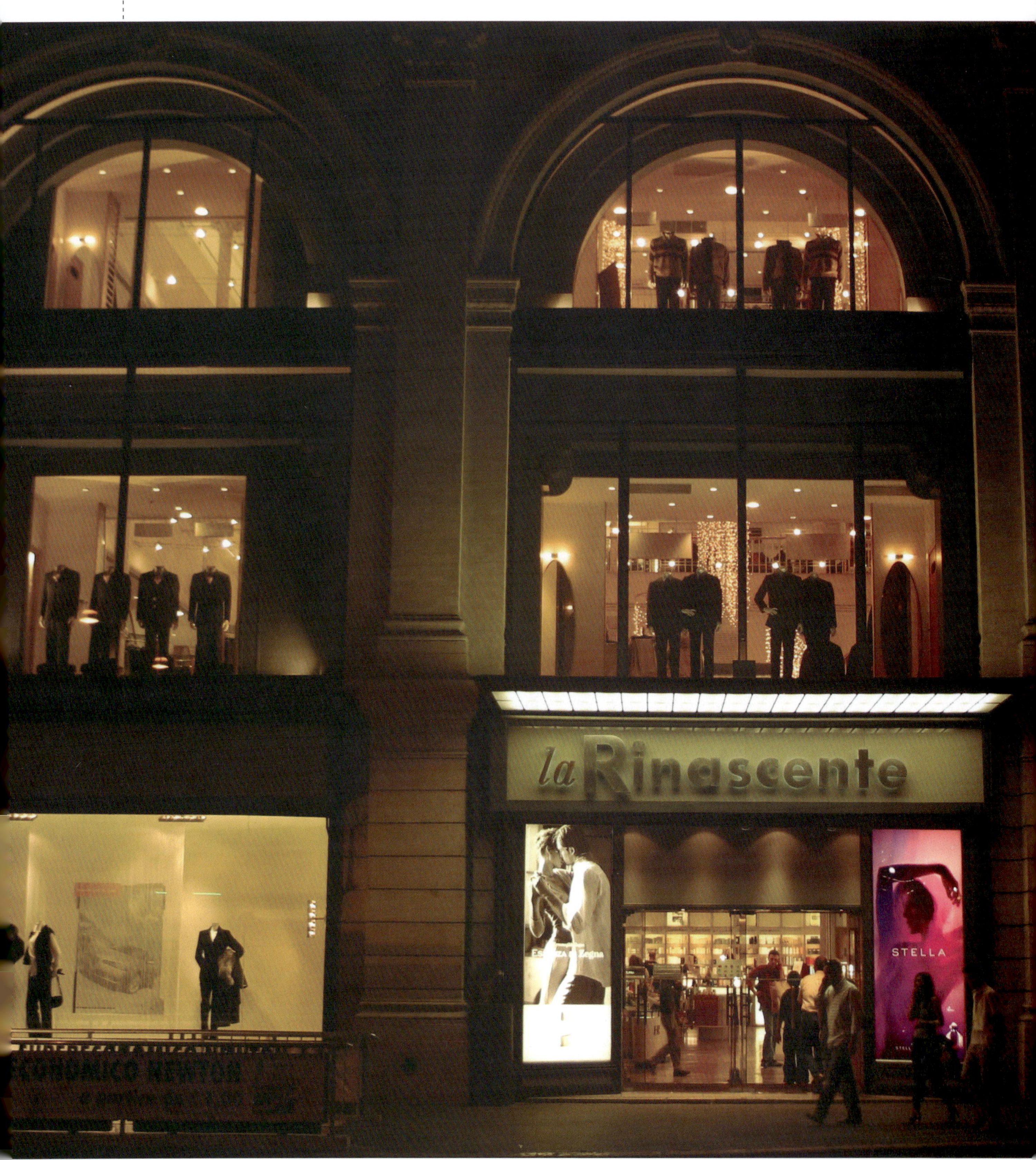

ABOVE: La Rinascente, the oldest shopping mall in Rome
OPP PAGE: (LEFT) Vintage La Rinascente advertisments
(RIGHT) Umberto Brustio, President of La Rinascente, presides over the reopening of the Milan branch, 1950

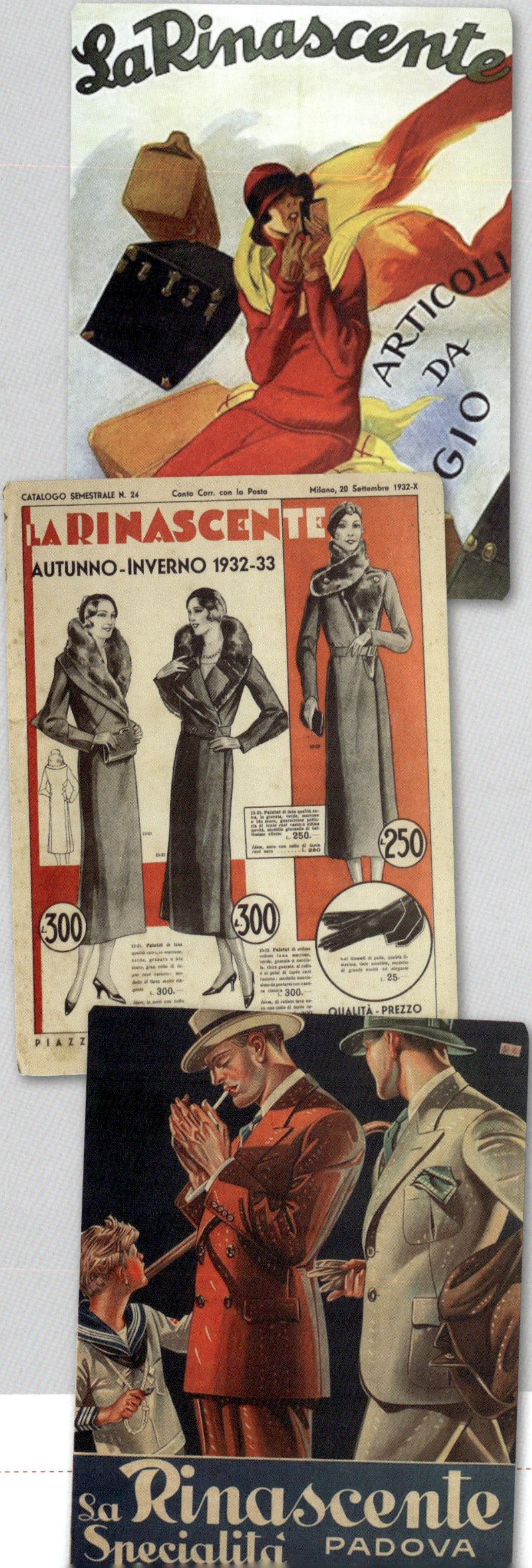

Milan to study medicine. However, after three years of medical studies, Armani made a life-changing decision and enlisted in the Italian army. During his service, he worked in a military hospital, where he encountered first-hand the contrast between the human form and the rigid uniforms worn by service personnel. He began to develop an eye for structure, fabric and the connection between movement and clothing.

On exiting the army and having decided that medicine was not for him, Armani sought work in Milan, the emerging centre of Italy's fashion industry. Through a stroke of luck, he landed a job as a window dresser at La Rinascente, a prestigious Milanese department store where he was, for the first time,

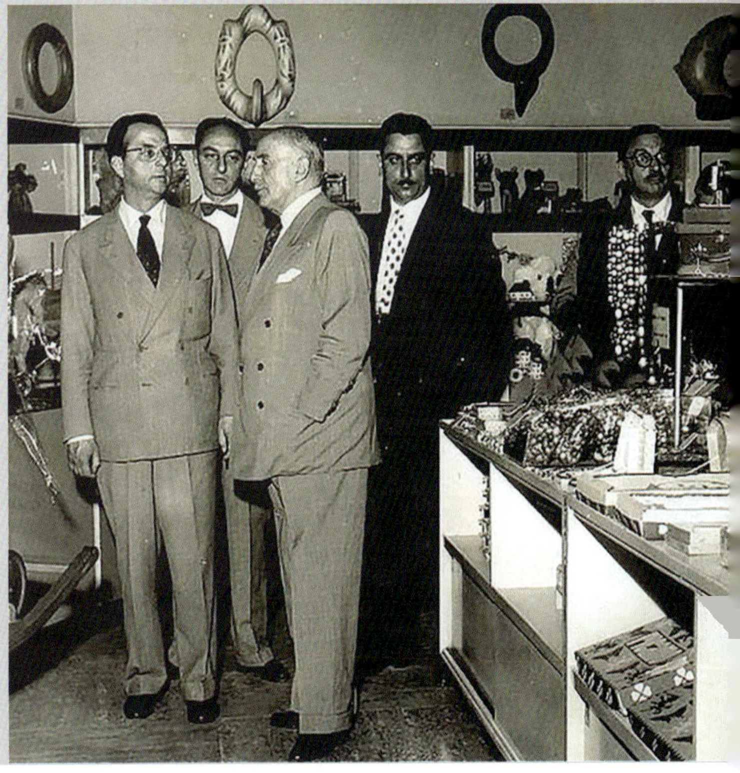

exposed to elegance and style. The world of fabrics, cuts and colours fascinated him. His keen sense of aesthetics caught the attention of the store's buyers. Before long, Armani had become a fashion buyer and merchandiser, travelling across Europe to source the latest trends.

By the early 1960s, the name of Giorgio Armani was beginning to be known within fashion circles. His growing expertise led him, in 1964, to a pivotal role at the fashion house of Nino Cerruti. Cerruti entrusted him with the selection of fabrics for his collection designs and began working with Giorgio. In this way, Armani learned the practices of the designer's craft: fabric selection, cutting, tailoring, and marketing. He began to develop his own personal style as a designer, introducing elements of foreign fashion and trends into the Milanese universe and to Italian consumers. It was at Cerruti that Armani's signature aesthetic—soft, unstructured tailoring that would go on to redefine masculinity—began to take shape. While designing menswear, he discarded the fashion for stiff, boxy suit silhouettes, and opting instead for lightweight fabrics that allowed fluidity and movement. His designs spoke of effortless sophistication, marking the beginning of a revolution in menswear. For nearly a decade, Armani perfected his craft under Cerruti's mentorship while taking on freelance design projects for brands such as Zegna and Hilton. However, by the early 1970s, Armani was wanting to go it alone. He had the vision, the experience, and most importantly, an unwavering belief that fashion could be redefined.

Encouraged by his partner Sergio Galeotti, an architectural draftsman who recognised Armani's talent and entrepreneurial potential, in 1975 Armani founded Giorgio Armani S.p.A., operating initially out of a modest apartment in Milan. His and Galeotti's ambition was to create a brand that merged tailoring with comfort, luxury with accessibility, and Italian craftsmanship with global appeal.

Armani's first collection debuted with menswear, featuring his now-iconic deconstructed jacket—a soft, unlined blazer that challenged traditional rigid tailoring. Unlike the heavily padded shoulders and stiff fabrics of the time, Armani's jackets moved naturally with the body, creating an effortless yet polished look. It was a soft sartorial revolution but one that caught the attention of style-conscious men across Italy and beyond. Buoyed by success, Armani launched his first womenswear collection in 1976, applying the same philosophy of fluidity and modernity. His designs liberated women from stiff, overly structured clothing, offering instead sleek, neutral-toned suits that exuded power and confidence—an aesthetic that would later become the uniform of the 'power woman'. Nineteen Seventy Nine saw the launch of a luxury ready-to-wear line called 'Armani Collezioni' that would appeal to and be accessible to all generations. As the 1980s dawned, Giorgio Armani's influence was rapidly spreading across Europe and beyond...

OPP PAGE: Giorgio Armani Spring 1978 Ready-to-Wear runway

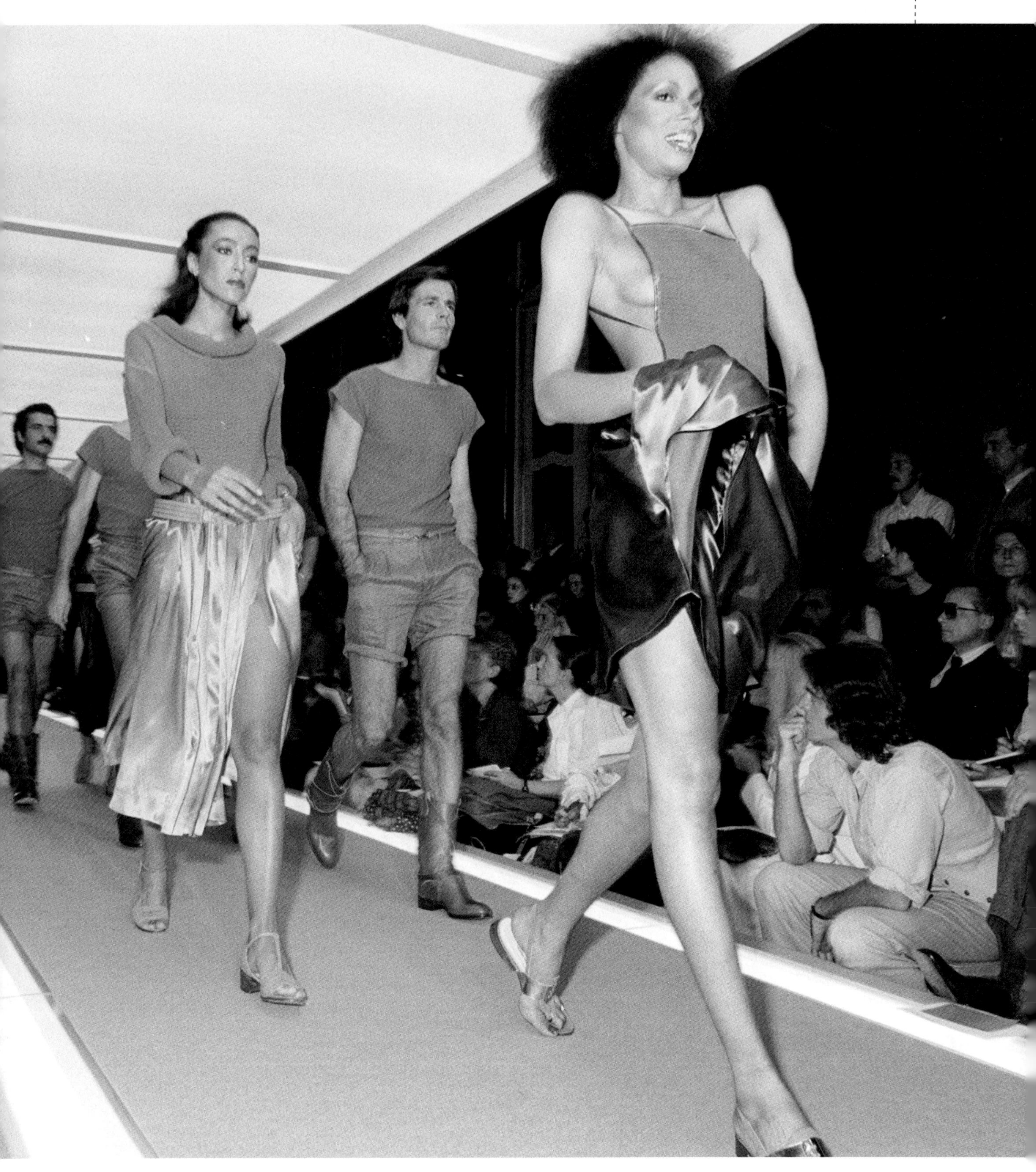

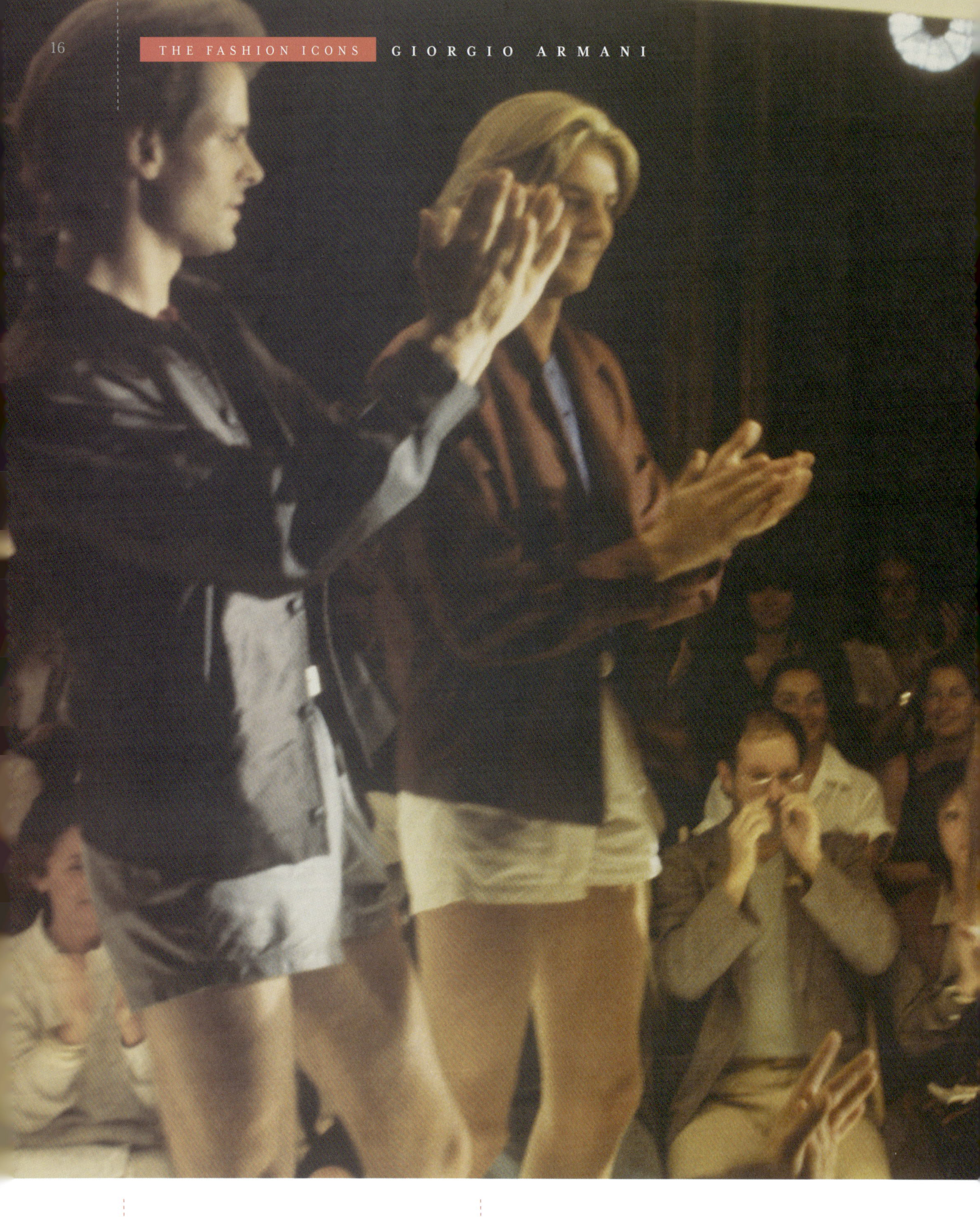

ABOVE: Giorgio Armani receiving applause after a
fashion show in 1978

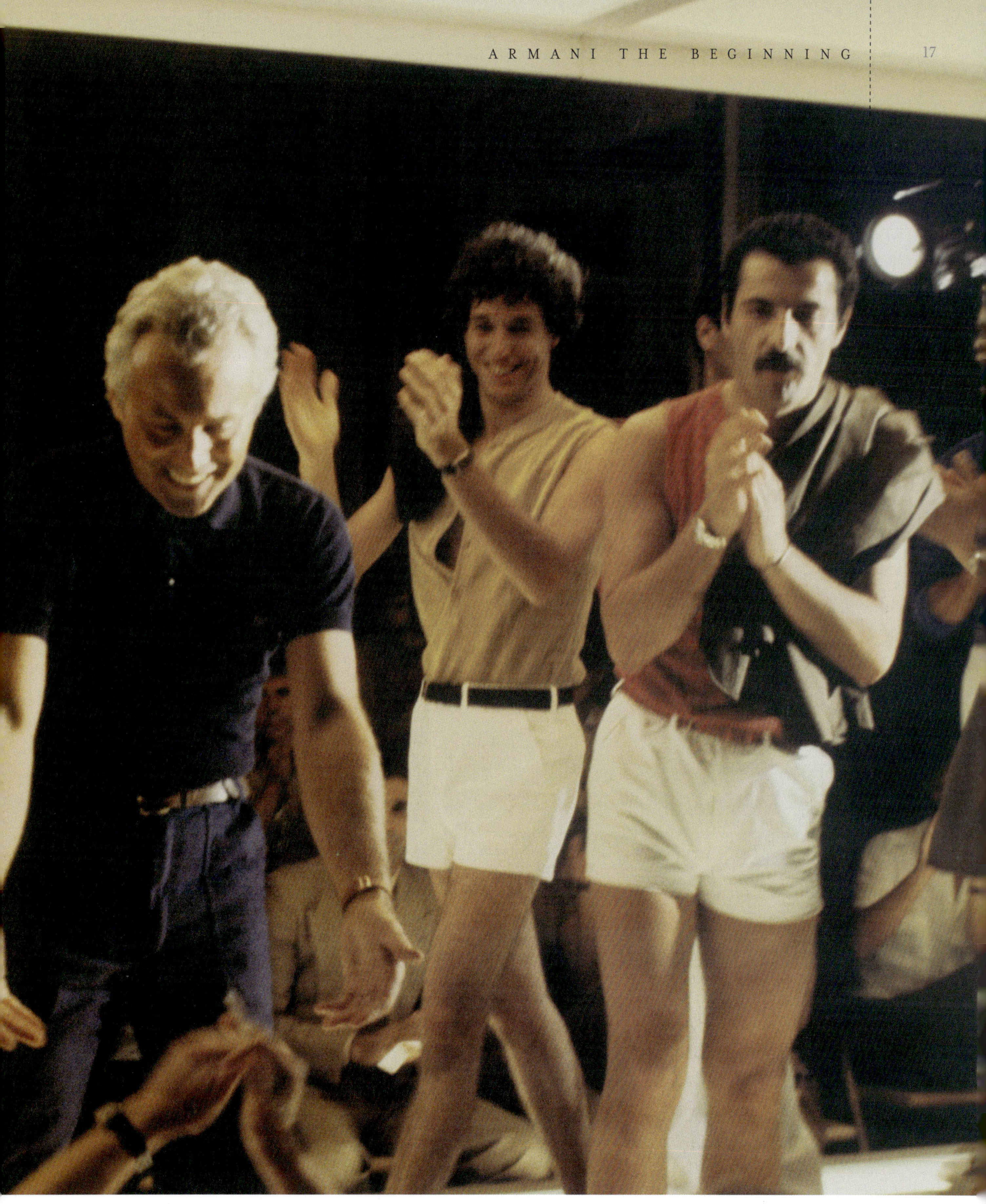

ARMANI GOES GLOBAL

"The world is changing and so is fashion"
Giorgio Armani

By the 1980s, Giorgio Armani had already established himself as a visionary in the fashion industry. His unstructured suits, neutral colour palettes and effortless elegance had revolutionised menswear and womenswear alike. But Armani was never one to be content with limited success—he had a bigger vision. The designer didn't just desire to create fashion, he wished to build an empire. From the runways of Milan to the skyscrapers of New York, the red carpets of Hollywood, and the busy streets of Tokyo, Armani expanded his brand beyond clothing, turning his name into a symbol of global luxury.

Armani's first international breakthrough came in 1980 when he dressed the actor Richard Gere in the film 'American Gigolo'. The movie introduced the world to Armani's sleek, minimalist suits, and almost overnight, Armani became the go-to designer for Hollywood's elite. The American fashion industry,

RIGHT: Richard Gere in *American Gigolo*, 1980

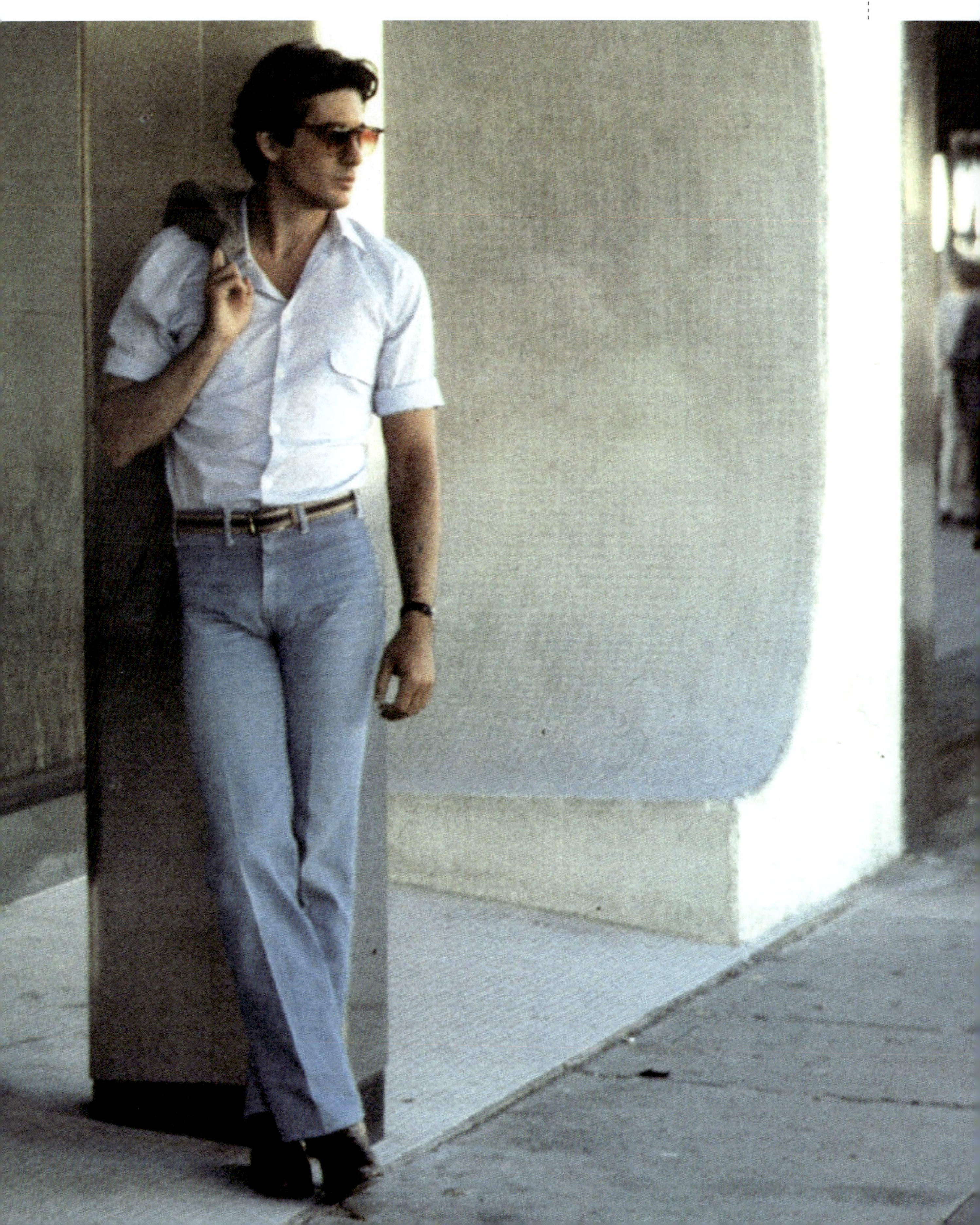

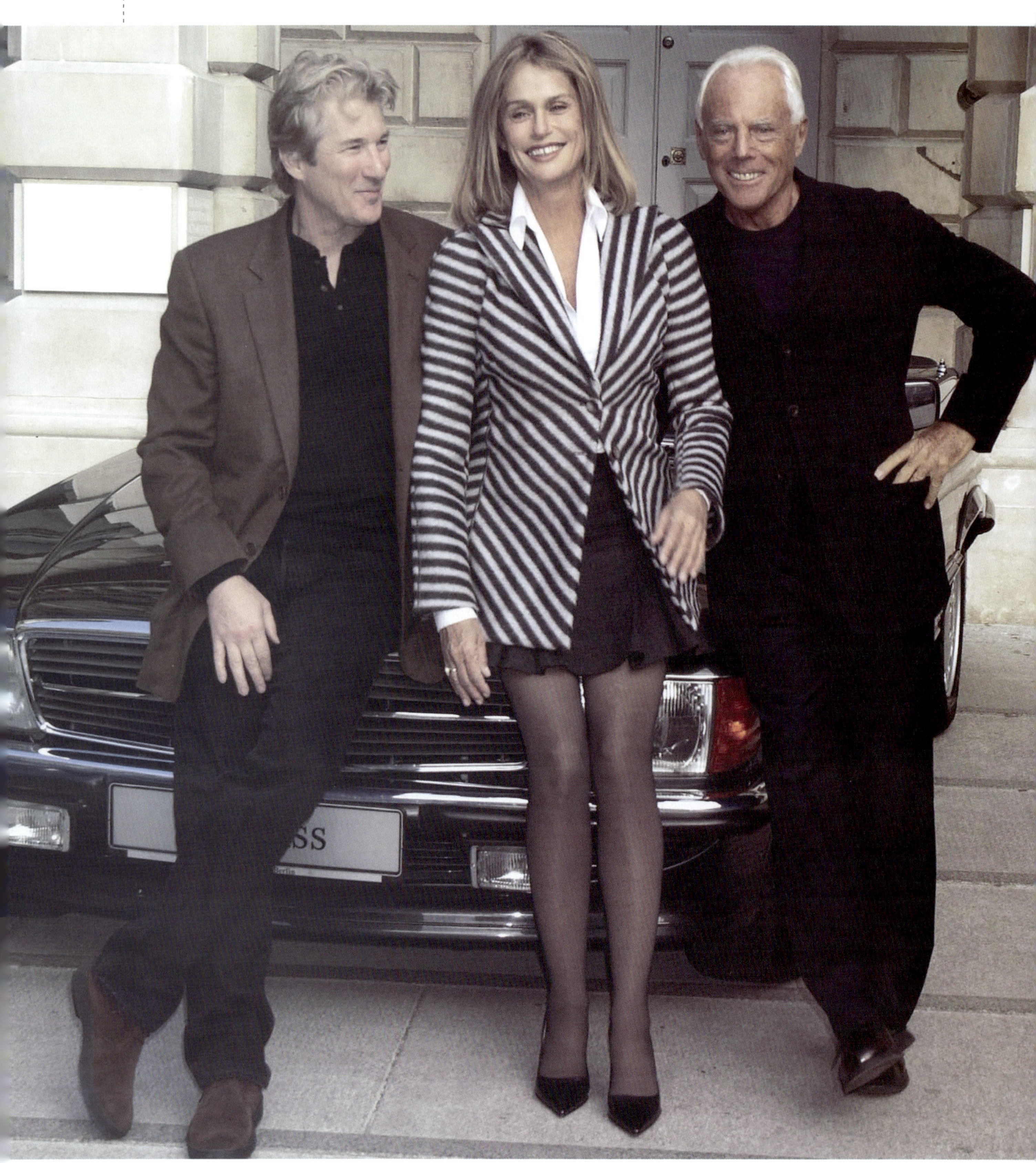

ABOVE: *American Gigolo* actors Richard Gere and Lauren Hutton pose with Giorgio Armani at the "Giorgio Armani Retrospective" exhibition showcasing the film's iconic Armani wardrobe at the Royal Academy, London, 2003

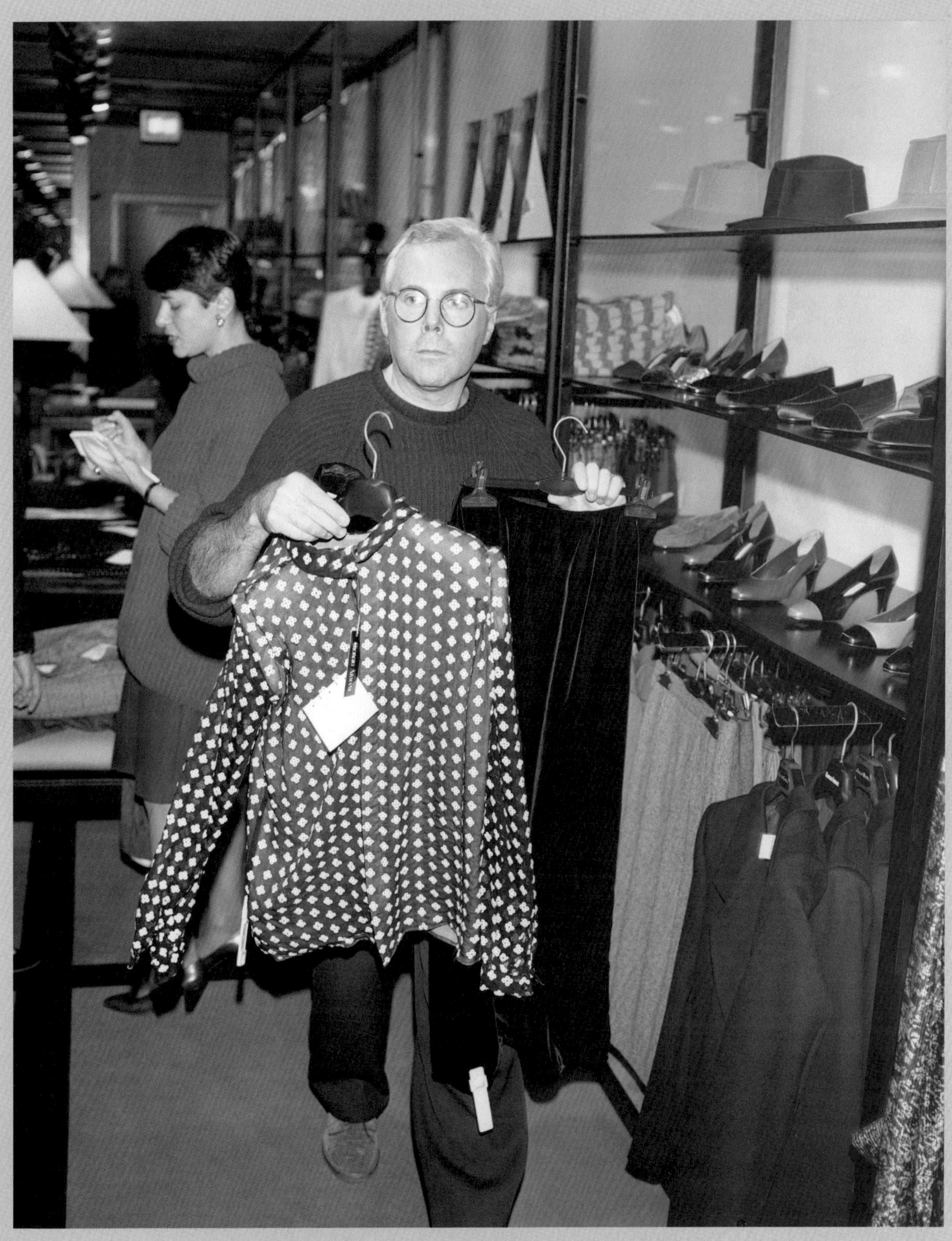

ABOVE: Giorgio Armani at work in his Madison Avenue store in November, 1984

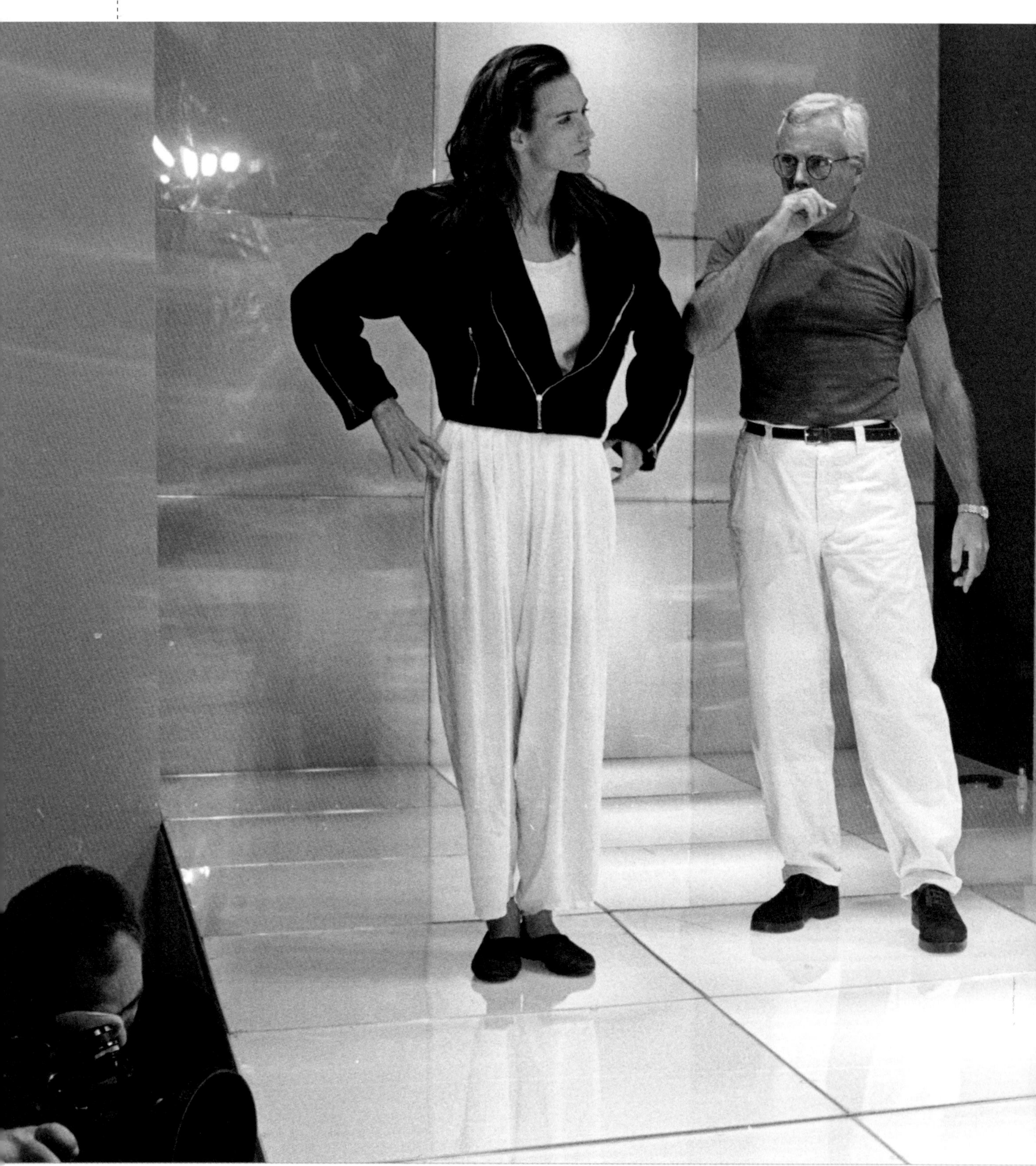

ABOVE: Giorgio Armani and executive Gabriella Forte direct models during a rehearsal for Armani's promotional dinner and fashion show in Los Angeles, 1988

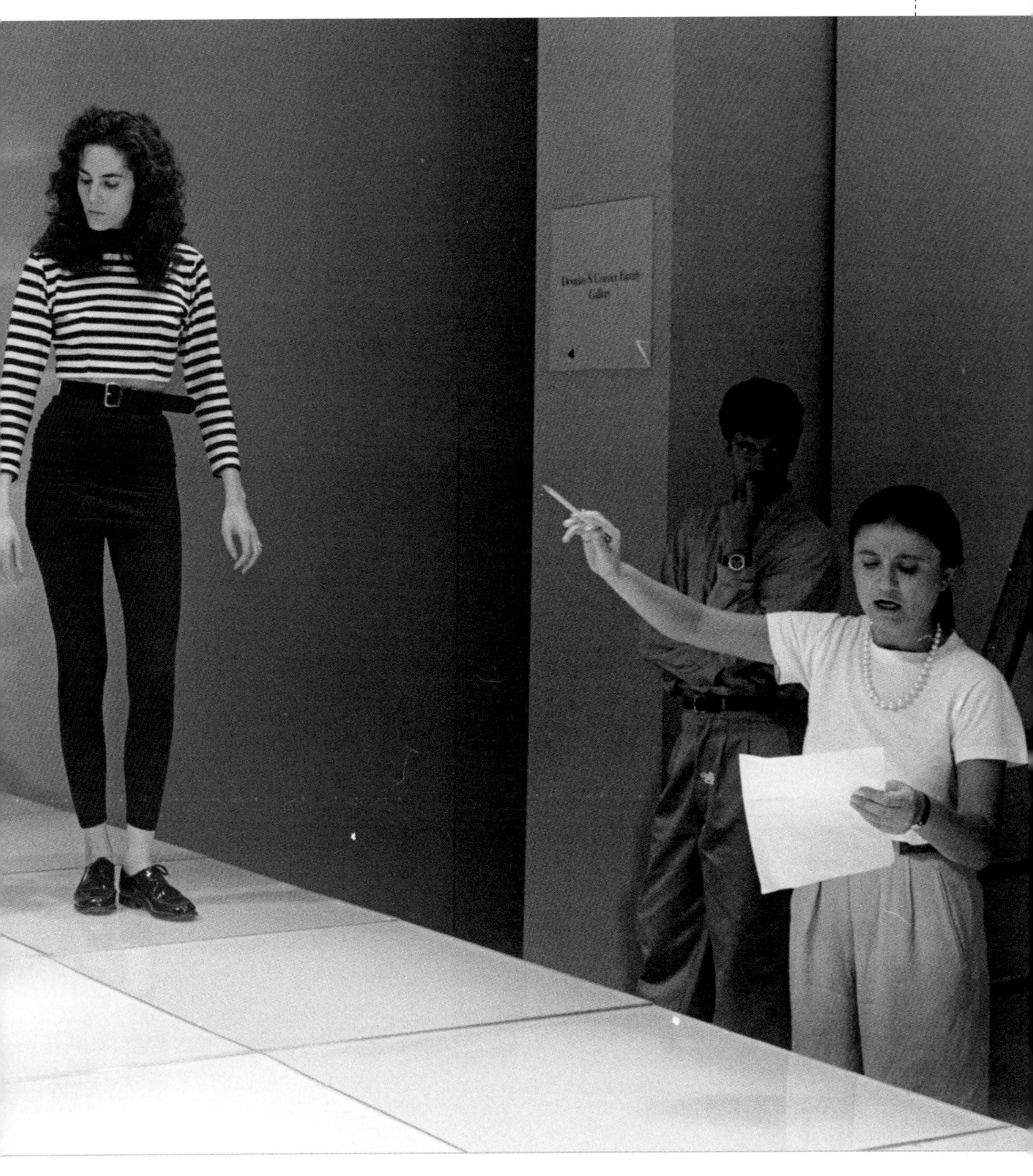

traditionally dominated by names like Ralph Lauren and Calvin Klein, had never seen Italian luxury like this before. Armani's designs weren't just elegant, they were modern, wearable, and effortlessly cool. He became the preferred designer for celebrities, businessmen, and even politicians, cementing his brand in the United States. He opened his first US boutique in Beverly Hills, Los Angeles in 1981 and by the end of the decade his suits had become a status symbol both in Hollywood and on Wall Street, New York. With growing demand, Armani expanded his presence in New York, Miami and Chicago, opening flagship stores that brought Italian luxury into the lives and closets of US consumers.

The House of Armani launched its first fragrance in the early '80s with the debut of Armani Eau Pour Homme, a classic citrusy, woody scent for men. This marked the beginning of Giorgio Armani's fragrance line, which has since expanded into numerous iconic collections for both men and women. In 1981 the House revolutionised the fashion industry again by launching Emporio Armani, a more affordable and youthful brand aimed at trendy, style-conscious consumers across Europe, Asia, and the US. Emporio Armani's eagle logo became an instant symbol of cool, and it wasn't long before Emporio Armani boutiques started popping up in Paris, London, and Tokyo. By the mid-1980s, Giorgio Armani had recognised Asia as the next frontier for luxury fashion. Japan, with its love for tailored suits and high-end craftsmanship, became one of his key markets. Success in Hong Kong and Singapore paved the way for luxury expansion and Giorgio making inroads into China. As China's luxury market exploded in the 2000s, Armani rapidly expanded into cities like Shanghai, Beijing, and Guangzhou, capturing the attention of China's new wave of wealthy consumers. Today, Armani has over 100 stores across China, making it one of his most lucrative markets.

ABOVE: 1980s advertisement for Armani Eau Pour Homme

OPP PAGE: Emporio Armani store on Canton Road, Hong Kong

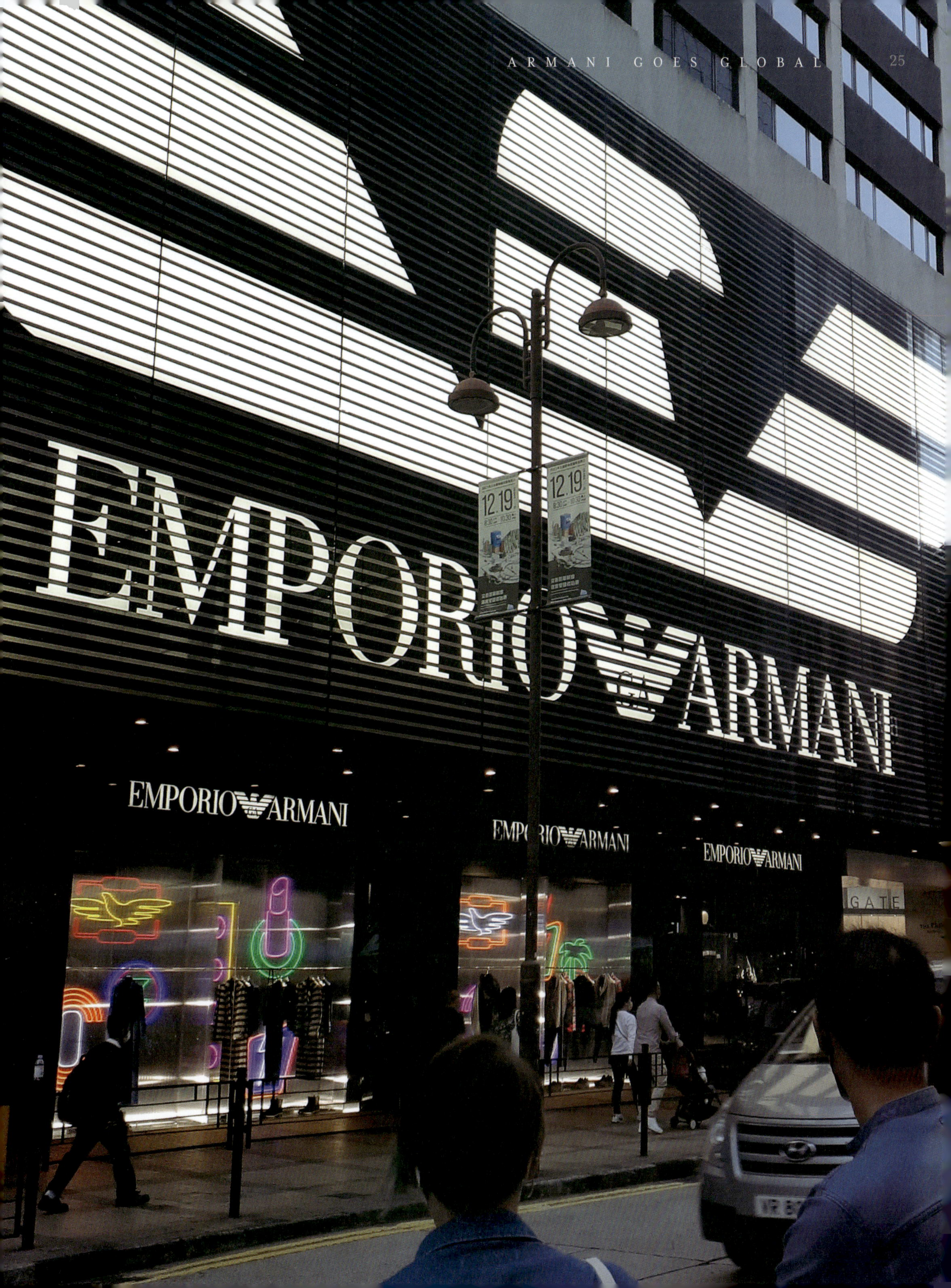
EMPORIO ARMANI
EMPORIO ARMANI
EMPORIO ARMANI
EMPORIO ARMANI
12.19
12.19
GATE

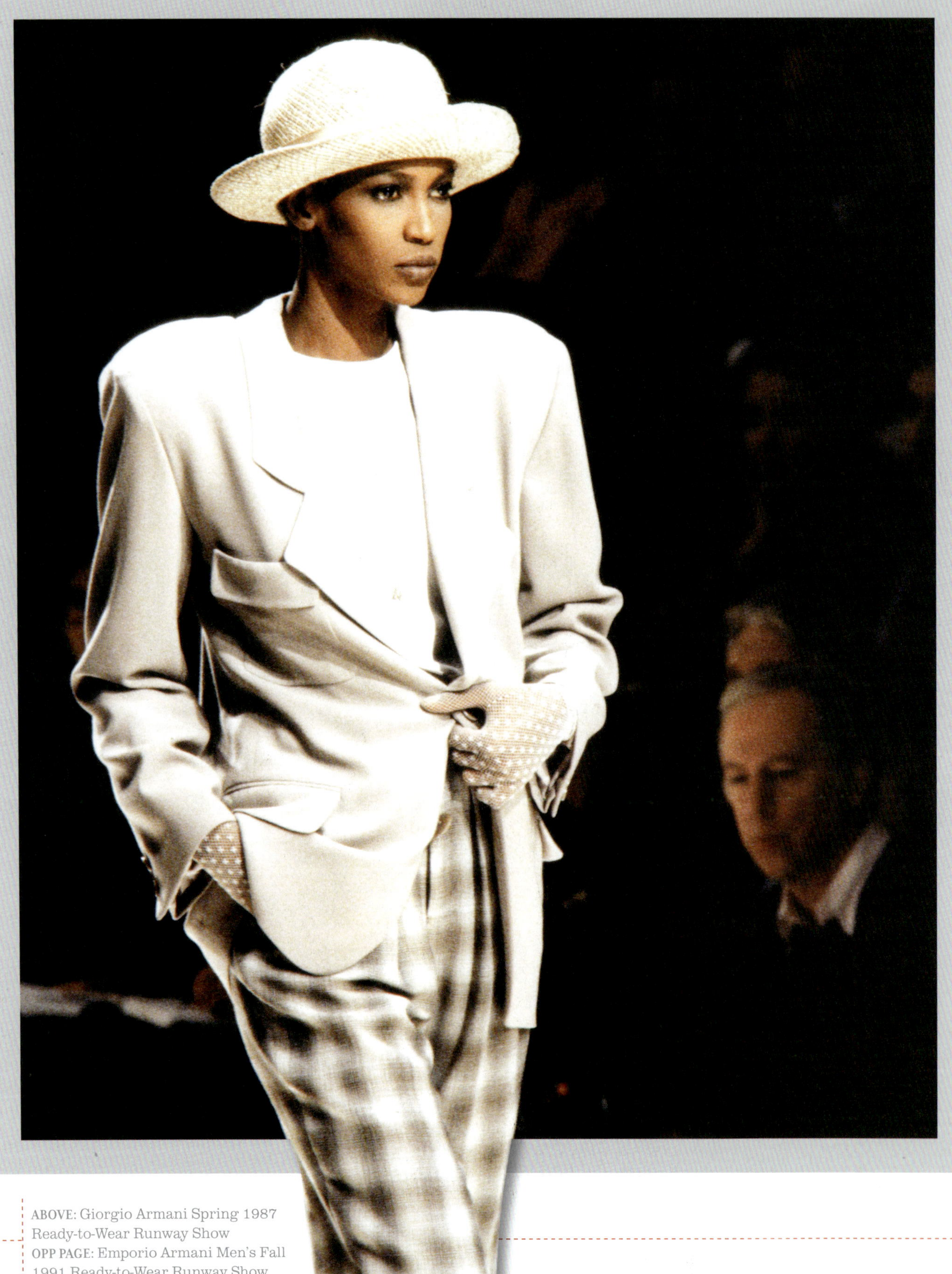

ABOVE: Giorgio Armani Spring 1987
Ready-to-Wear Runway Show
OPP PAGE: Emporio Armani Men's Fall
1991 Ready-to-Wear Runway Show

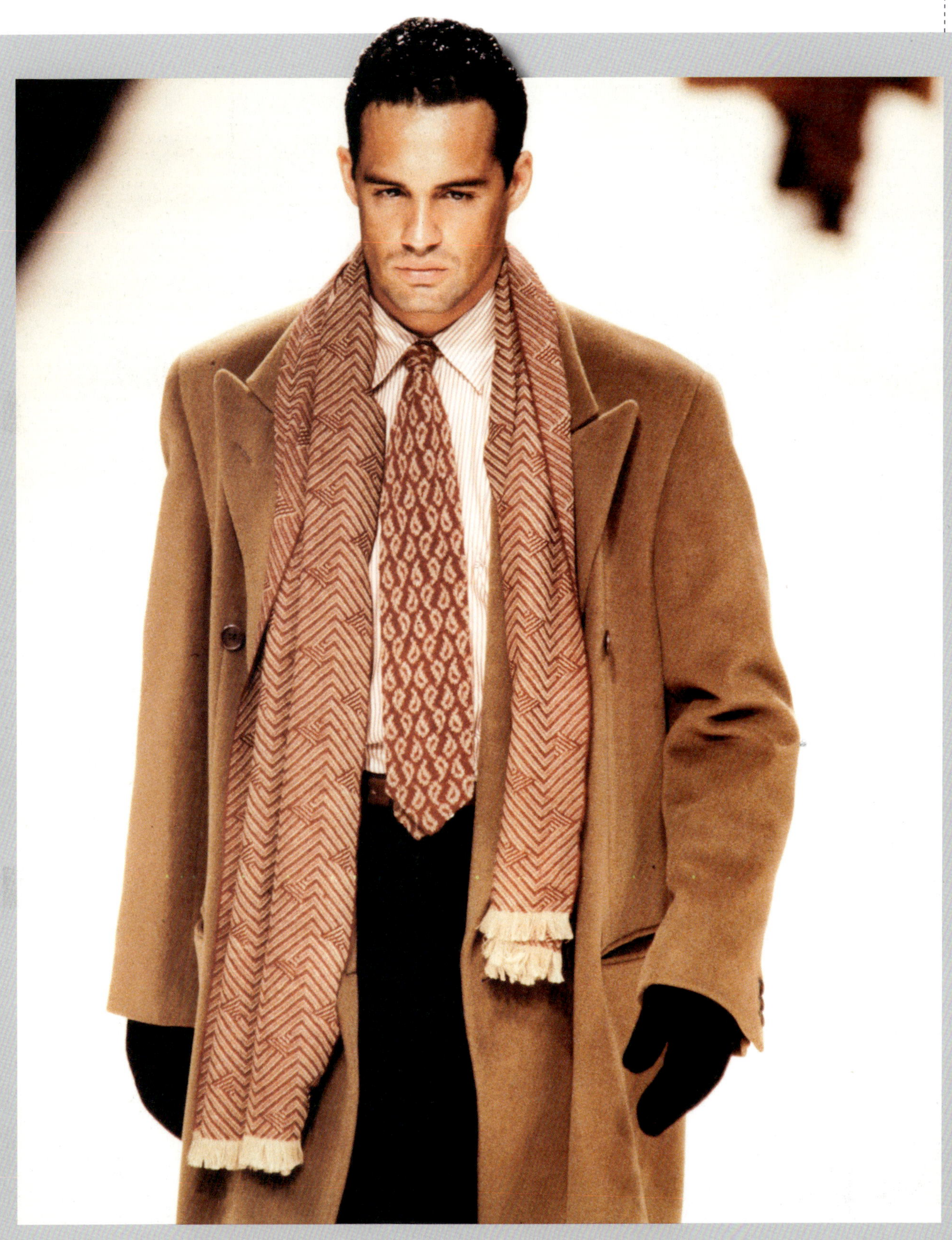

In 1991, Armani launched Armani Exchange (A|X), his most accessible and casual brand to date. Unlike his luxury lines, A|X was inspired by street fashion, urban culture and music—appealing to a younger, more diverse audience. The brand expanded worldwide, becoming a massive success in London, Paris, and Latin America—and a fashion staple in the hip-hop and urban streetwear communities.

A|X positioned Armani as a multi-dimensional designer, proving he could master not just high fashion but also mass-market appeal. As Armani's influence grew, so did his ambition to create a complete luxury lifestyle brand. He didn't just want people to wear Armani—he wanted them to live Armani. In 2000, Armani Casa—his ranch of high-end furniture, interior design and home décor—was launched. Also, at the dawn of the new century, the Armani make-up line first saw the light of day. Under the name Giorgio Armani Beauty in partnership with L'Oréal Luxe, the brand quickly became known for its luxurious, lightweight and skin-like formulas, with products like the Luminous Silk Foundation becoming cult favourites. Since its launch, Armani Beauty has expanded into a full range of foundations, lipsticks, eyeshadows and more—maintaining a focus on elegance, innovation and professional-grade performance. Ten years later, in 2010, Armani unveiled Armani Hotel Dubai and Armani Hotel Milan, redefining luxury hospitality. The company have also compiled a stunning real estate portfolio with Armani-styled residences for sale and rent in Miami, Dubai, Beijing, Mumbai and the Philippines.

These expansions have transformed Armani from a fashion designer into a global lifestyle mogul. Today the brand is one of the largest privately-owned fashion empires in the world, with a presence in over 60 countries and more than 500 stores worldwide. Armani generates billions in revenue but the man himself has remained fiercely independent, refusing—time and time again—to sell his company. From a small apartment in Milan in 1975 to a global fashion and lifestyle empire, Giorgio Armani has transformed his name into one of the most powerful and recognised brands in the world. His ability to blend luxury with accessibility, modernity with timelessness and Italian heritage with global appeal has made him a pioneer in the fashion industry. But even with all his success, Armani remains deeply involved in his brand, personally overseeing collections and maintaining his uncompromising vision of elegance. His expansion has not just been about selling clothes but creating a world where Armani represents the pinnacle of style, refinement and global luxury. And as the world of fashion evolves, Armani's empire stands as a testament to his vision, perseverance and total mastery of design. This perfectionism even extends to our four-legged friends. In 2024, he launched the Armani Pet Collection—a range of luxury dog clothing and accessories for the pampered pooch!

OPP PAGE: Model wears A/X Armani Exchange T-shirt during the 1992 Ready-to-Wear runway Show

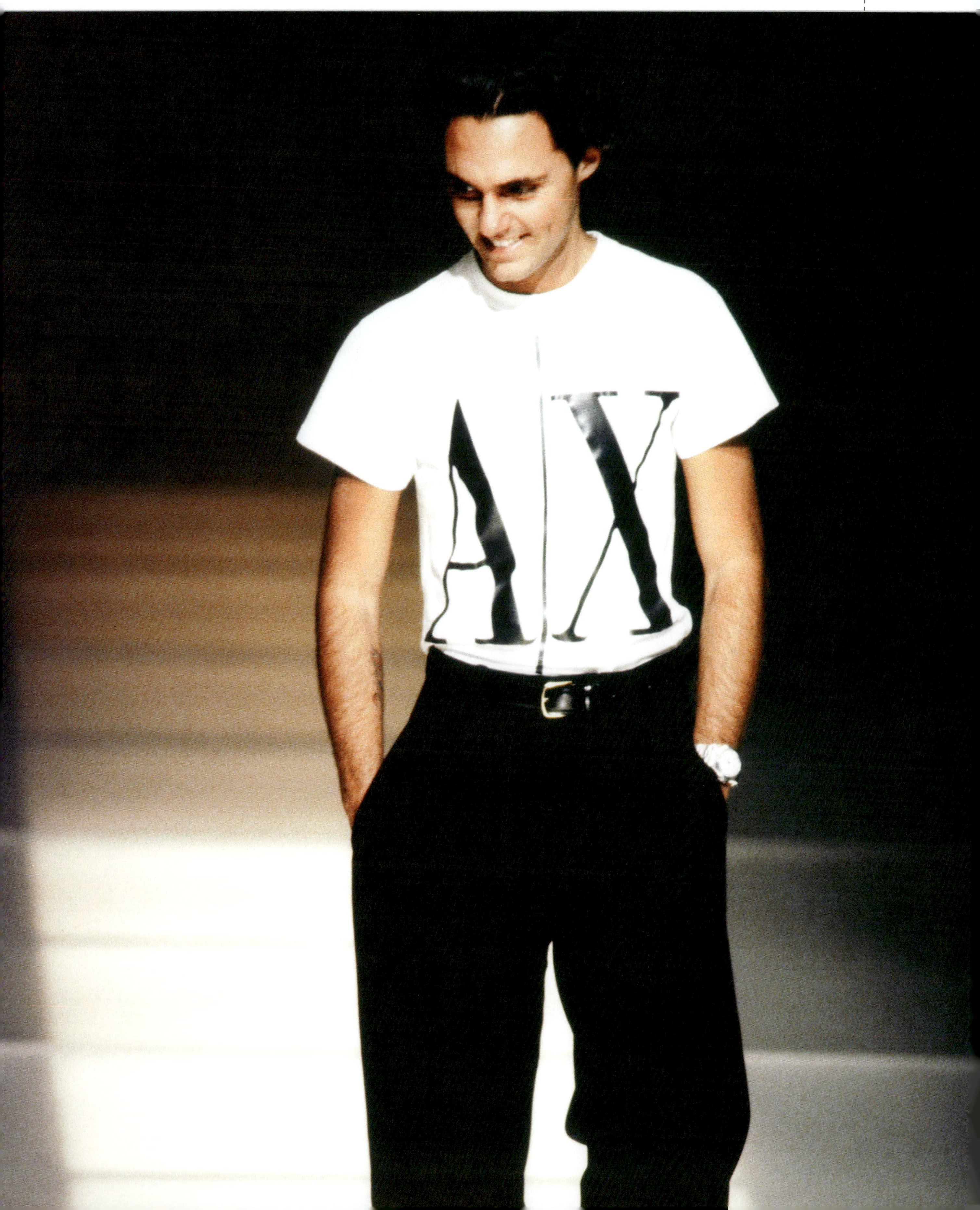

ARMANI MENSWEAR

"Less is more"
The Giorgio Armani mantra

When Giorgio Armani first entered the fashion arena as a menswear designer, tailoring was rigid, structured, and formal. The suits of the early 1960s and early 70s were stiff, heavily padded, and restrictive, reflecting an outdated perception of masculinity. Armani believed this needed to change. With a background in menswear design at Nino Cerruti, Armani had developed a keen understanding of fabric, cut and movement. His vision was clear and simple yet revolutionary—to create suits that embodied effortlessness, sophistication, and comfort while maintaining an aura of classic masculinity. His deconstructed tailoring, use of luxurious fabrics and neutral tones introduced a new kind of elegance— one that would redefine men's fashion for decades to come.

When Armani founded Giorgio Armani S.p.A. in 1975, one of his first major innovations was the unstructured jacket—a soft, lightweight item with natural shoulders and relaxed cuts. Out went heavy

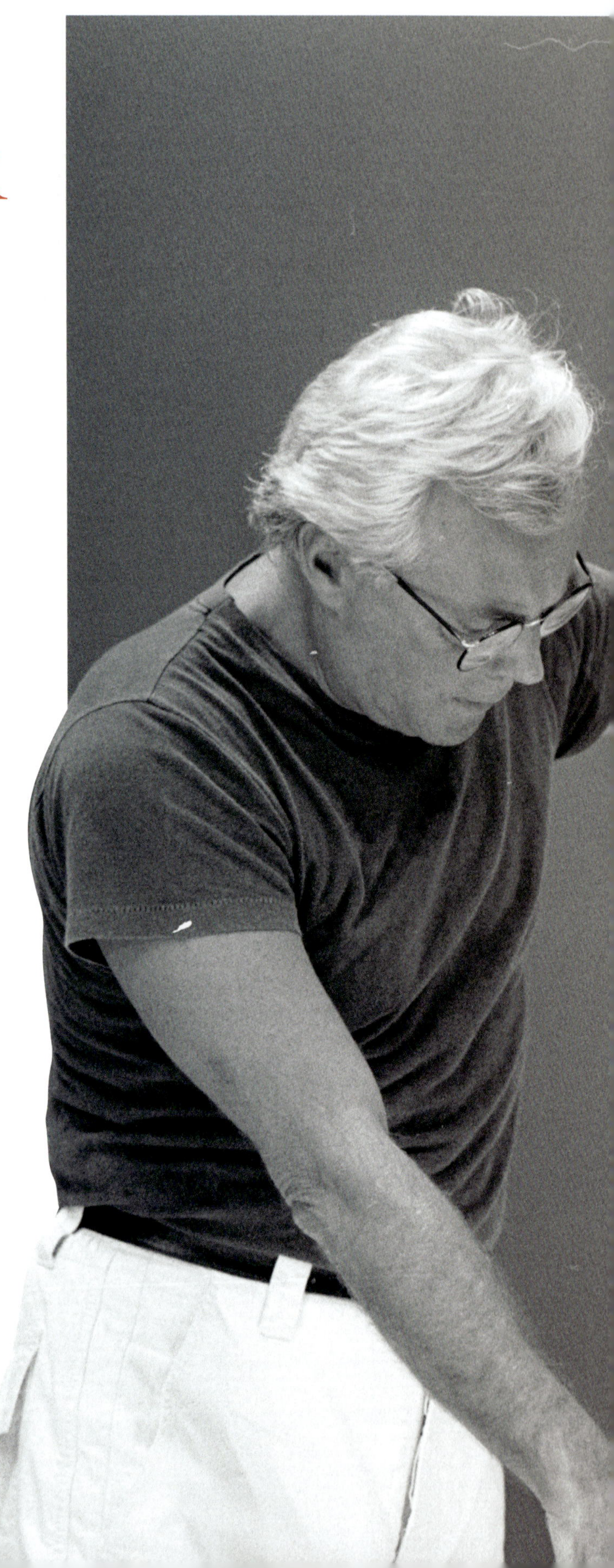

RIGHT: Rehearsals before the Giorgio Armani Fall 1988 runway show

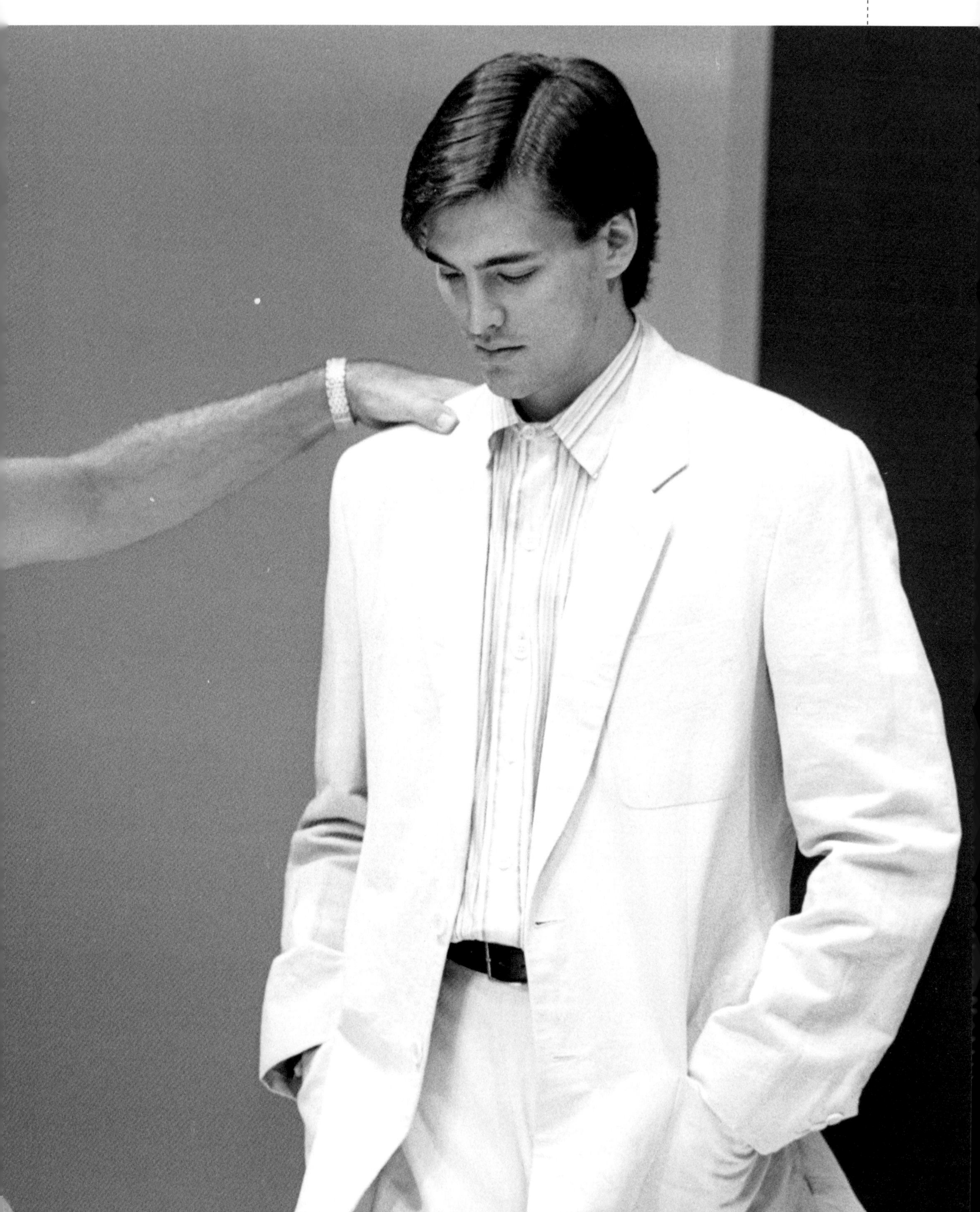

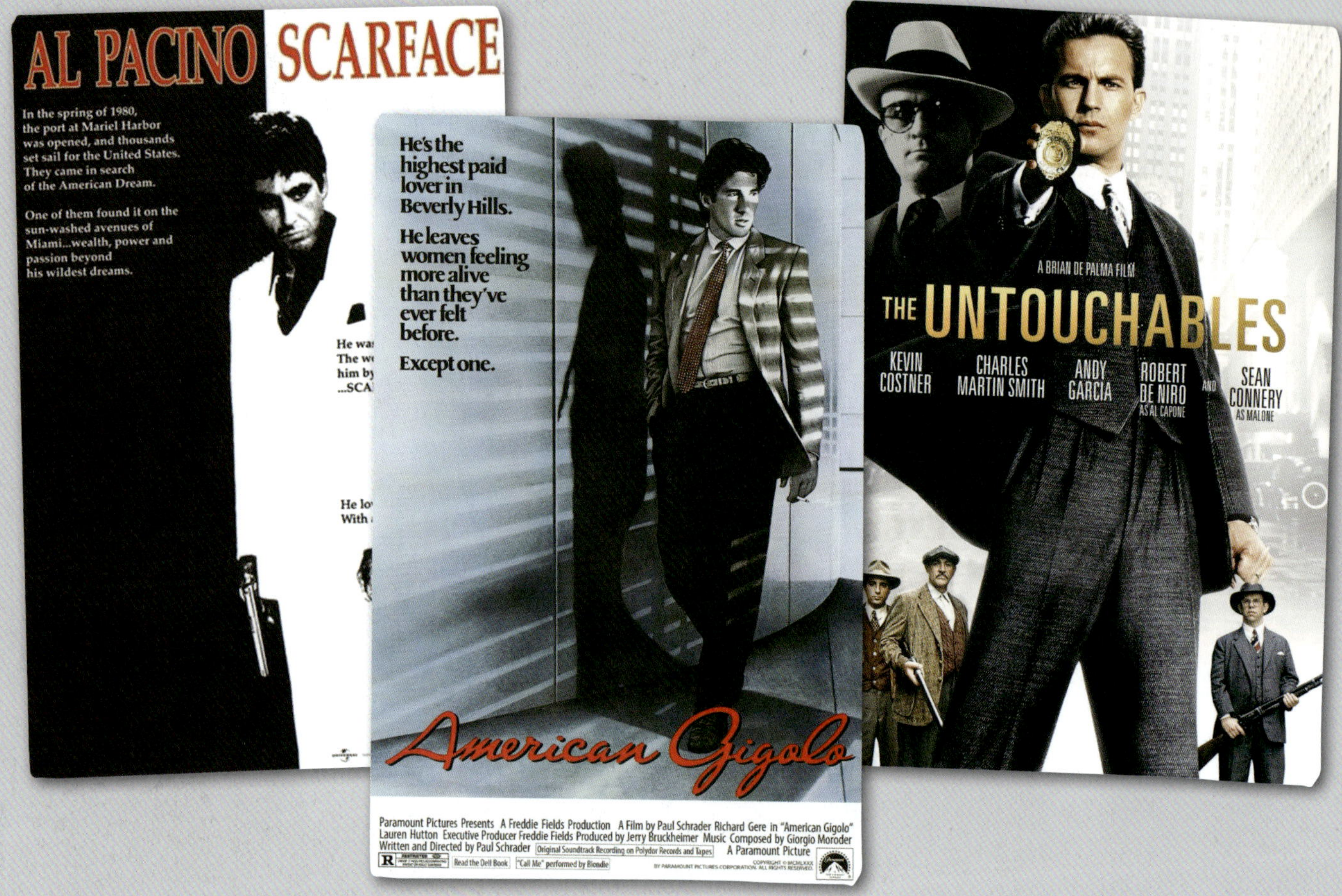

fabrics, rigid padding and stiff linings; in came lighter materials like silk, linen and fine wool blends in neutral, subtle shades. Armani menswear moved with the body rather than restrict it. The Armani suit skyrocketed in popularity after it was featured in the film *American Gigolo* (1980) in which star Richard Gere wore the designer's sleek, modern suits throughout the film. The character's effortless style—tailored yet relaxed—became the new template for modern masculinity. Other Armani Suit icons included Al Pacino in *Scarface* (1983) and Robert De Niro in *The Untouchables* (1987). Over 30 years on, George Clooney & Leonardo DiCaprio are both modern-day ambassadors of Armani tailoring. By the late 1980s, Armani suits had become the suit of choice for Hollywood stars, Wall Street businessmen, and European aristocrats, proving that power and refinement could coexist in fashion.

Today, Armani is still one of the most sought-after menswear brands in the world. Whether it be through the classic suits, luxury casualwear, overcoats, footwear or cologne, Armani menswear remains the ultimate symbol of modern yet elegant and suave masculinity.

ABOVE: Movie posters for *American Gigolo, Scarface* and *The Untouchables*

OPP PAGE: Giorgio Armani Autumn/Winter 2018–19 runway show at Men's Fashion Week in Milan, 2018

THE CLASSICS

THE ARMANI SUIT

Introduced in the 1980s, Armani revolutionised menswear by softening the structure of suits, creating a relaxed yet refined silhouette with GA's signature soft-shoulder tailoring. Tailored from luxurious fabrics like cashmere, wool, linen and silk blends, and with a neutral, understated palette, both Armani's single-breasted and double-breasted suits remain staples in his menswear collections.

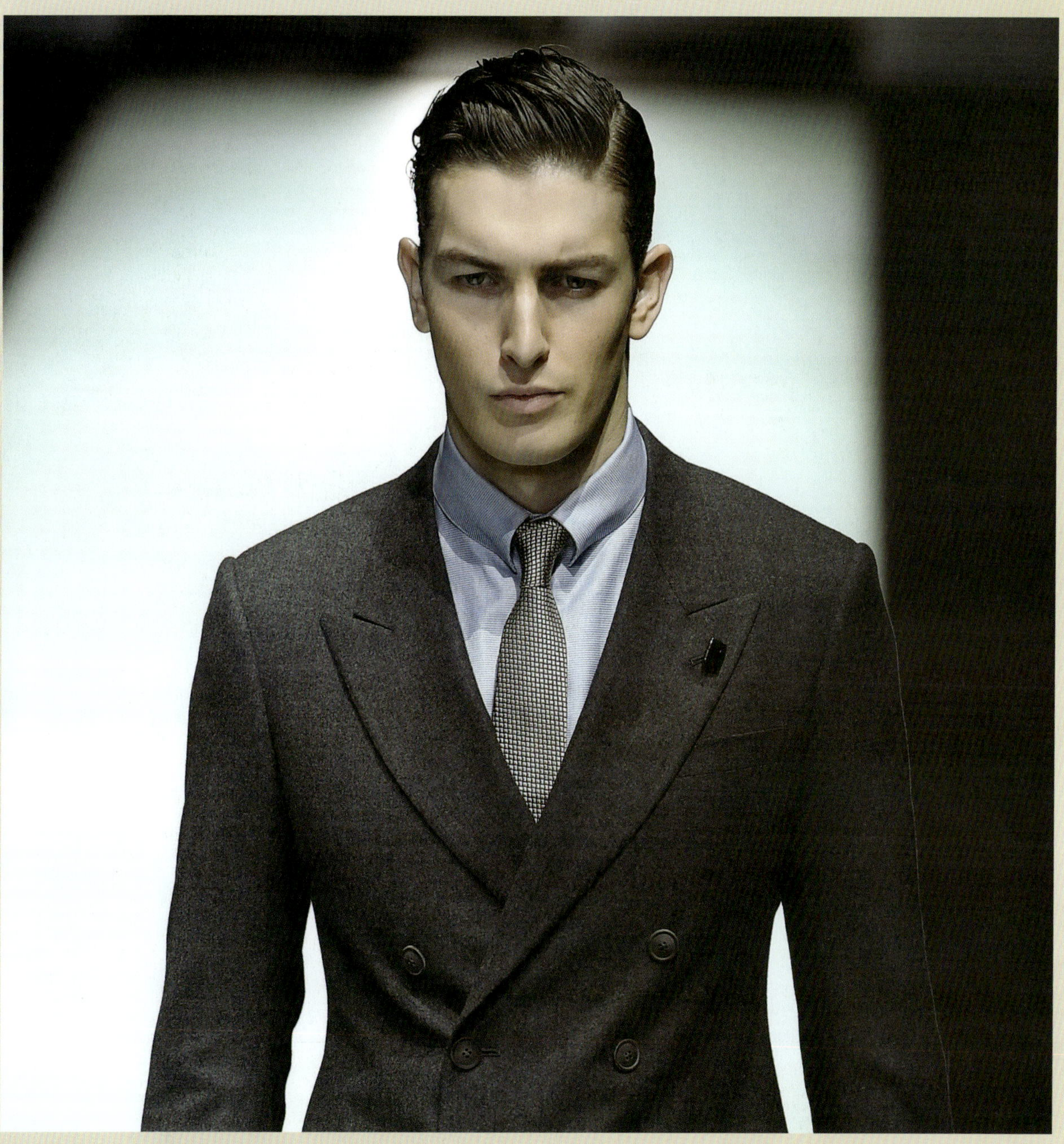

THE UNSTRUCTURED BLAZER

Armani is known for his lightweight, deconstructed blazers which offer comfort without compromising sophistication. Often made from linen, jersey or fine wool for a sleek, modern feel, the unstructured blazer is perfect for formal and smart-casual occasions alike.

THE TURTLENECK SWEATER

Often made from cashmere or merino wool, the understated yet luxurious Armani turtleneck is a timeless alternative to a shirt and adds a certain cosmopolitan, European flair. A signature look when paired with an Armani blazer or overcoat.

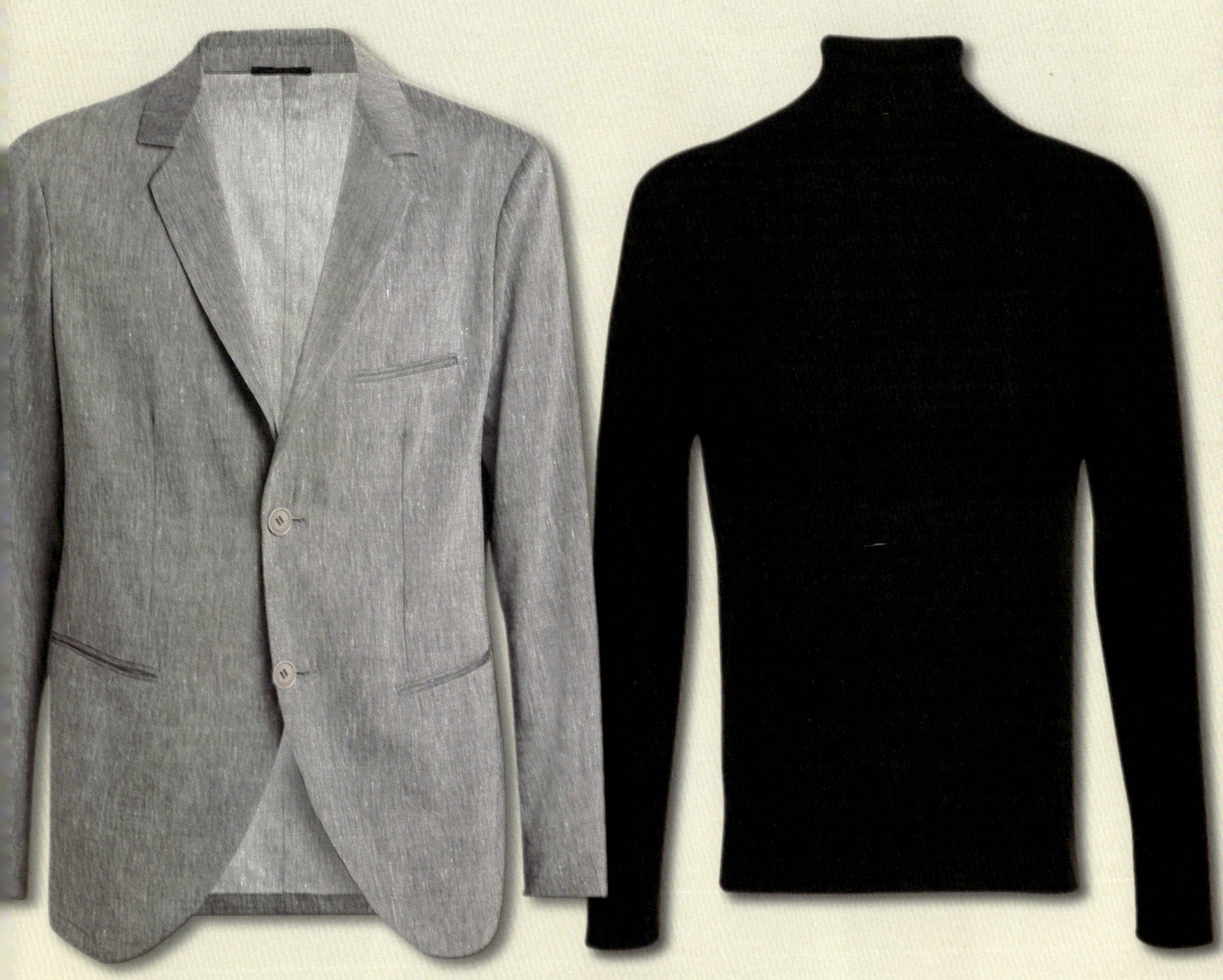

OPP PAGE: Model walks the runway at the Giorgio Armani Spring/Summer show during Men's Fashion Week in Milan, 2018

THE ULTIMATE WHITE SHIRT

Famous for is flawless fit and premium cotton fabric, Armani's perfect white shirt is a menswear essential. It looks equally good whether paired with a suit, blazer or worn open-necked for a more casual feel. Ever versatile, TUWS is available in classic spread, point or mandarin collars.

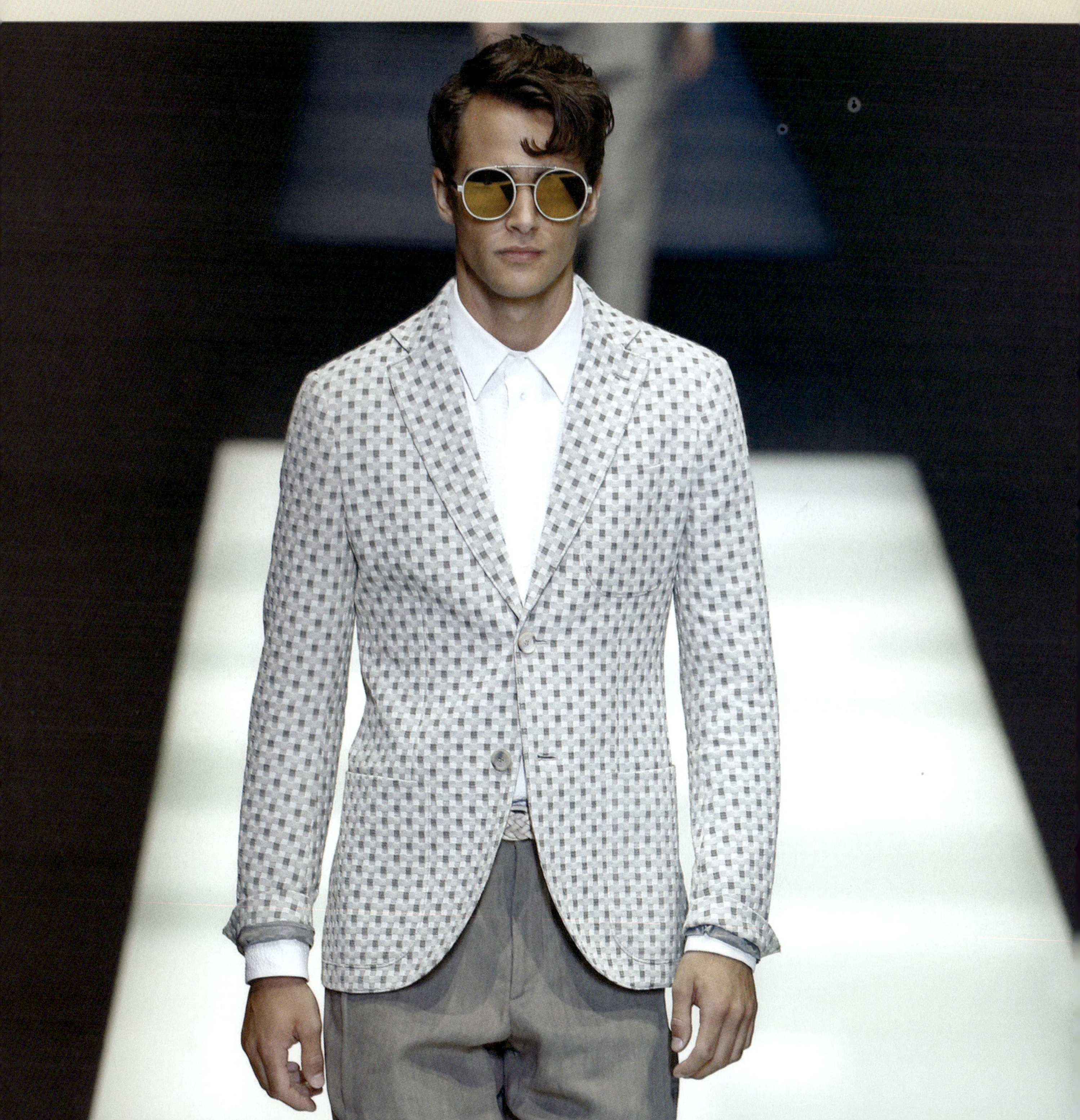

SLIM-FIT WOOL OR LINEN TROUSERS

A wardrobe essential, Armani trousers are known for their clean lines and impeccable tailoring with classic styles including pleated or flat-front pants in wool, linen or cotton. As always with Armani, they come in neutral, understatedly elegant shades.

THE TRENCH COAT

Designed with sleek, minimal detailing and exuding an air of quiet sophistication, the Armani Trench remains a truly timeless outerwear staple. Often made from luxurious wool or water-resistant fabric.

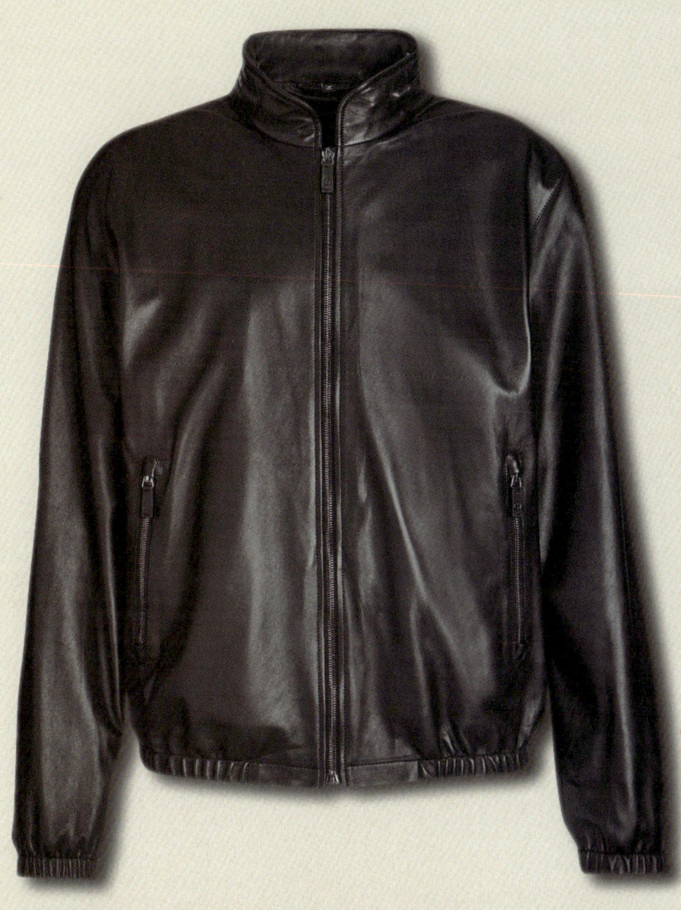

THE GIORGIO ARMANI LEATHER JACKET

Often crafted in buttery-soft lambskin or suede in neutral tones, and famous for its sleek, minimalist design, the Armani leather jacket is a symbol of refined masculinity. Pair with a turtleneck and tailored trousers for the ultimate smart-casual, uber-sophisticated look.

THE CASHMERE OVERCOAT

Another iconic Armani staple, the cashmere overcoat is usually tailored with a clean, structured fit and comes in classic shades such as camel, navy, and charcoal grey. Elevates any winter look, whether layered over a suit or casual knitwear.

LEATHER LOAFERS & DRESS SHOES

Armani's shoes for men include classic penny loafers, Derby shoes and Oxford styles in premium Italian leather. Often in black, brown, or deep burgundy, they are designed for both formal and smart-casual wear.

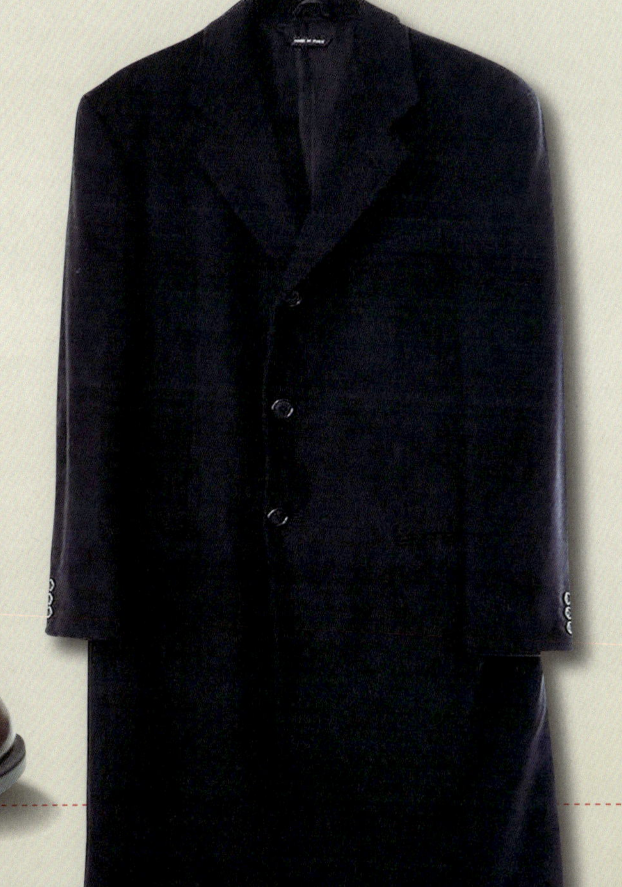

THE ARMANI POLO SHIRT

A luxurious upgrade to the classic polo, featuring soft Pima cotton or silk-blend fabrics, Armani's version features a slim yet relaxed fit, perfect for casual yet classy dressing.

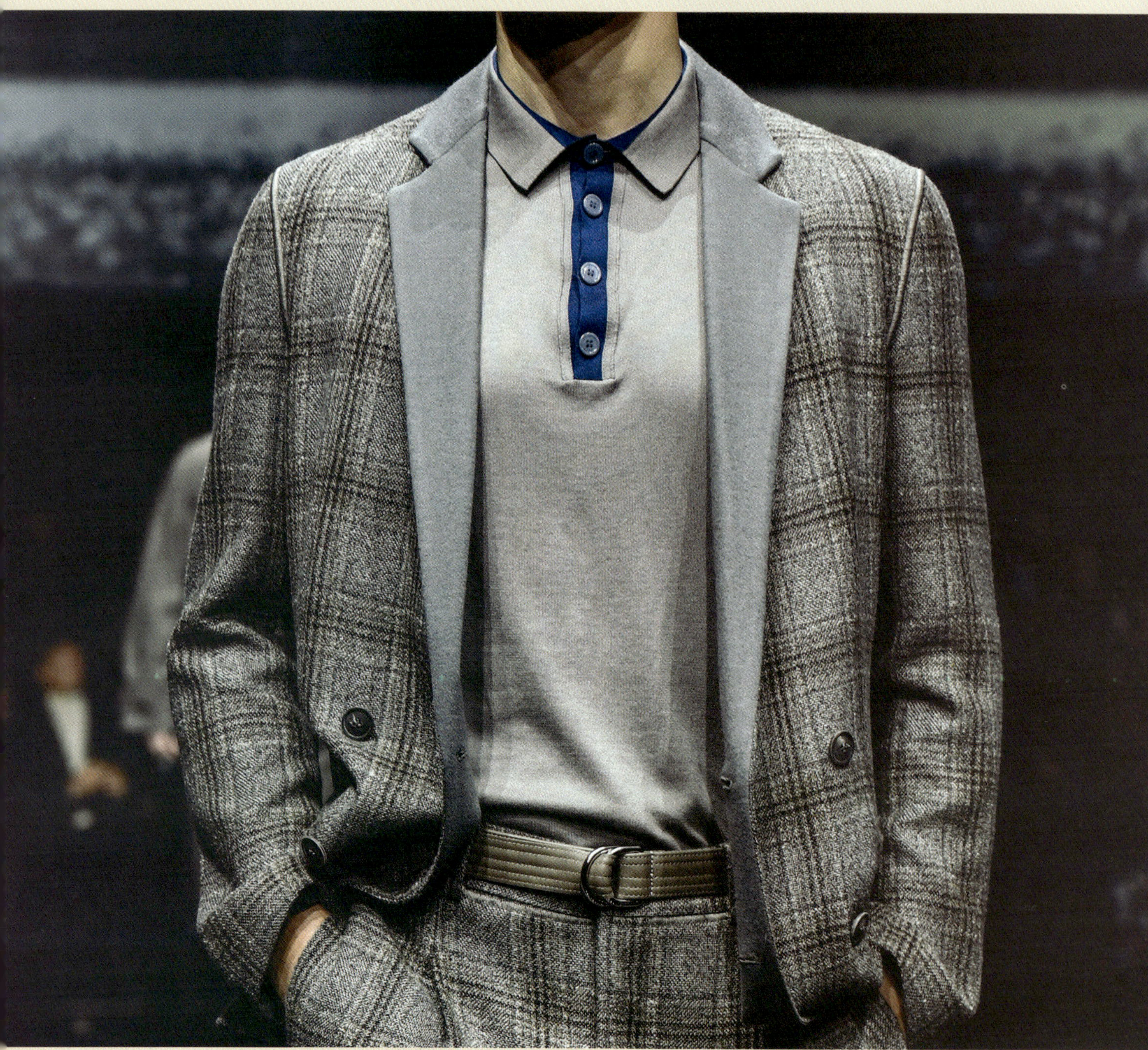

ABOVE: Giorgio Armani's Men's Autumn/Winter 2020–21 collection
OPP PAGE: Rafael Nadal reveals his Armani Jeans campaign at Macy's Herald Square, New York City, August, 2011

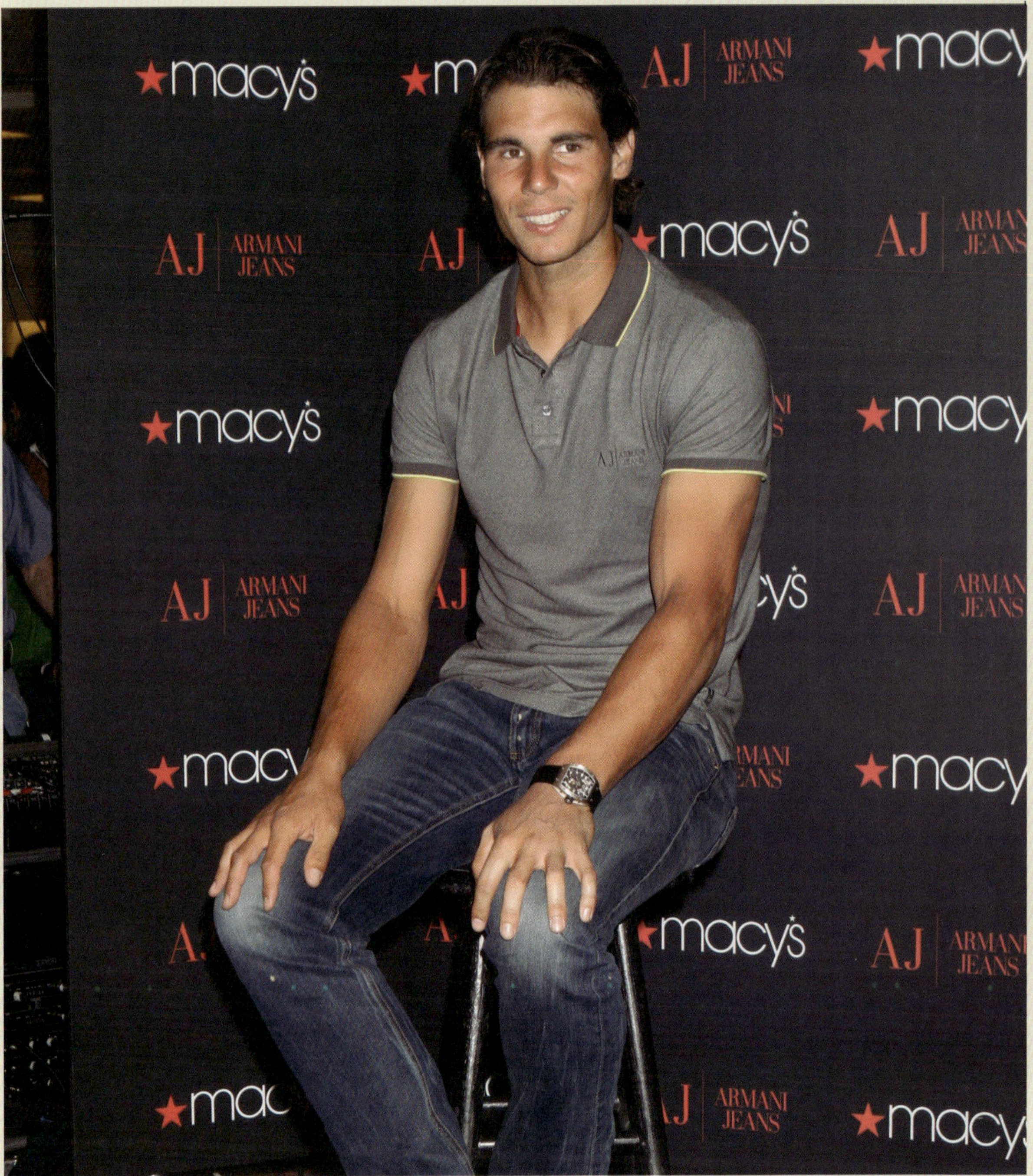

TAILORED DENIM & CLASSIC CHINOS

Armani's jeans and chinos are designed with a sophisticated and slim silhouette, making them ideal for smart-casual wear. Dark-wash denim remains a classic—offering versatility and understated elegance.

ELEGANT KNITWEAR & CARDIGANS

Fine cashmere and merino wool sweaters, V-neck or crew-neck styles, are Armani classics—with his slim-fitting cardigans adding a touch of sophistication to casual outfits.

THE SIGNATURE SUNGLASSES

Classic aviators, round frames and wayfarers are Armani staples—often featuring sleek, minimalist designs with subtle branding.

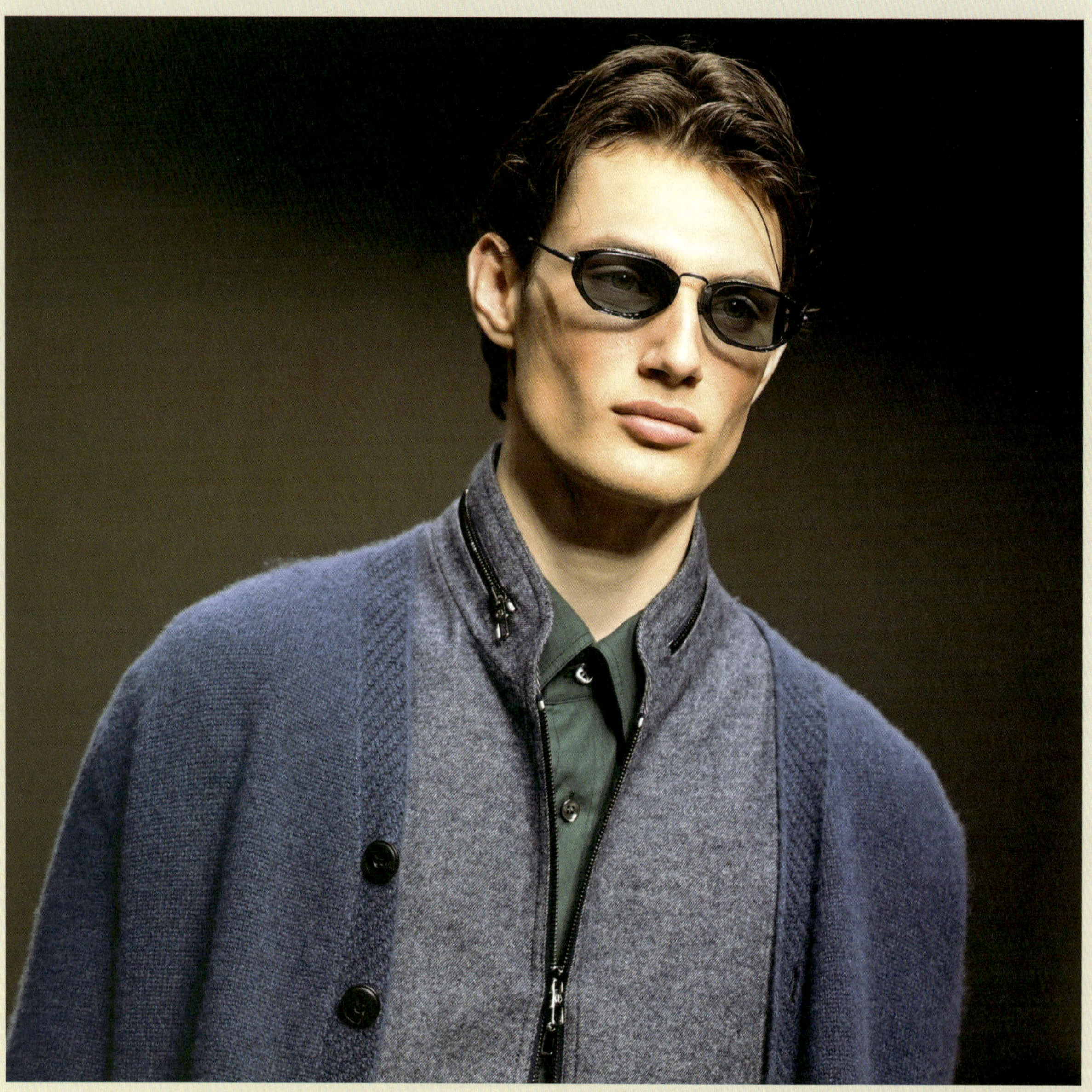

ABOVE: Giorgio Armani Autumn/Winter 2025-26 collection show at Men's Fashion Week in Milan, 2025
OPP PAGE: Giorgio Armani Eyewear Campaign in UK Magazine

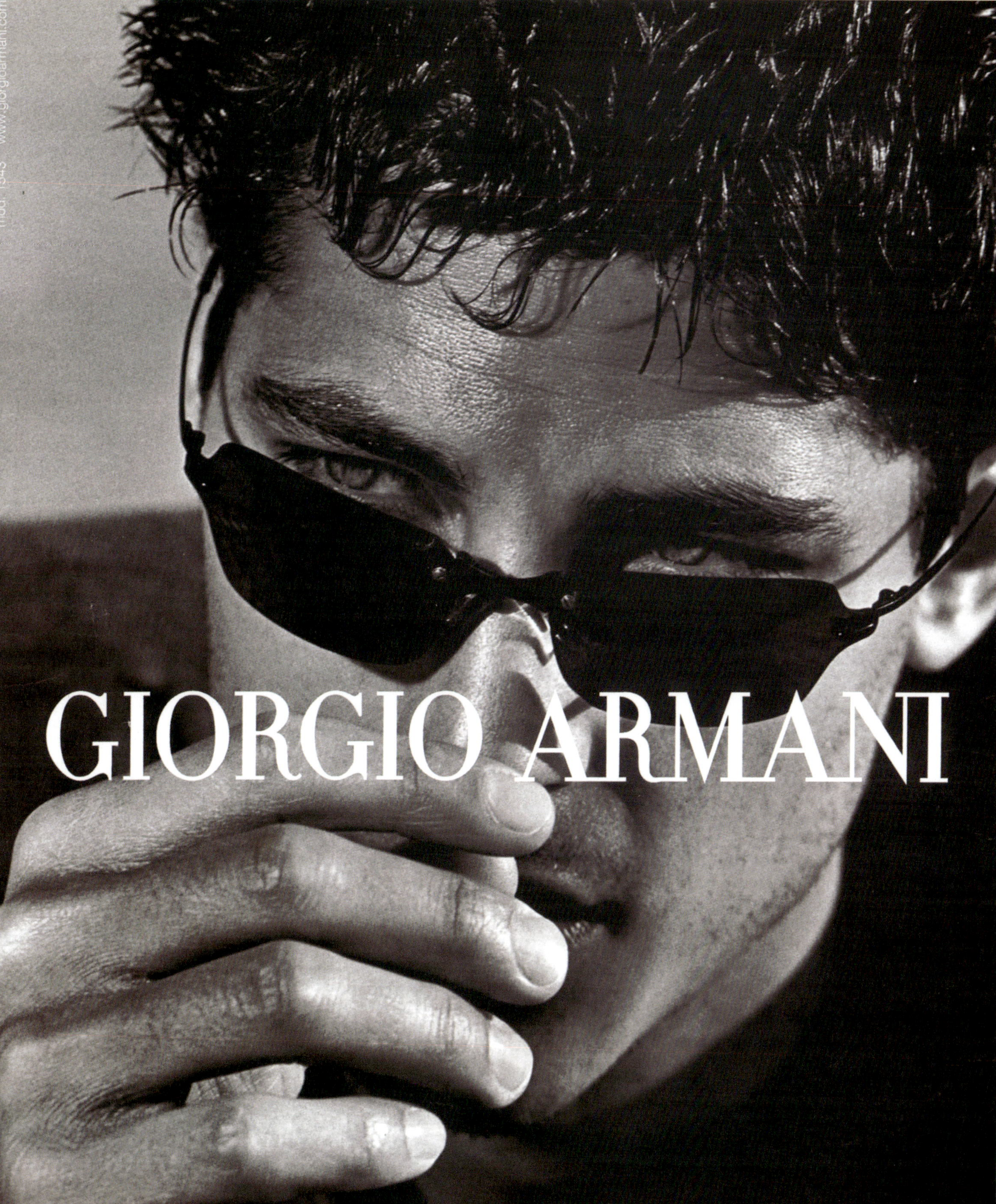
GIORGIO ARMANI

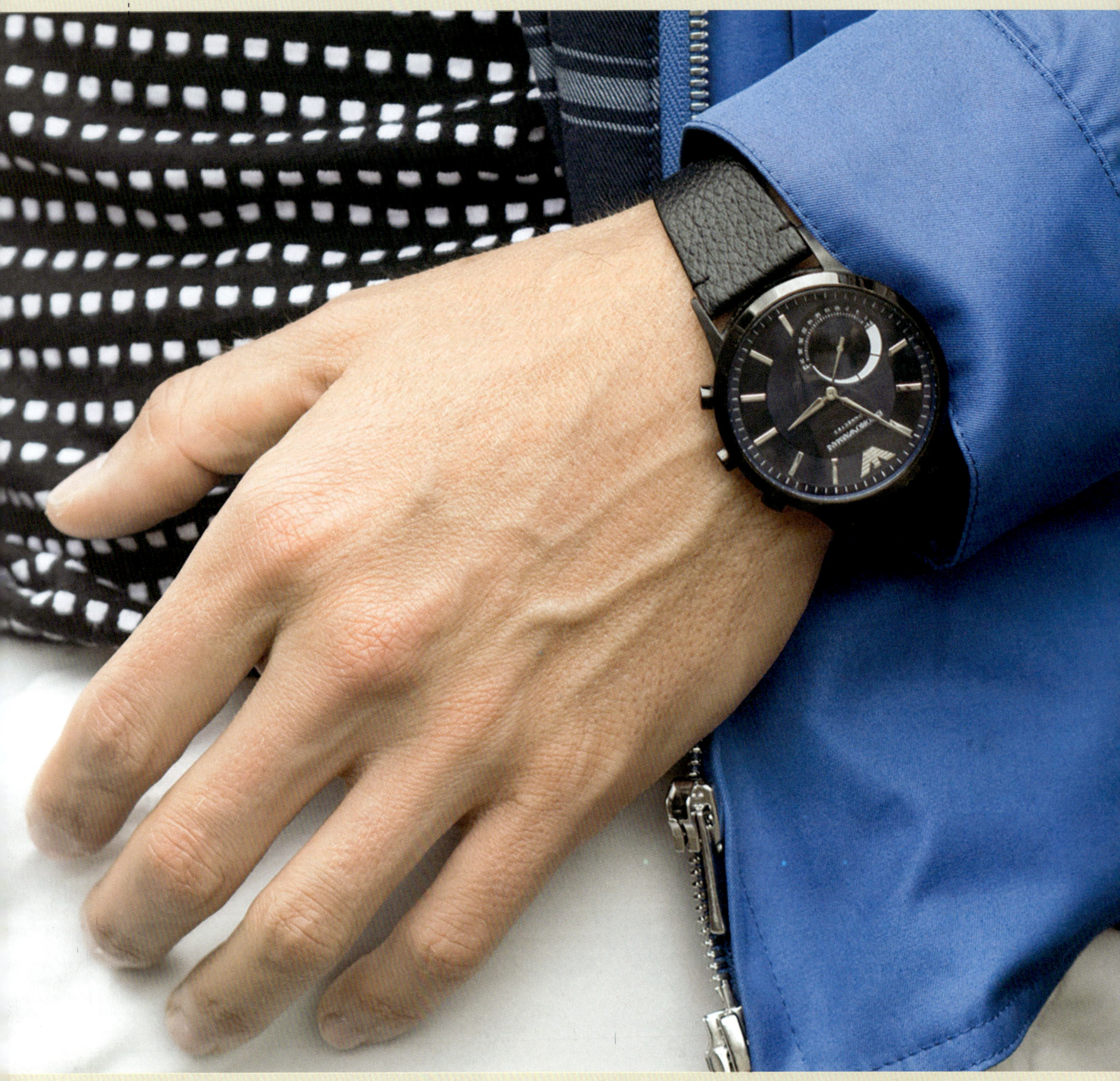

THE ARMANI WATCH

While not as famous as Swiss brands, Armani watches feature classic and modern designs that complement the brand's aesthetic.

ABOVE: TV presenter Darren Kennedy wears an Armani watch at London Fashion Week, 2018

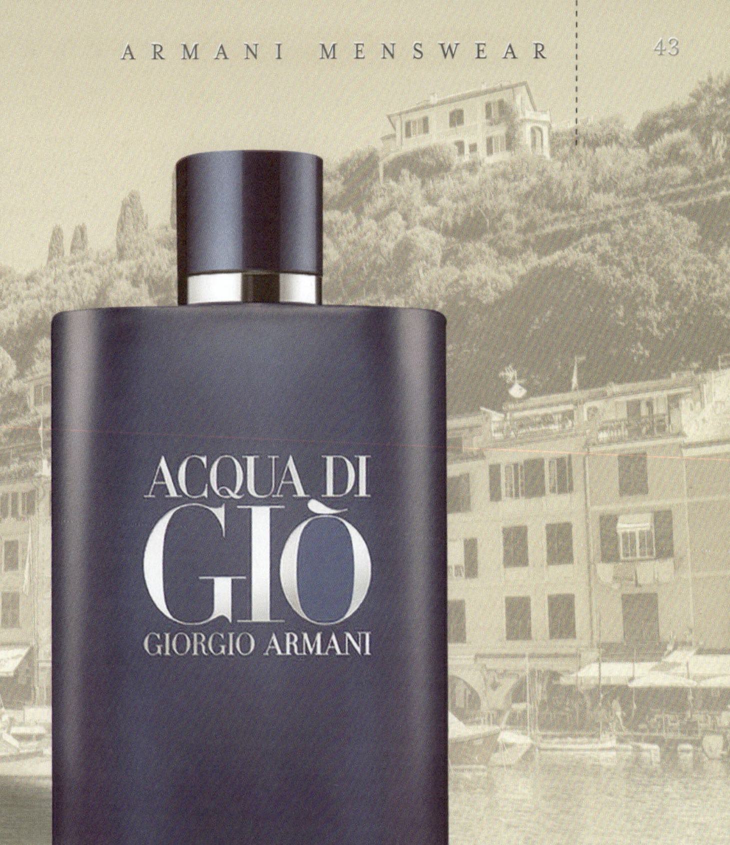

ARMANI MEN'S COLOGNES

The finishing touches to classic Armani menswear are the brand's signature men's fragrances, which began in 1984 with Armani Eau Pour Homme. The brand's official UK website currently lists 33 men's fragrances, including various versions and concentrations of popular lines like Acqua di Giò—the cologne of choice for actor Chris Hemsworth, and Armani Code.

THE GIORGIO ARMANI TIE

Think silk, subtle patterns and a refined colour palette, the GA necktie is a staple in any man's wardrobe. Perfect for both business and formal occasions.

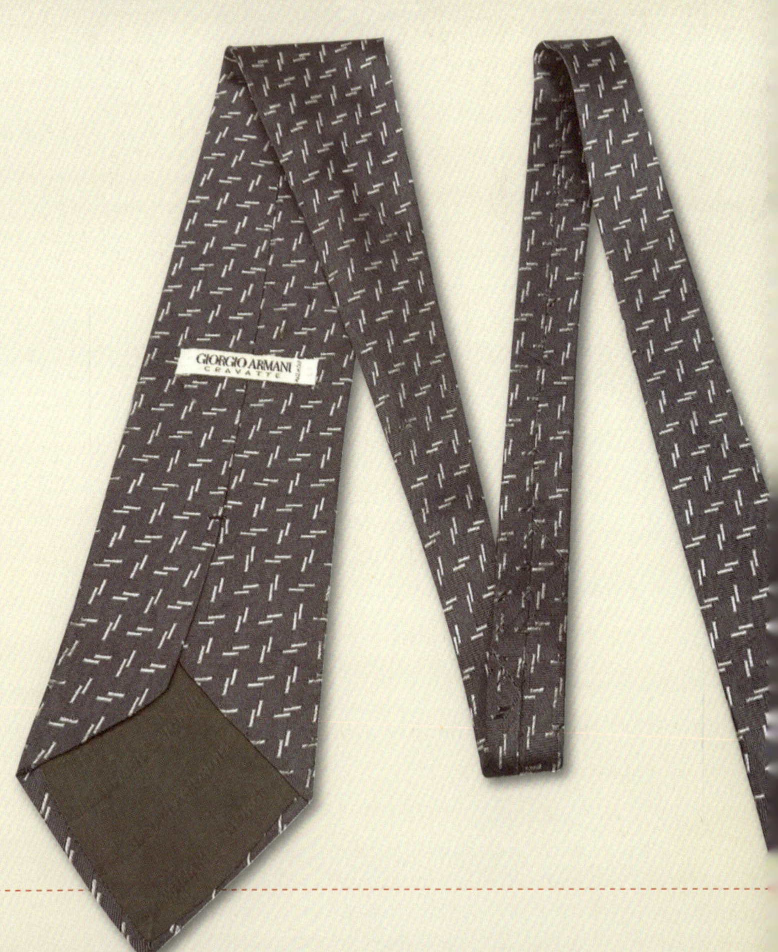

ARMANI WOMENSWEAR

"I don't like women who follow fashion in the sense of becoming victims of it. I like women who have elegance, who have allure, who use fashion, rather than the other way around"
Giorgio Armani

By the time Giorgio Armani had established himself as a master of menswear, his influence on women's fashion was only just beginning to take shape. Unlike many designers who embraced extravagant, ultra-feminine silhouettes throughout the 1970s and '80s, Armani took a radically different approach. His vision was not to embellish but to refine—to empower rather than overwhelm. Armani's women's collections became a defining force in modern fashion, blending masculine strength with feminine grace, and giving women a wardrobe that exuded confidence, elegance, and ease. From 'power suits' to the red-carpet gowns, he has reshaped the way women dressed for work, leisure, and luxury.

When Armani launched his first women's collection in 1976, his approach was revolutionary. At a time when women's fashion was still dominated by tight-fitting, ultra-feminine silhouettes, Armani redefined

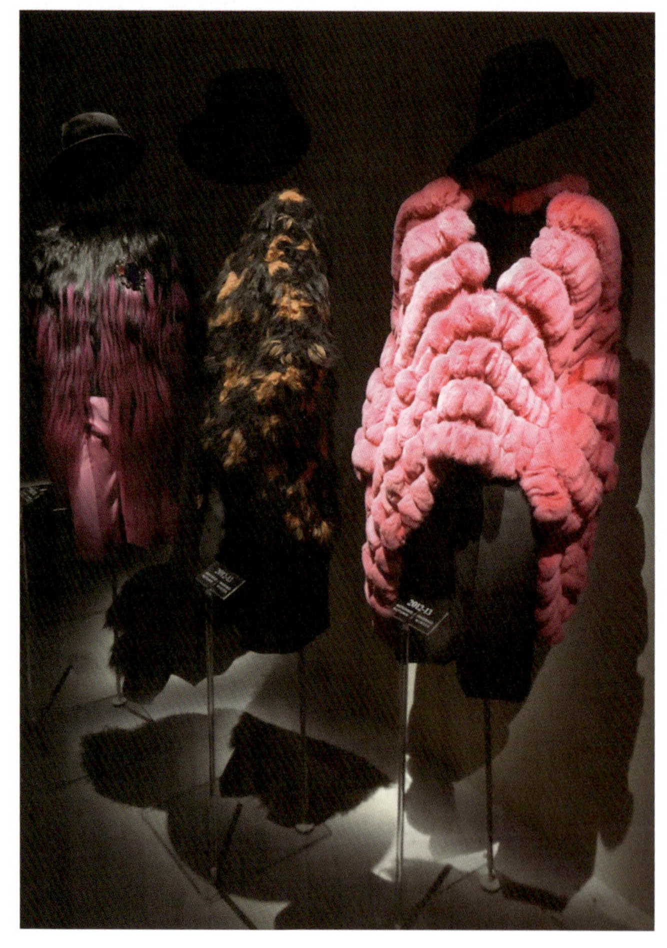

ABOVE RIGHT: A collection at Armani/Silos, the fashion art museum in Milan, Italy
OPP PAGE: A model wears an outfit from the Giorgio Armani Spring/Summer collection, 2008

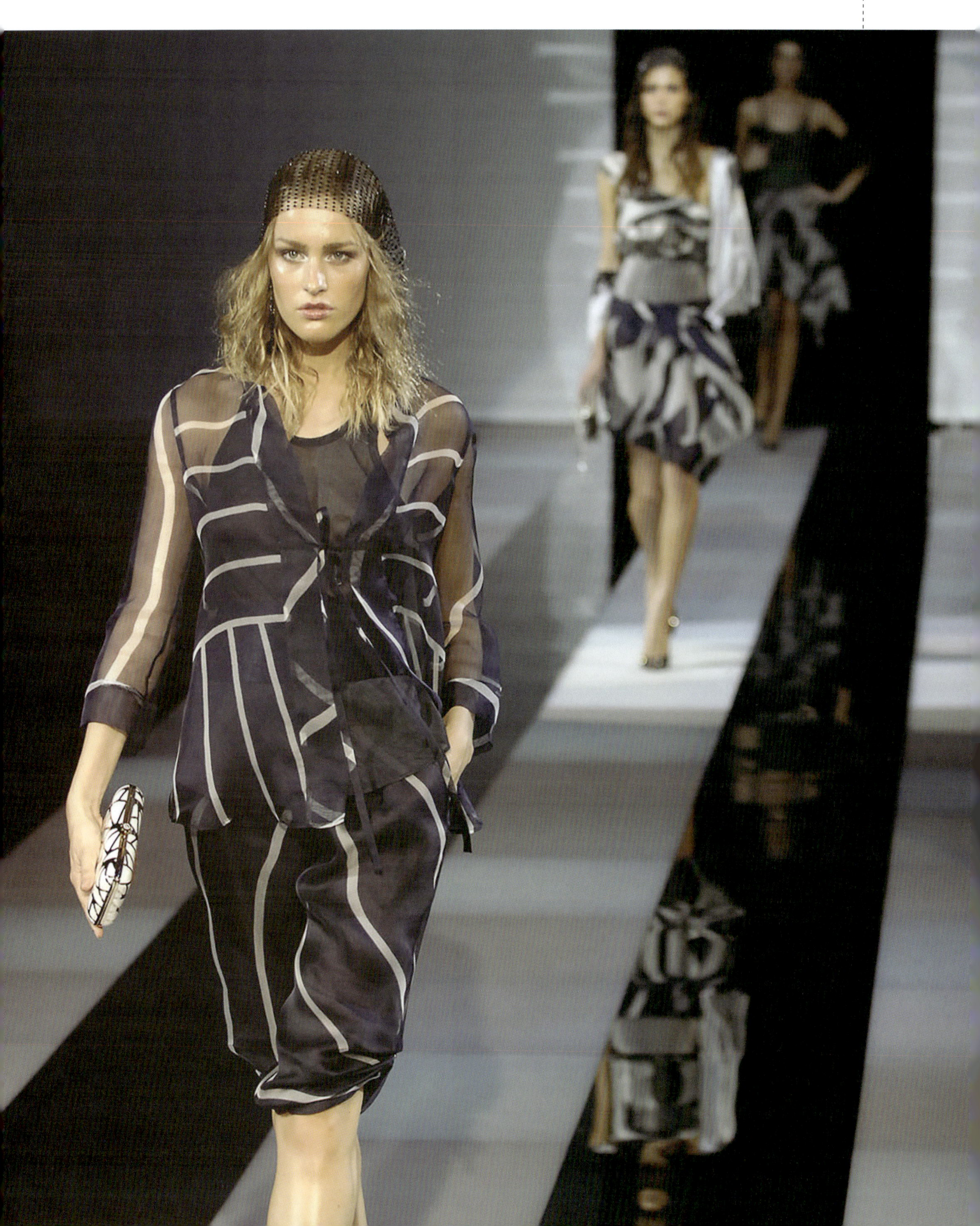

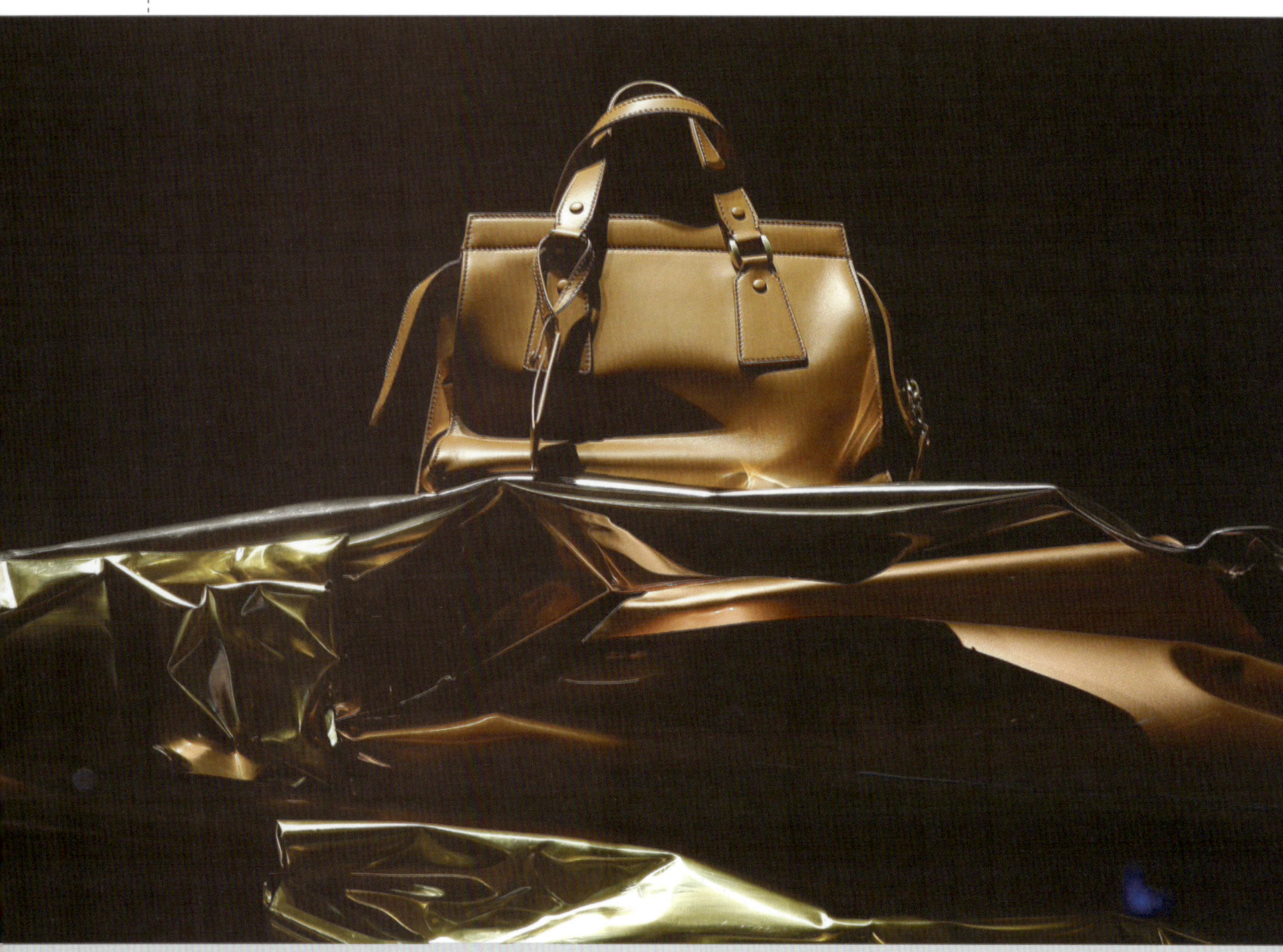

it. Taking inspiration from his menswear collections and altering the designs for the female form, he invented the 'Power Suit'. His signature neutral palette came into play—no flashy, feminine tones, rather navy, black, grey and beige in lightweight fabrics like wool, linen, and silk blends that allowed movement and comfort. The designs were minimalist, clean and sleek. This was a suit designed for the modern working woman, someone who wanted to be taken seriously in the boardroom but was unwilling to sacrifice style for professionalism. Actress Diane Keaton was one of the first high-profile women to wear Armani—specifically in the Oscar winning film *Annie Hall*. A few years later in 1983 Michelle Pfeiffer wore Armani in the movie *Scarface*, doing much the same for the label's womenswear as Richard Gere had achieved for Armani menswear in *American Gigolo*. The late Princess Diana was always at her effortlessly elegant best in an Armani suit. Throughout the 1980s and '90s, female power dressing became

ABOVE: Giorgio Armani's 'Le Sac 11' bag at the Antonia Giacinti boutique during its presentation in Milan, 2015
OPP PAGE: Model on the runway at the Giorgio Armani Spring 2024 Ready-to-Wear Runway Show

synonymous with Armani, and soon, his jackets, trousers, and blazers became the go-to choice for strong, independent women.

While Armani's suits became a corporate staple, his eveningwear wowed Hollywood red-carpets. Unlike the extravagant, over-the-top gowns of his contemporaries, Armani designed understated yet breathtakingly elegant evening dresses. Gowns that draped effortlessly over the body in luxurious fabrics—silk, satin, velvet, and chiffon in classic colour choices such as black, deep jewel tones and soft pastels. Armani's eveningwear remains a favourite among A-list celebrities, with his designs often defining timeless Hollywood glamour.

A great outfit is never complete without perfect accessories and fragrance, and Armani's womenswear empire extends far beyond clothing. The brand excels in creating sleek, leather totes and structured handbags; elegant high-heeled shoes for evening looks, loafers for the business wardrobe, and stylish trainers and flats for casual luxury. The label has developed a fine line of minimalist gold and silver jewellery in addition to classic time pieces which balance elegance and modernity. Best-selling women's fragrances include 'Si'—a modern, feminine floral scent worn by Cate Blanchett; 'My Way'—fresh and floral, worn by Zendaya; and the sensual, mysterious 'Armani Code for Women,' worn by Adriana Lima.

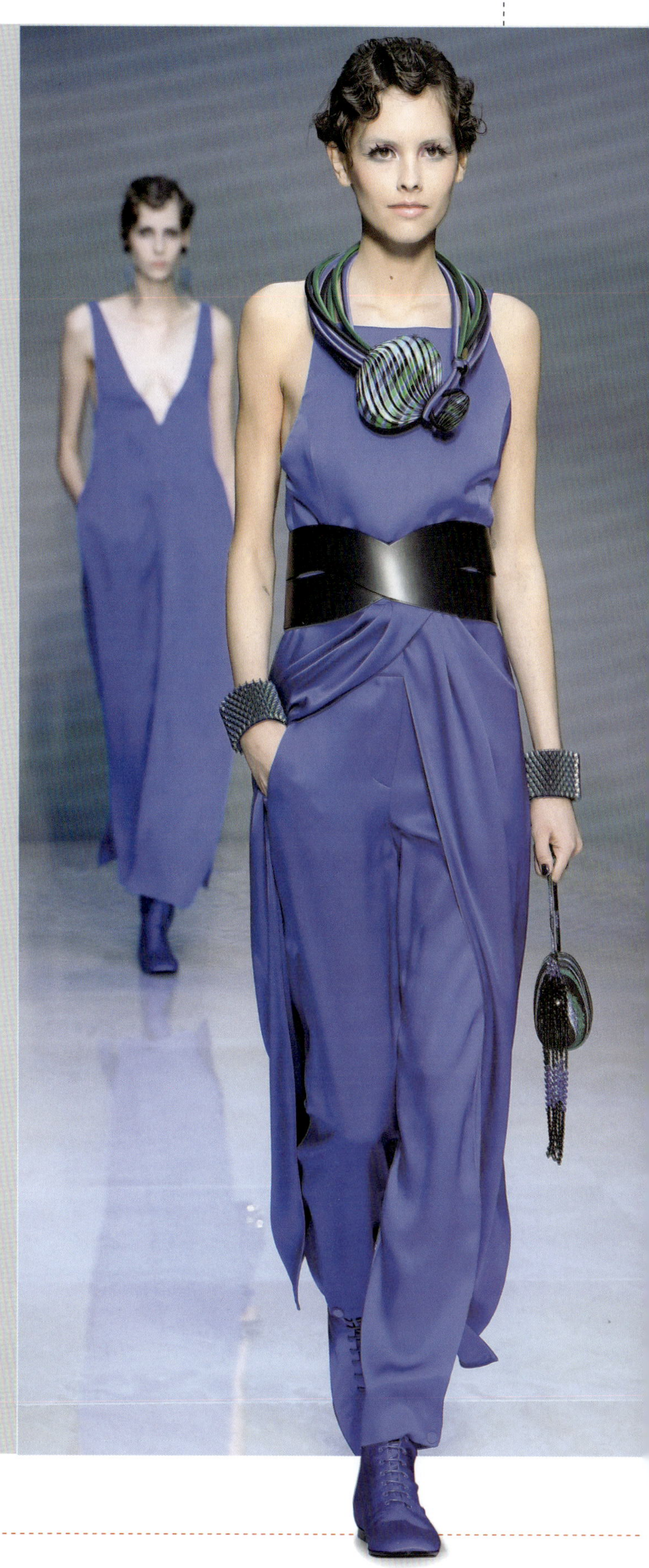

THE CLASSICS

Armani's womenswear classics embody timeless elegance, sophisticated tailoring and effortless luxury.

THE ARMANI POWER SUIT

A signature of Giorgio Armani's since the 1980s, the power suit features sharp tailoring, soft shoulders and a relaxed fit. Often crafted in neutral tones like beige, grey, navy and black.

SILK BLOUSES & SOFT SHIRTS

Armani blouses are known for their fluidity and understated luxury. Often made from silk or satin, they drape beautifully and pair seamlessly with both trousers and skirts.

MINIMALIST EVENING GOWNS

Giorgio Armani evening wear collections showcase exquisite designs with clean lines, luxurious fabrics and subtle embellishments. Think sleek, floor-length gowns with refined detailing such as beading and embroidery.

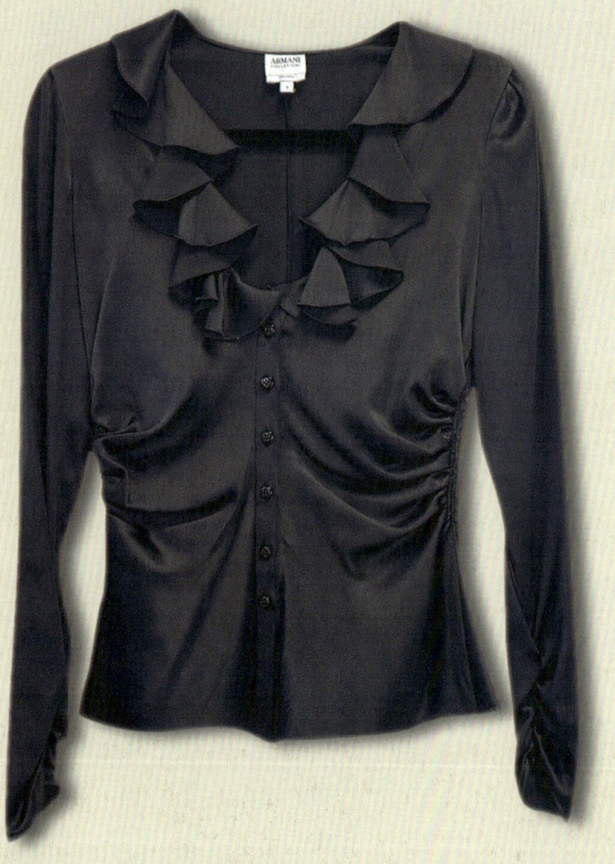

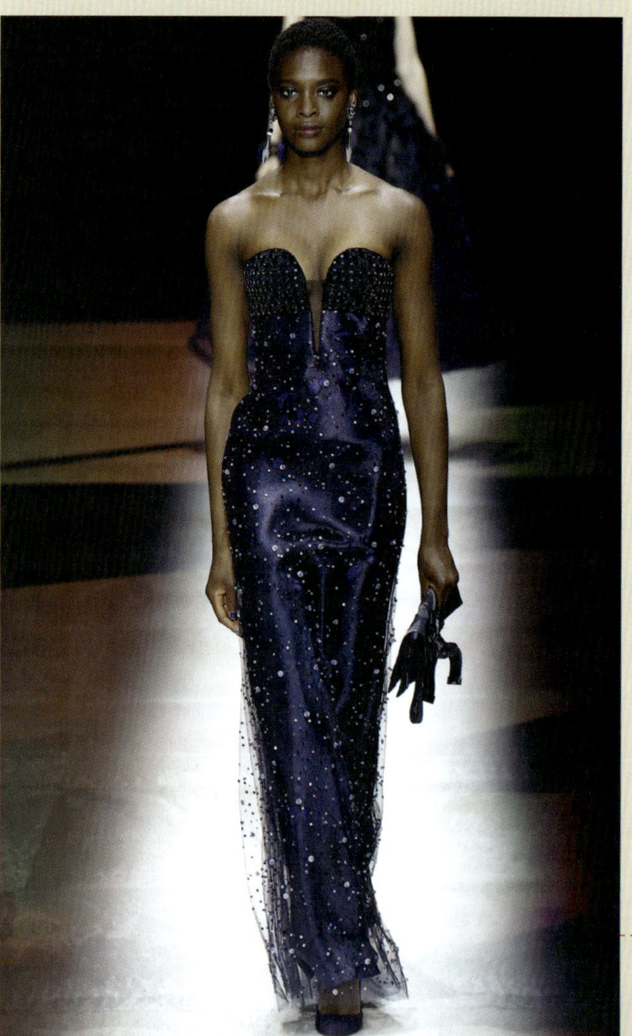

RIGHT: Armani Haute Couture Autumn/Winter 2022-23
OPP PAGE: Katherine Langford wears a classic Armani suit to the L'Oréal Paris Women of Worth Celebrations, 2022

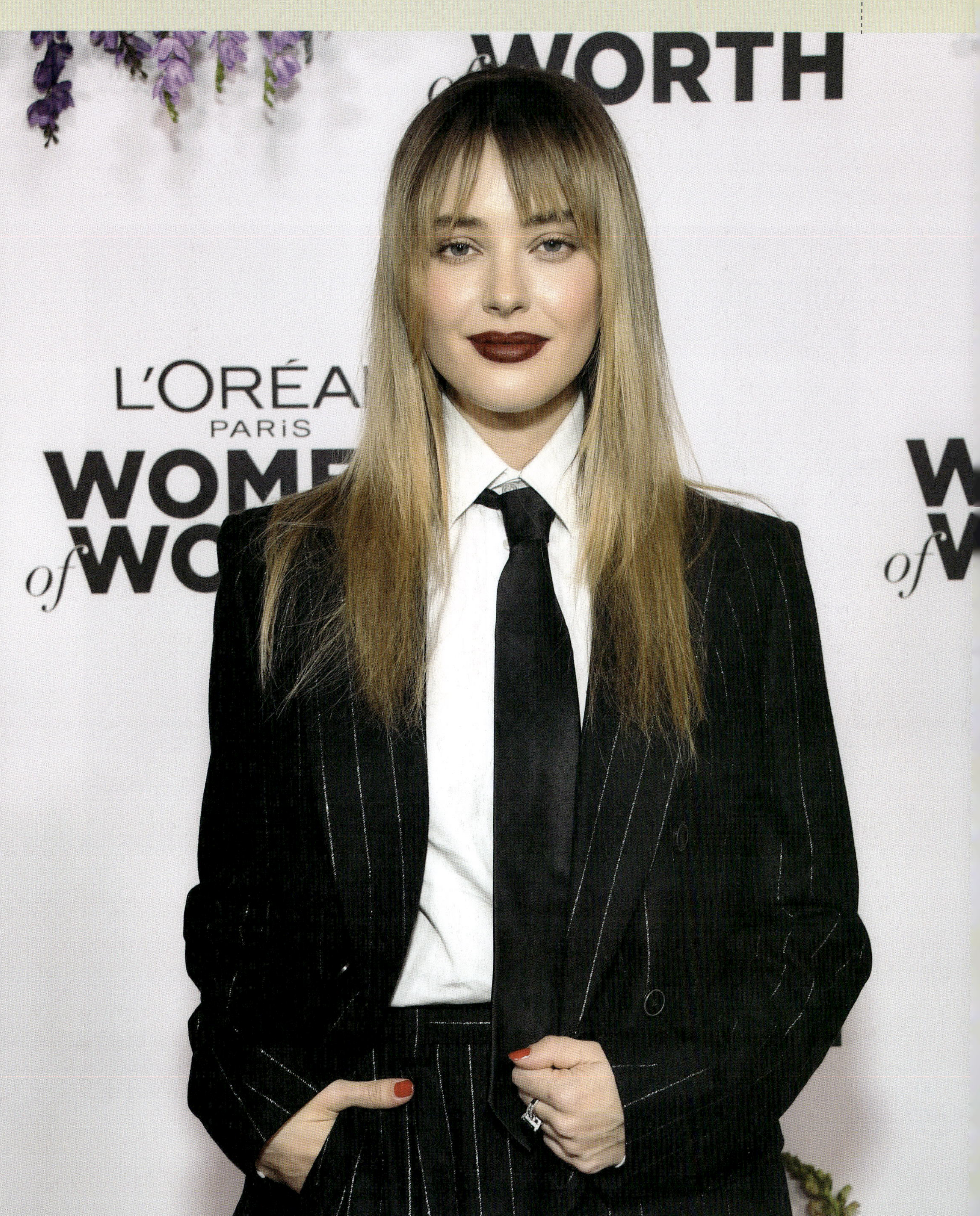
WORTH
L'ORÉAL
PARIS
WOMEN
of WORTH

CLASSIC WOOL & CASHMERE COATS

Elegant, structured outerwear is a staple in Armani's womenswear collections. Tailored wool coats and minimalist trench coats in neutral tones add a polished touch to any look.

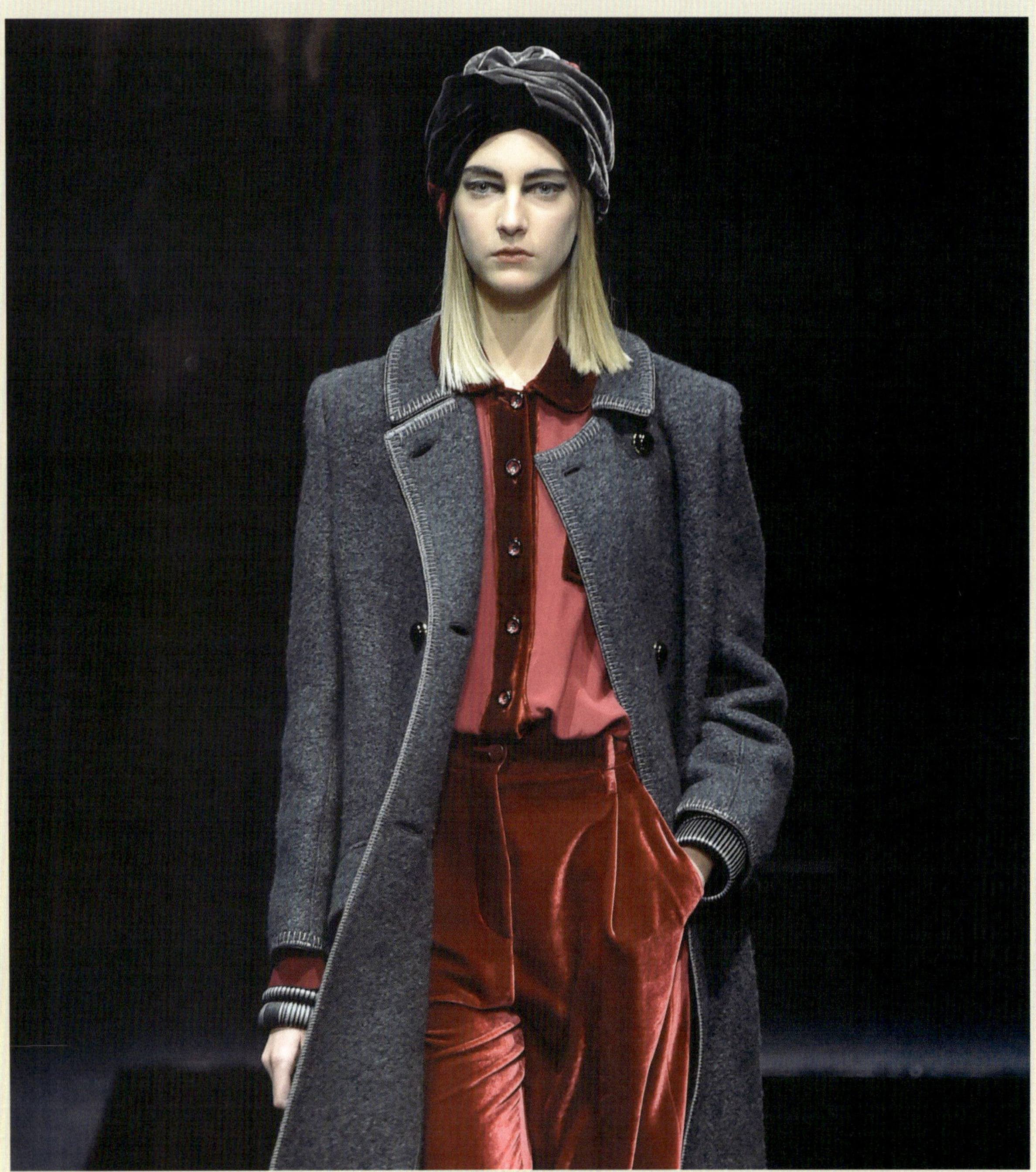

ABOVE: Giorgio Armani Pre-Fall 2020/21 Collection Show
OPP PAGE: Emporio Armani Runway, Milan Fashion Week, Womenswear Autumn/Winter 2014

WIDE-LEG TROUSERS

Relaxed yet structured, Armani's wide-leg trousers are a hallmark of his understated aesthetic. They provide effortless sophistication, whether styled with a fitted blazer or a soft knit.

TIMELESS BLAZERS

Armani is known for revolutionising women's blazers, making them both strong and feminine. His signature unstructured blazers, often in lightweight fabrics, are perfect for modern, sophisticated dressing.

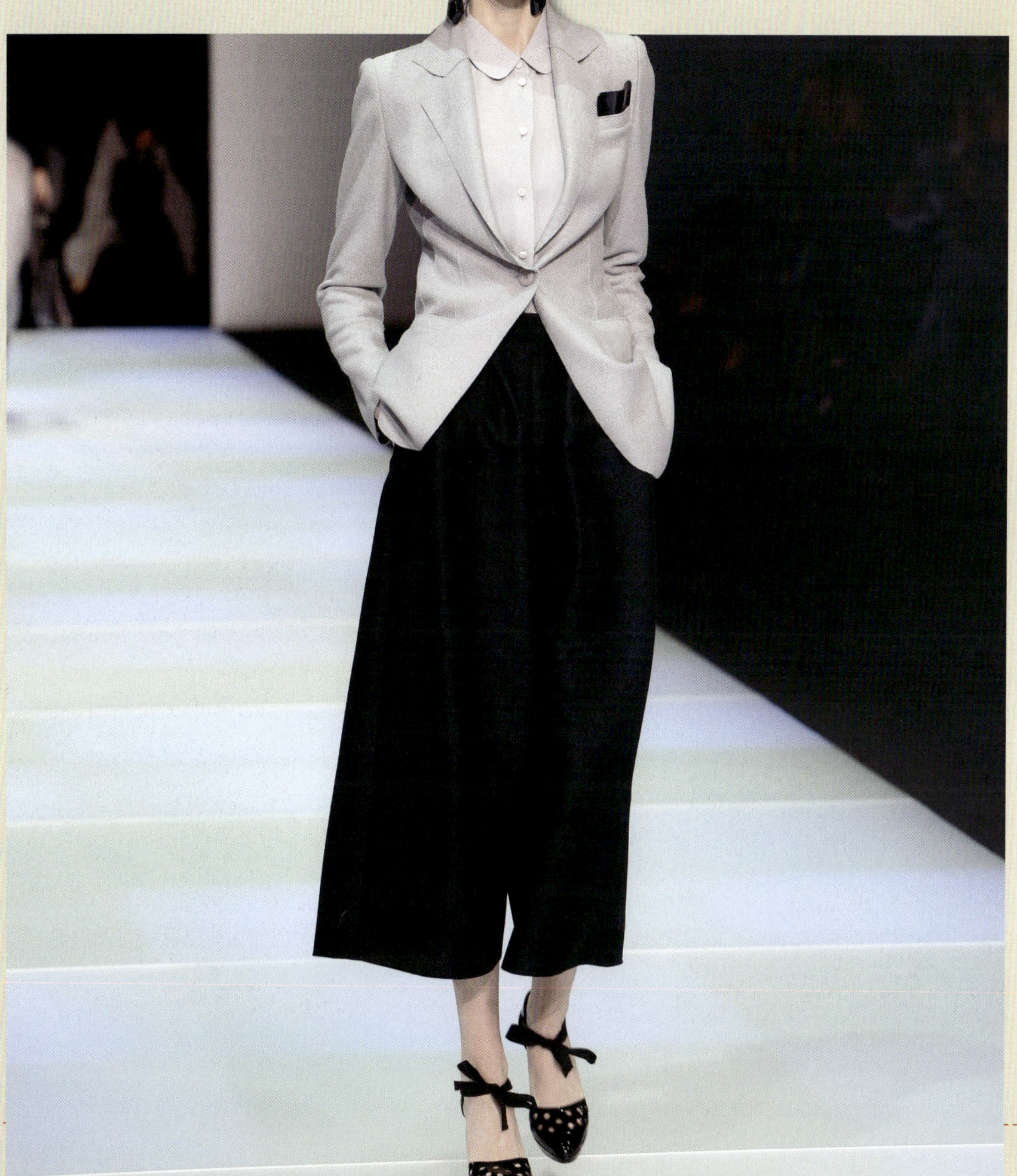

ARMANI LA PRIMA HANDBAG

A classic, structured handbag with a minimalist design, inspired by a 1995 archival piece, making it a staple in Armani's accessory collection.

SOFTLY DRAPED DRESSES

Whether knee-length or maxi, Armani dresses are known for their elegant draping, luxurious fabrics and neutral colour palettes.

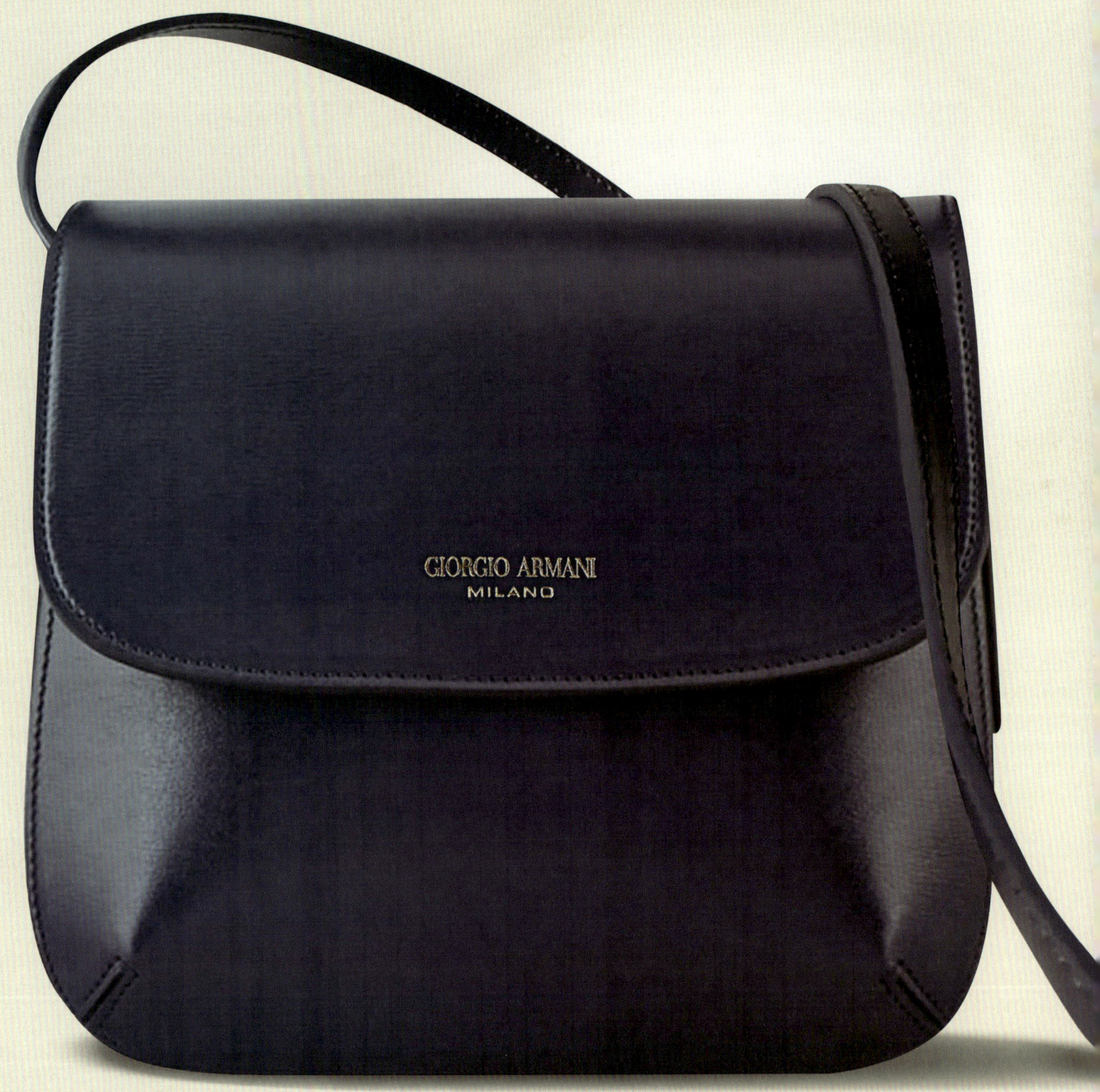

OPP PAGE: Anne Hathaway in a Giorgio Armani dress at the 75th Cannes Film Festival, 19 May, 2022

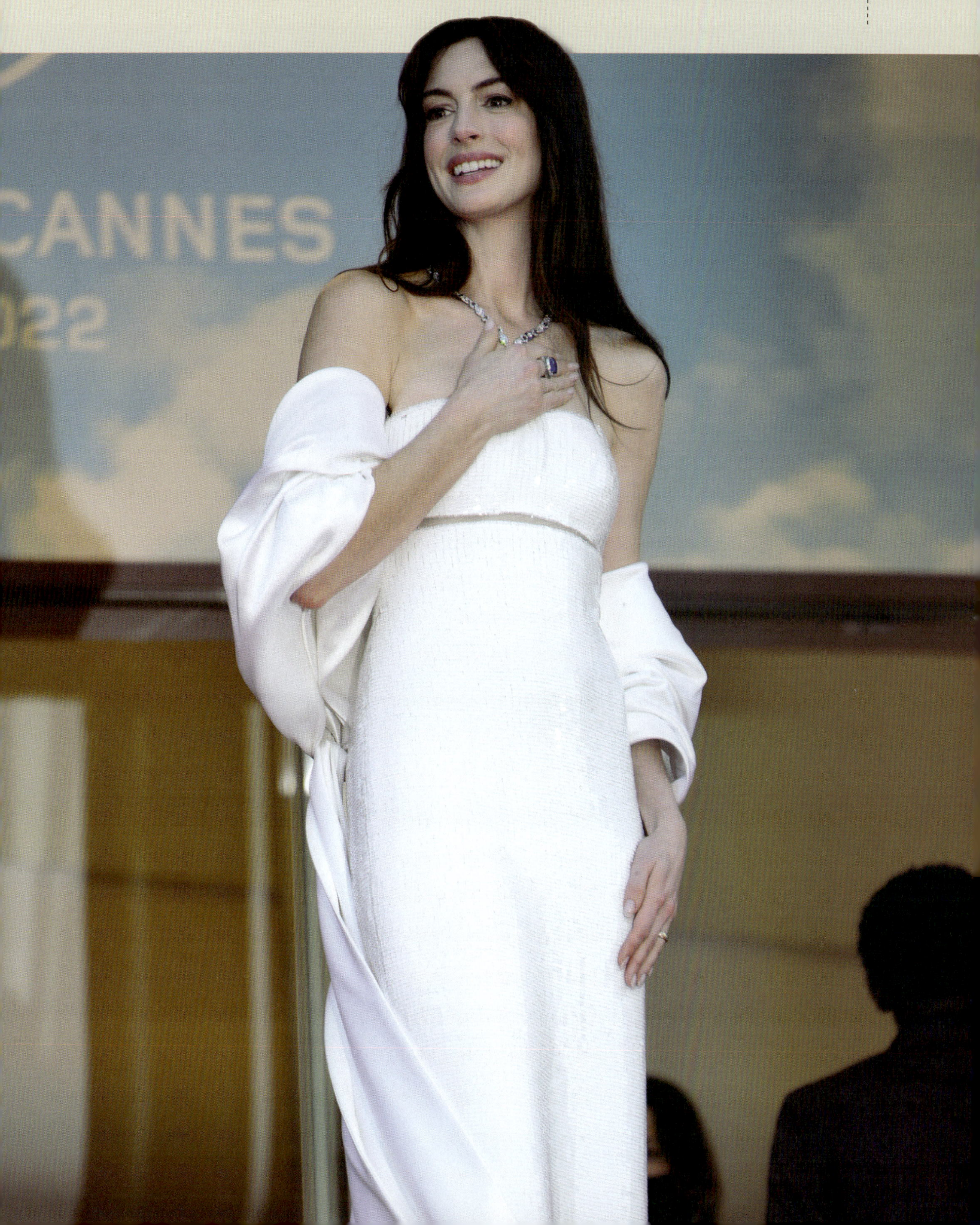
CANNES
022

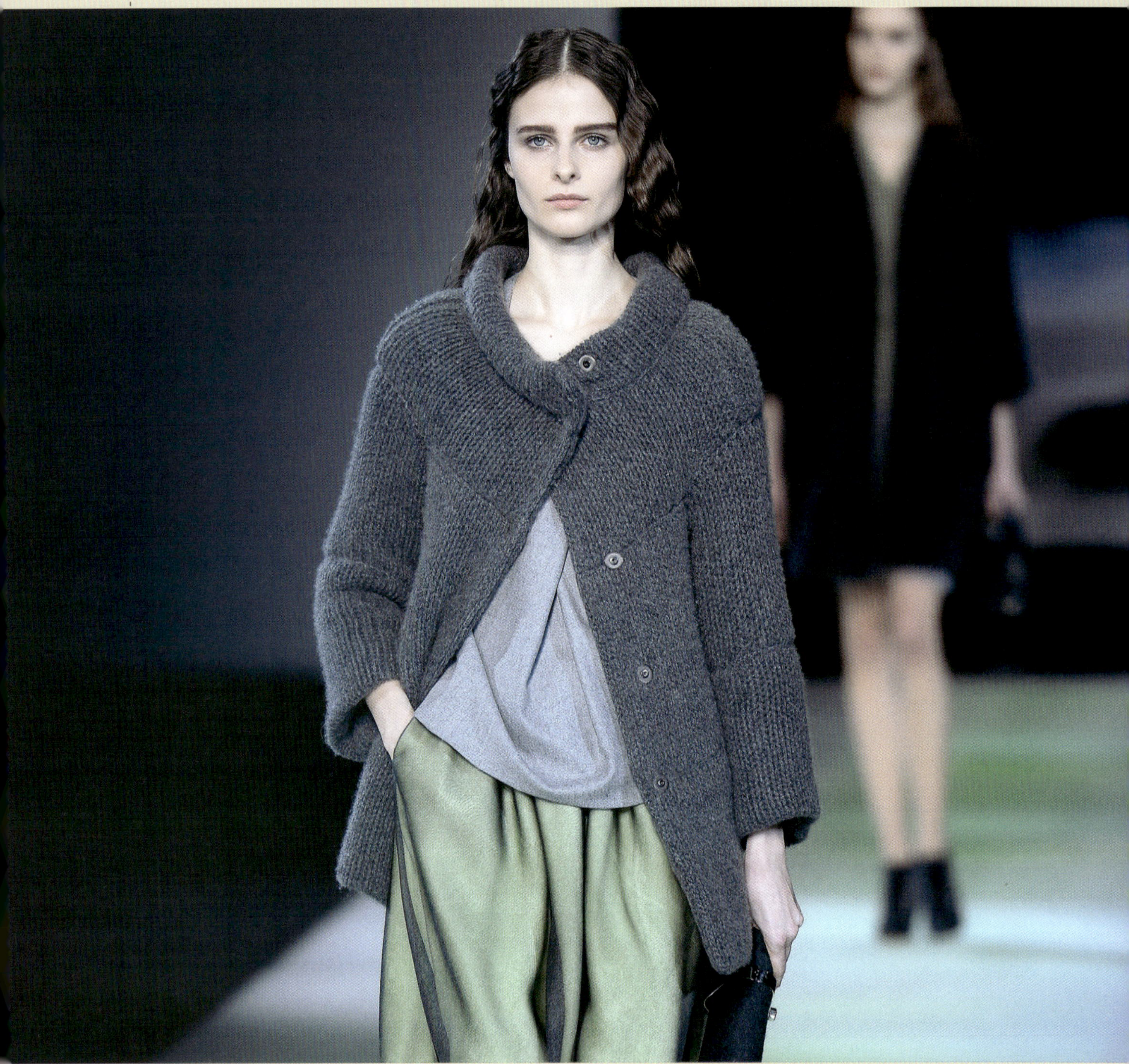

ELEGANT KNITWEAR

Sleek and sophisticated, Armani's knitwear often features asymmetrical cuts, fine cashmere, or silk blends—perfect for layering with tailored pieces.

ABOVE: Giorgio Armani Womenswear Autumn/Winter 2014 show at Milan Fashion Week

OPP PAGE: Giorgio Armani Autumn/Winter 2016 show at Milan Fashion Week

CLASSIC EVENING JACKETS

Armani is renowned for his opulent yet subtle evening jackets, featuring intricate beading, embroidery or velvet textures, adding a refined glamour to formal ensembles.

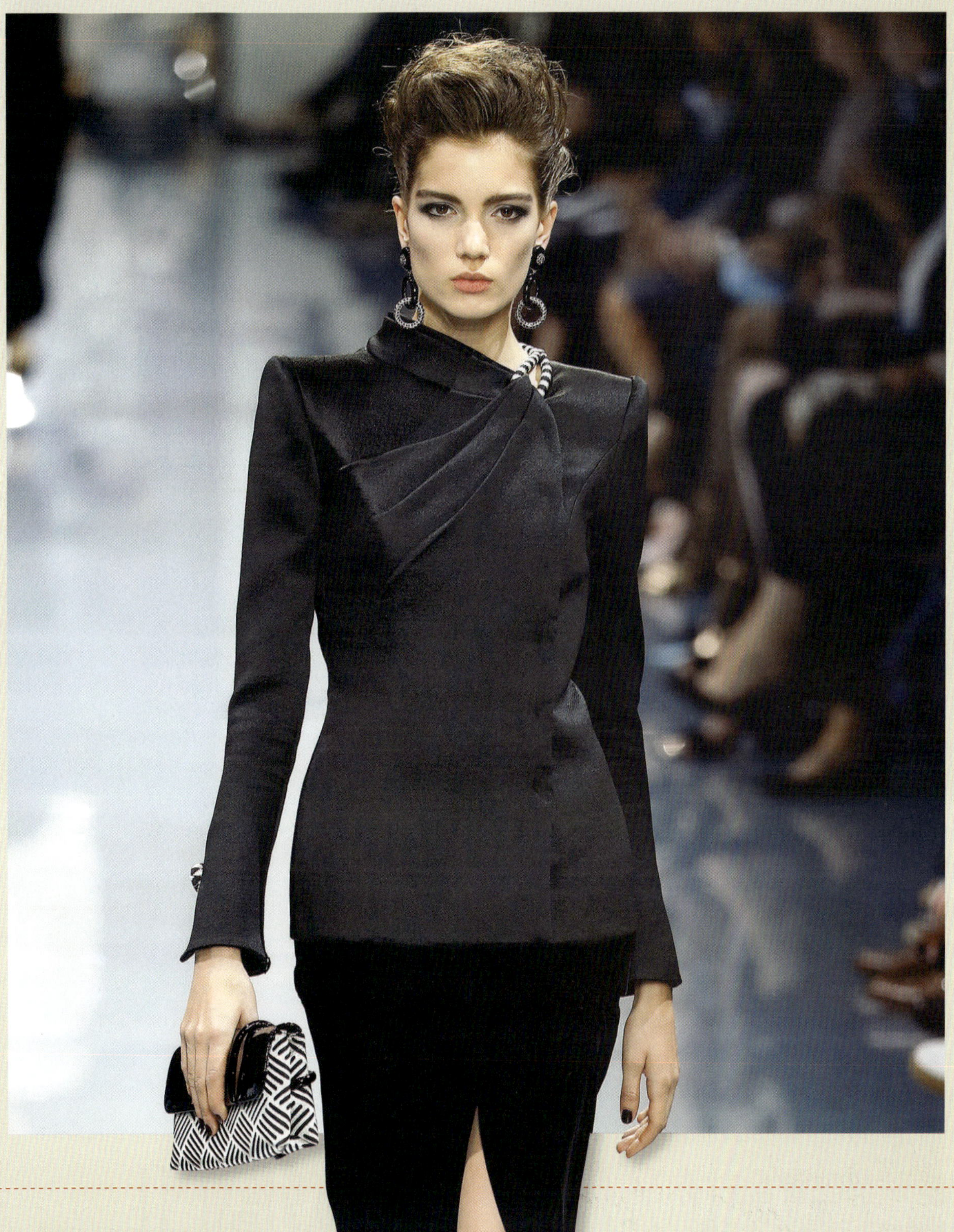

SUNGLASSES

From oversized and retro-inspired styles to cat-eye
and aviator designs for everyday glamour.

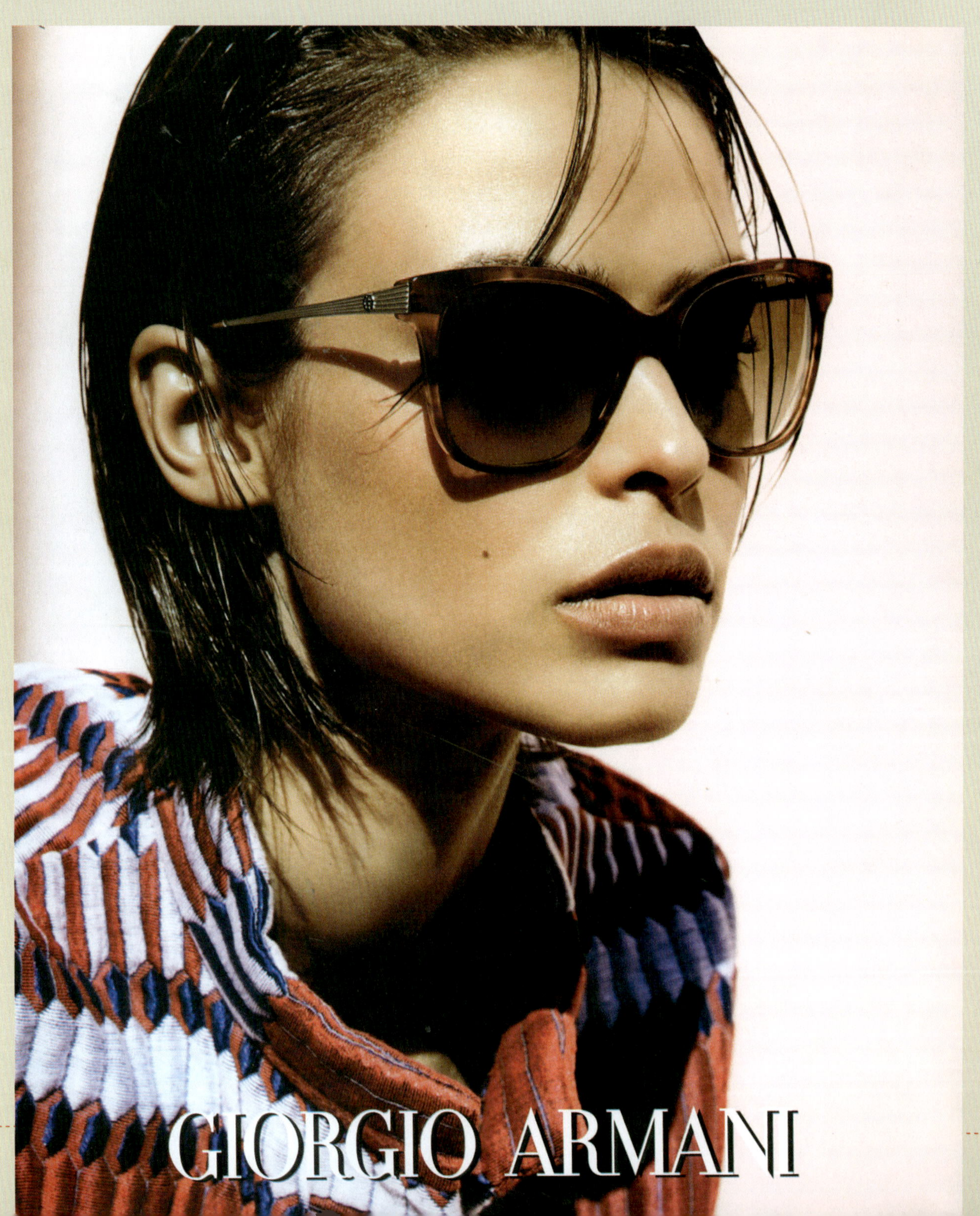

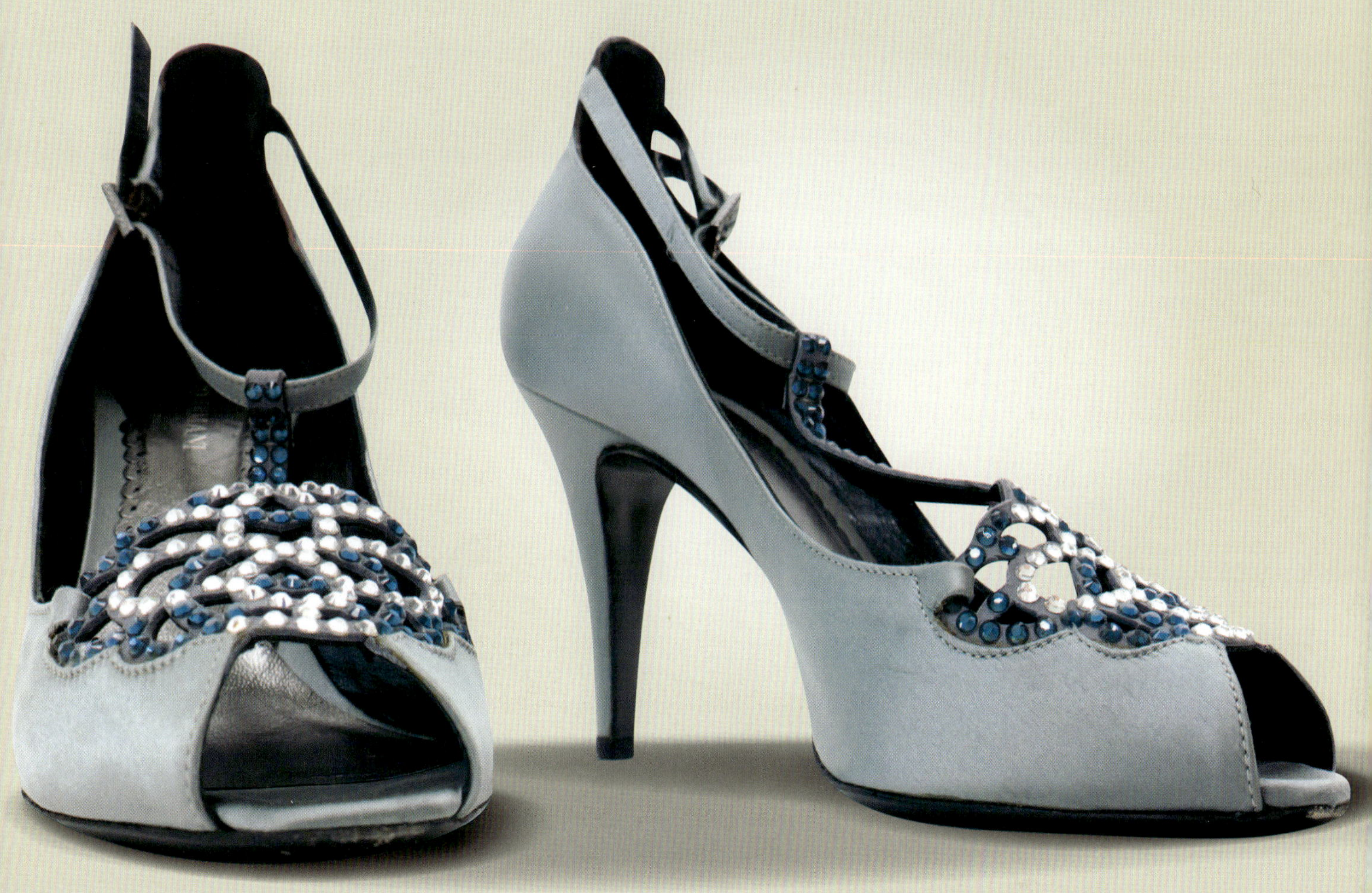

SHOES

While Giorgio Armani is best known for tailoring, his footwear collections also feature timeless styles that complement his clothing lines. Iconic Armani women's shoe styles include classic pointed-toe high heels, slingback heels, glamorous strappy sandals, comfortable yet stylish loafers and moccasins, sophisticatedly simple ballet flats, sexy kitten heels, stylish ankle boots and summer-perfect espadrilles.

From wardrobe essentials to signature scents, Armani has given women a complete lifestyle brand that represents modern luxury, understated glamour and effortless confidence. From the corporate world to the red-carpet, from streetwear to luxury living, Armani has mastered the art of dressing women for every stage of life. The Armani woman is confident, stylish and effortlessly chic—and thanks to Giorgio Armani, she will always be remembered rather than just noticed.

OPP PAGE: Giorgio Armani Eyewear Campaign in UK Magazine

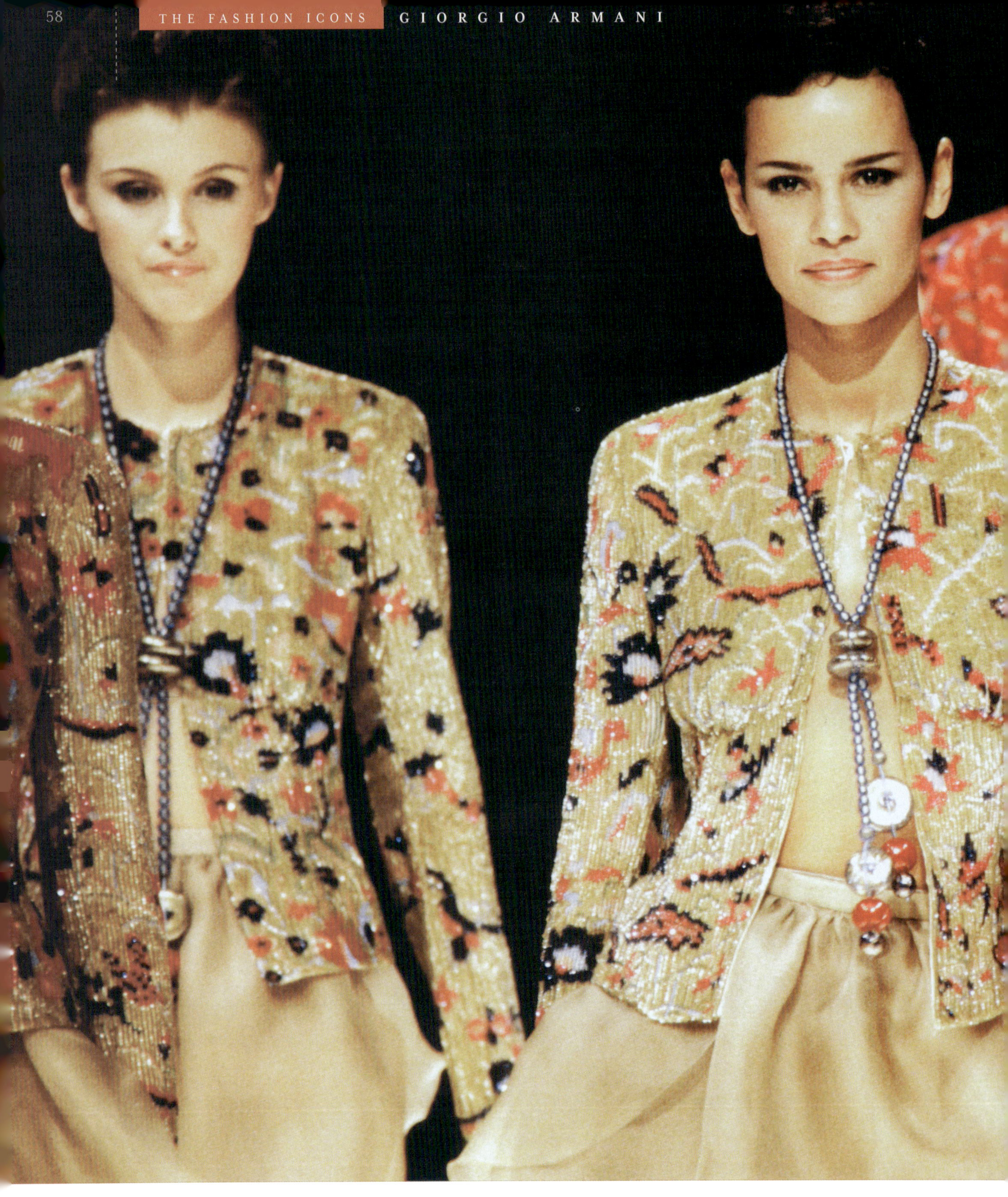

ABOVE: Models Trish Goff and Nadege du Bospertus at the Giorgio Armani Spring 1995 Ready-to-Wear Runway Show

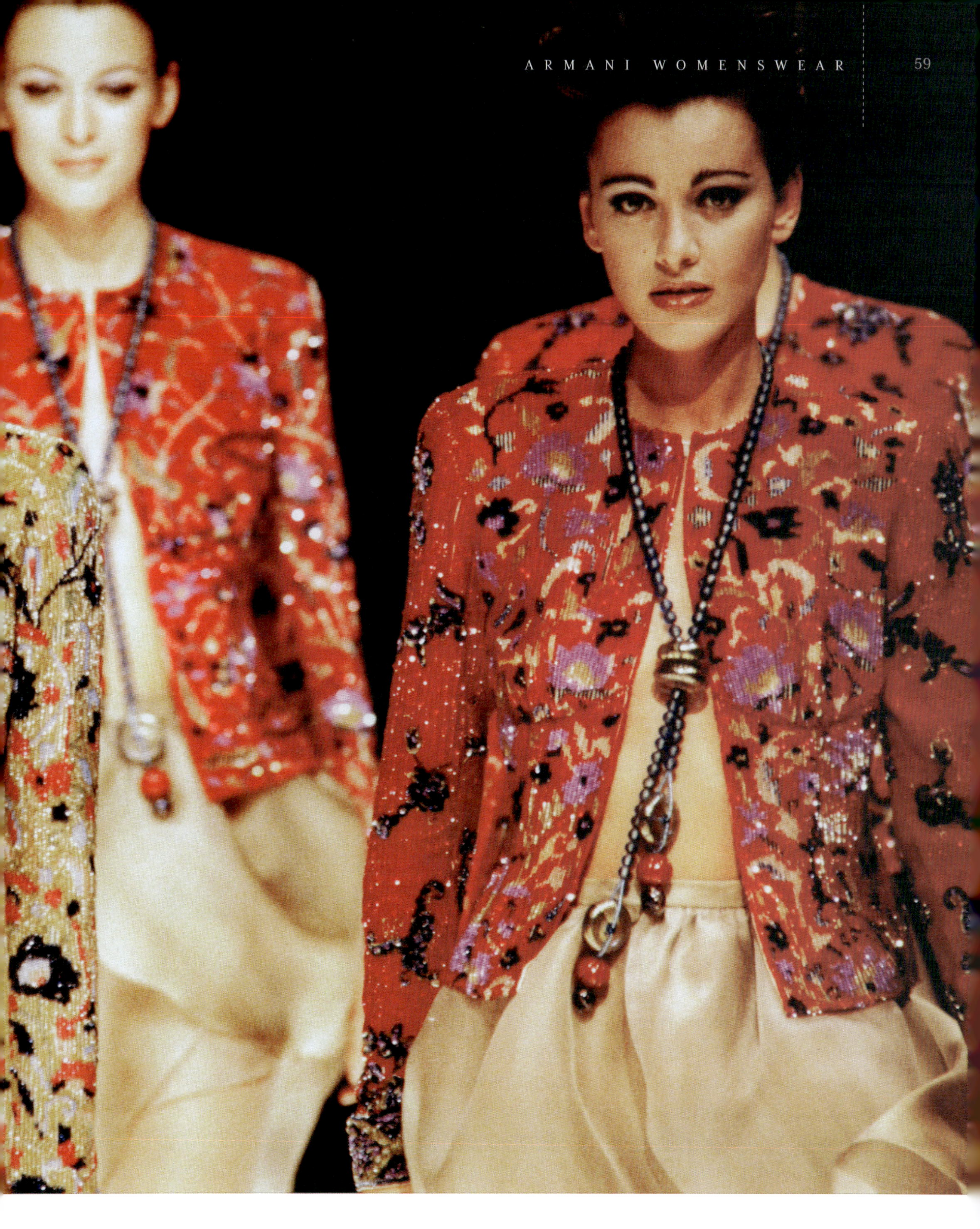

EMPORIO ARMANI

"Everyone is welcome"
Giorgio Armani

In 1981 Giorgio Armani launched Emporio Armani as a more accessible and youthful offshoot of the Armani brand. Focusing on urban and trend-focused fashion, the aim was to reach a younger, wider demographic. It would be a brand that embraced a contemporary aesthetic while maintaining the core sophistication of Armani and offer a more affordable alternative to the original high-end label. A wider clientele would engage with the Armani brand without compromising on quality or style.

The name 'Emporio' (Italian for 'emporium') reflected—and still reflects—the brand's inclusive spirit and its aim to serve as a marketplace for diverse lifestyles. From clothing to accessories, eyewear, watches, and fragrances, Emporio Armani offers a complete lifestyle experience—blending high fashion with everyday practicality. Its aesthetic is characterised by its ability to seamlessly merge elegance with functionality. The brand is celebrated for its sleek silhouettes, monochromatic palettes and subtle logo-centric designs. Pieces often feature the

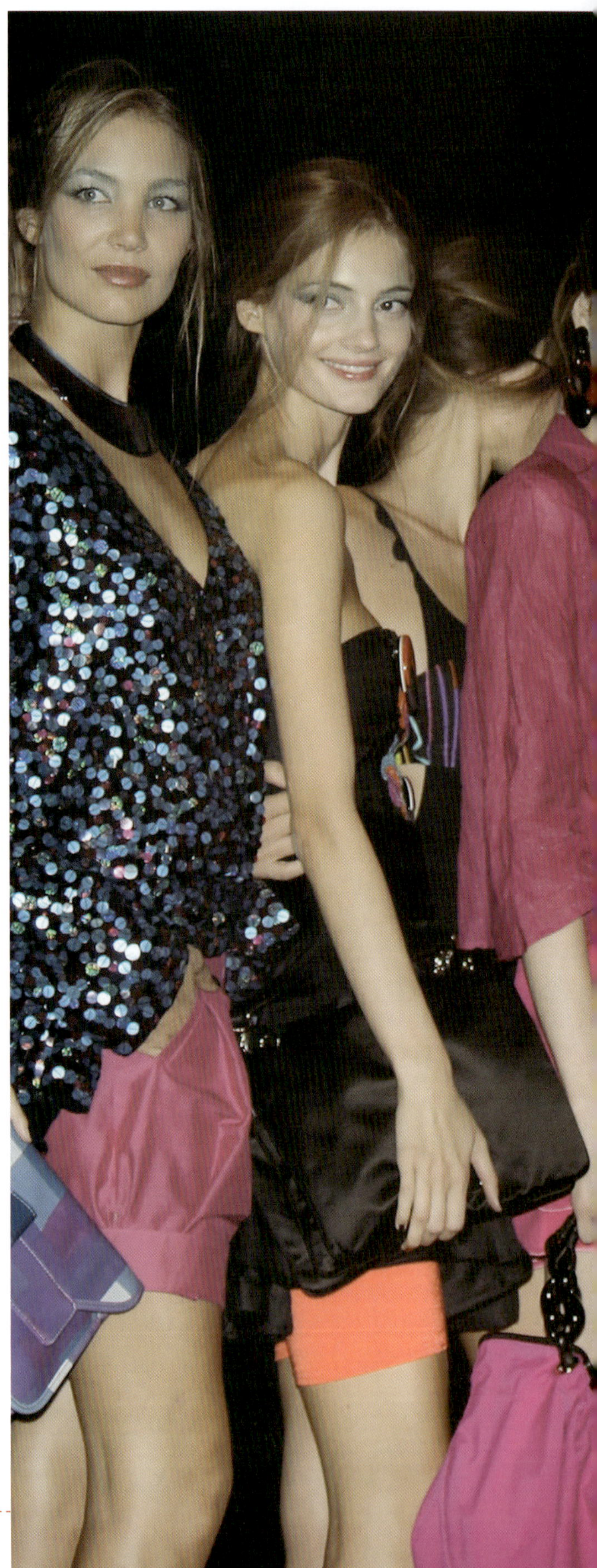

RIGHT: Giorgio Armani posing for the audience following the Emporio Armani Spring/Summer Womenswear show at Milan Fashion Week, 2010

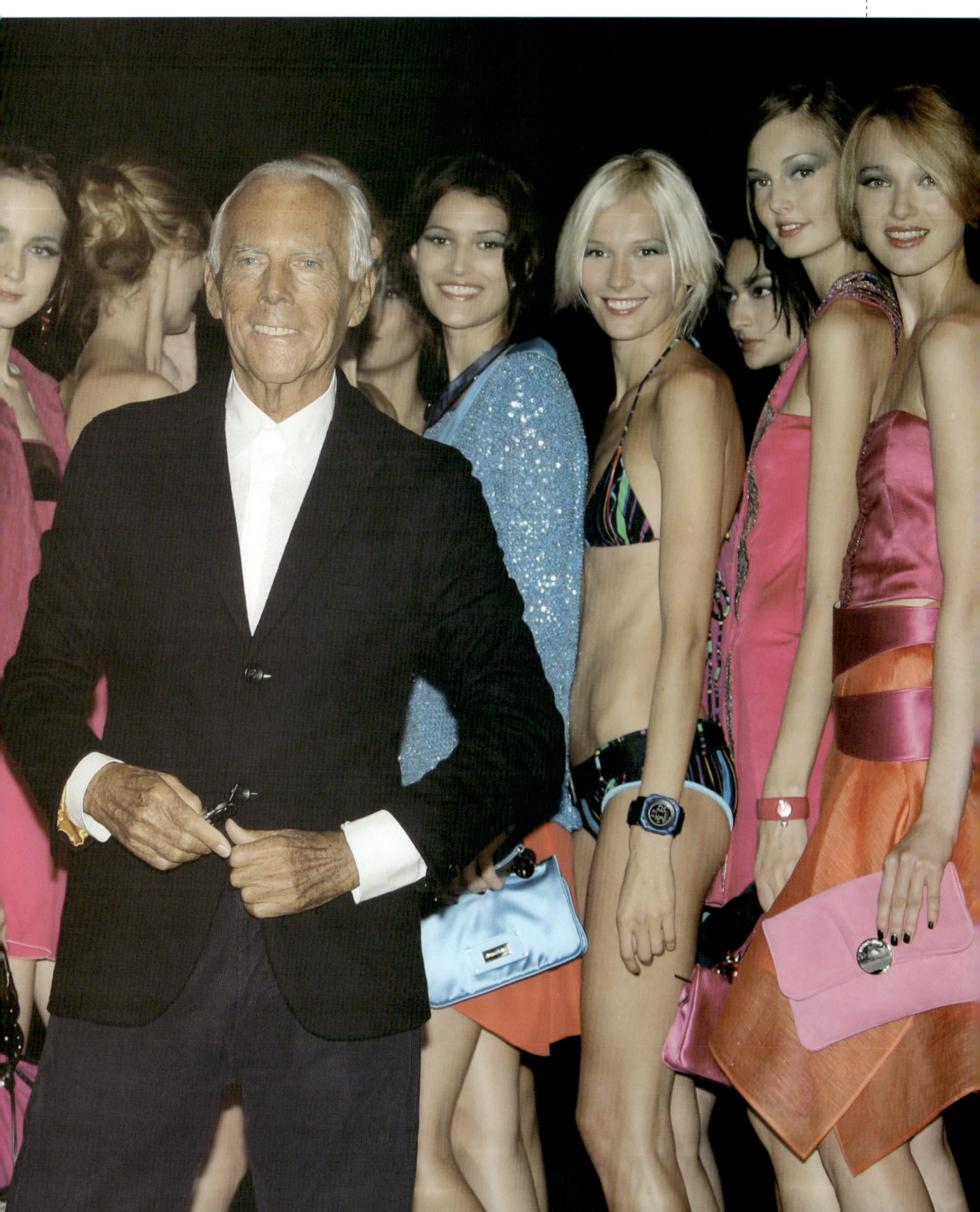

iconic eagle emblem, a symbol of freedom and aspiration that resonates with the brand's youthful ethos. Unlike the more formal and minimalist Giorgio Armani women and menswear lines, Emporio Armani is playful, fun and experimental. EA incorporates bold colours, contemporary cuts and innovative fabrics, making it a favourite among style innovators and celebrities. From tailored blazers and casual denim to sporty athleisure and evening wear, the brand caters to a broad spectrum of style requirements— thus ensuring its relevance in the lexicon of high yet accessible fashion.

The label has successfully carved out a global presence with flagship stores in major cities such as Milan, Tokyo, New York, and Dubai. These stores are not just retail spaces but designed to immerse customers in the Armani lifestyle. The brand's campaigns, often featuring top models and photographers, reinforce its status as a leader in contemporary fashion. One of the brand's most notable achievements was the Emporio Armani magazine, launched in the early 1980s. This publication was a pioneering effort to connect with the fashion-savvy audience and served as a platform for showcasing the brand's ethos. The magazine's sleek design and editorial content mirrored the aesthetic of Emporio Armani, further solidifying its cultural impact. The magazine ran until 1998. In 2017, it returned with a new issue celebrating the label and its achievements, and on the occasion of the 40th anniversary of Emporio Armani in 2021, Rosanna

Armani edited a collector's edition of the iconic magazine, '*THE WAY WE ARE*'.

Emporio Armani has long been associated with pop culture. The brand's sporty yet refined designs have made it a staple among athlete and musicians, models and actors. Celebrities like Cristiano Ronaldo, Rihanna and Megan Fox have been signed up either as campaign faces or red-carpet ambassadors. The line's focus on accessible luxury also resonates with younger audiences, who appreciate its balance of style and practicality. Emporio Armani's watches and fragrances, in particular, have become gateways for those desiring to become part of the EA world.

Wearing Emporio Armani is about more than just fashion—it's about embodying a lifestyle that embodies confidence, individuality and elegance. The brand's diverse offerings ensure that there is something for everyone, whether that be a tailored suit for a business meeting, a chic dress for an evening out, or comfortable leisure wear for a casual day relaxing. Emporio Armani's fashion shows, often presented in vibrant and youthful settings, capture the brand's spirit. These events celebrate the coming together of tradition and modernity, showcasing collections that are both innovative and timeless. Emporio Armani stands as a testament to Giorgio Armani's ability to adapt and innovate within the ever-changing landscape of fashion. By offering a blend of sophistication and accessibility, the brand has redefined modern luxury. It continues to inspire and empower individuals to express

OPP PAGE: A vibrant look from the Emporio Armani Autumn/Winter 2017–18 show during Milan Fashion Week, 2017

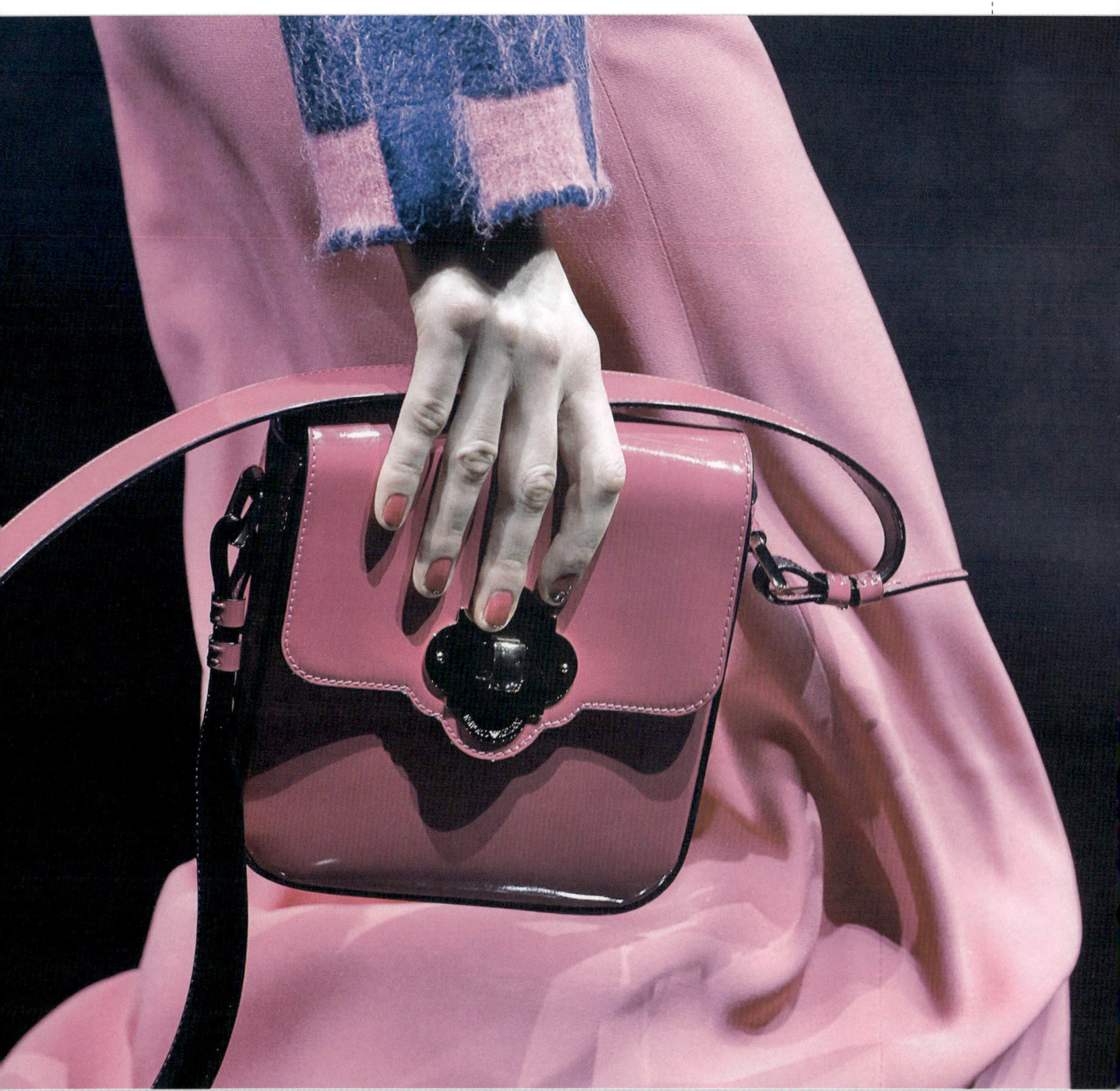

themselves through style, making it an enduring force in the global fashion arena. With its finger on the pulse of contemporary trends and a steadfast commitment to quality, Emporio Armani remains a beloved icon of versatile elegance while also producing enduring fashion investments.

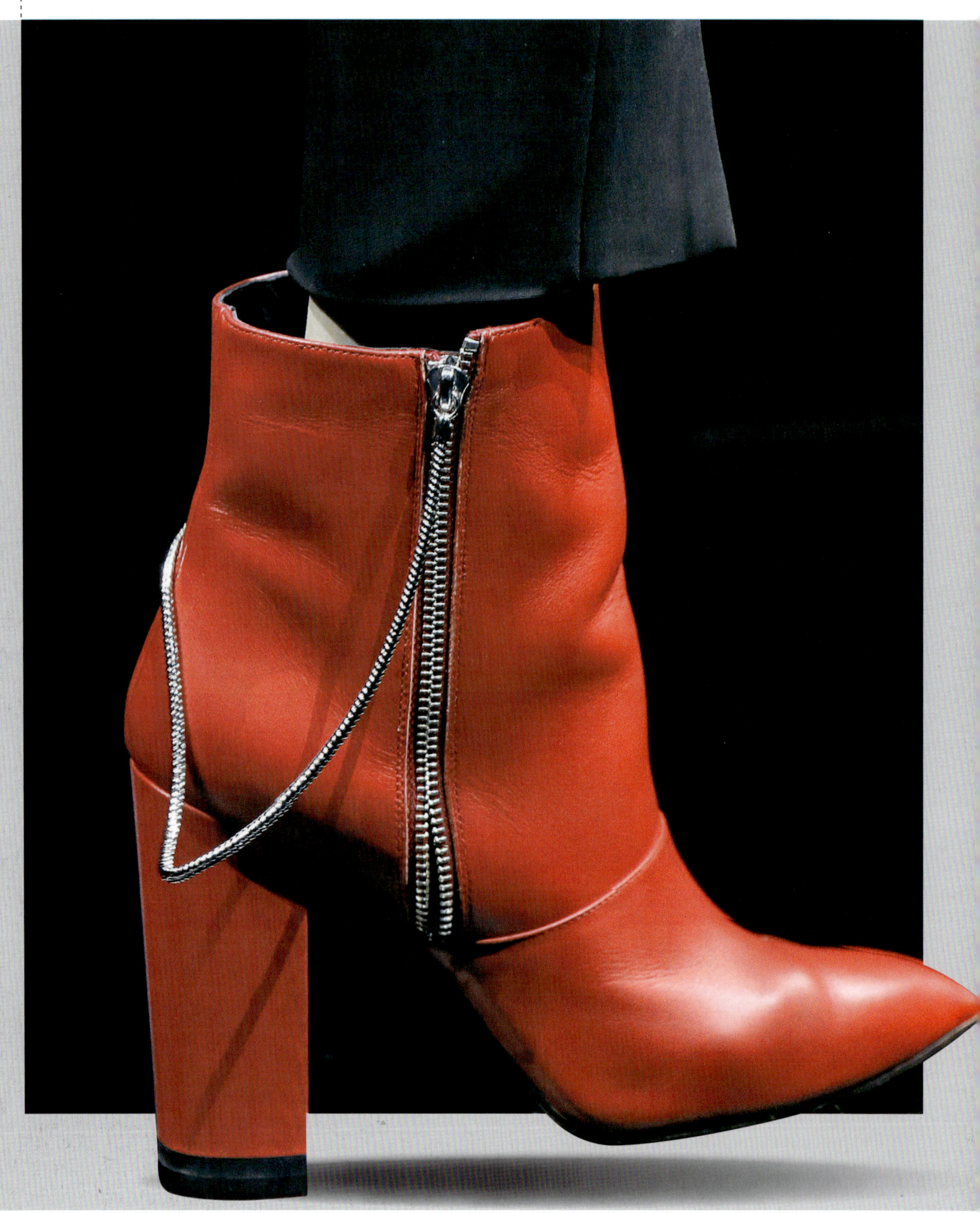

ABOVE: Boots on the runway at the Emporio Armani Autumn/Winter 2017-18 show during Milan Fashion Week, 2017

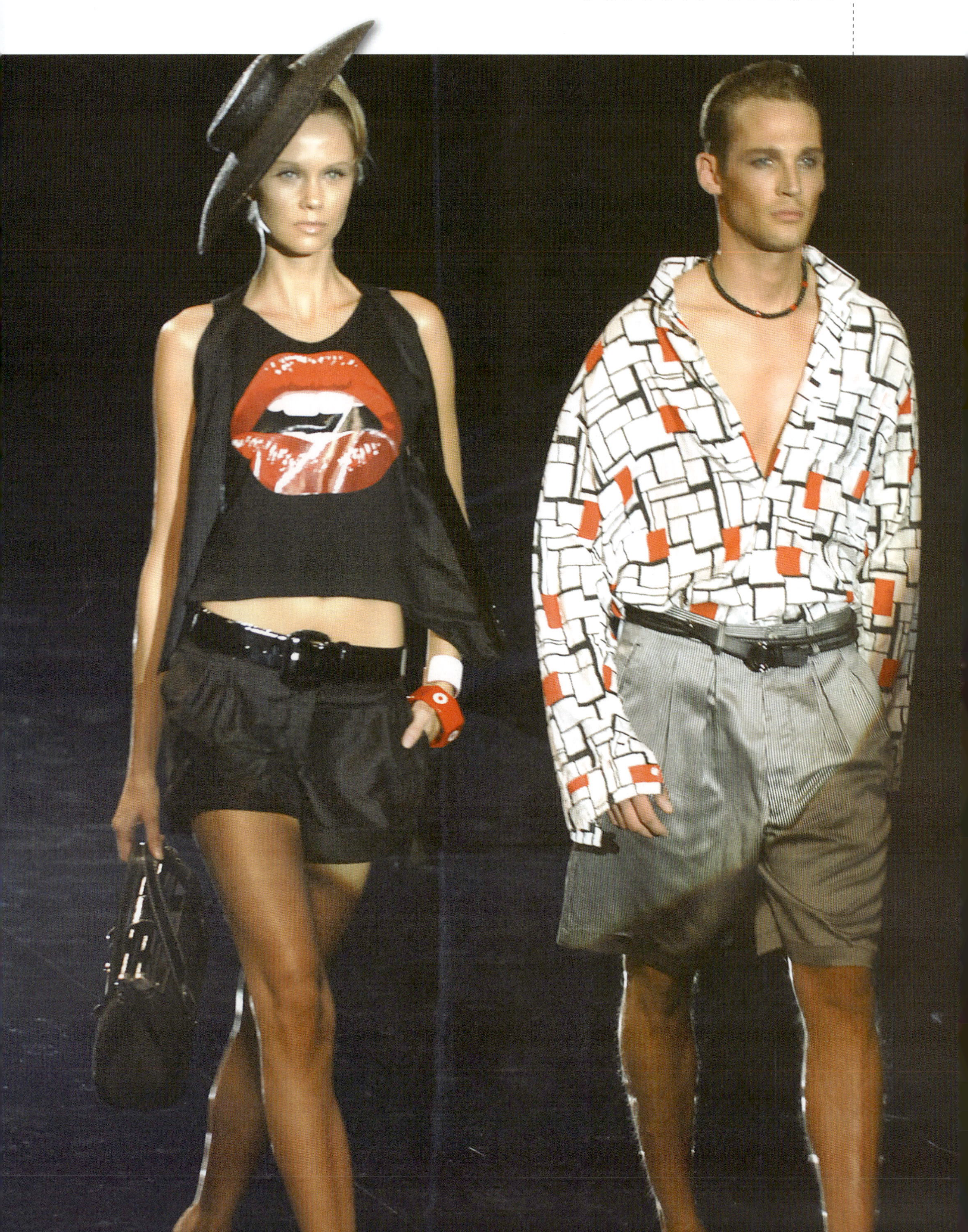

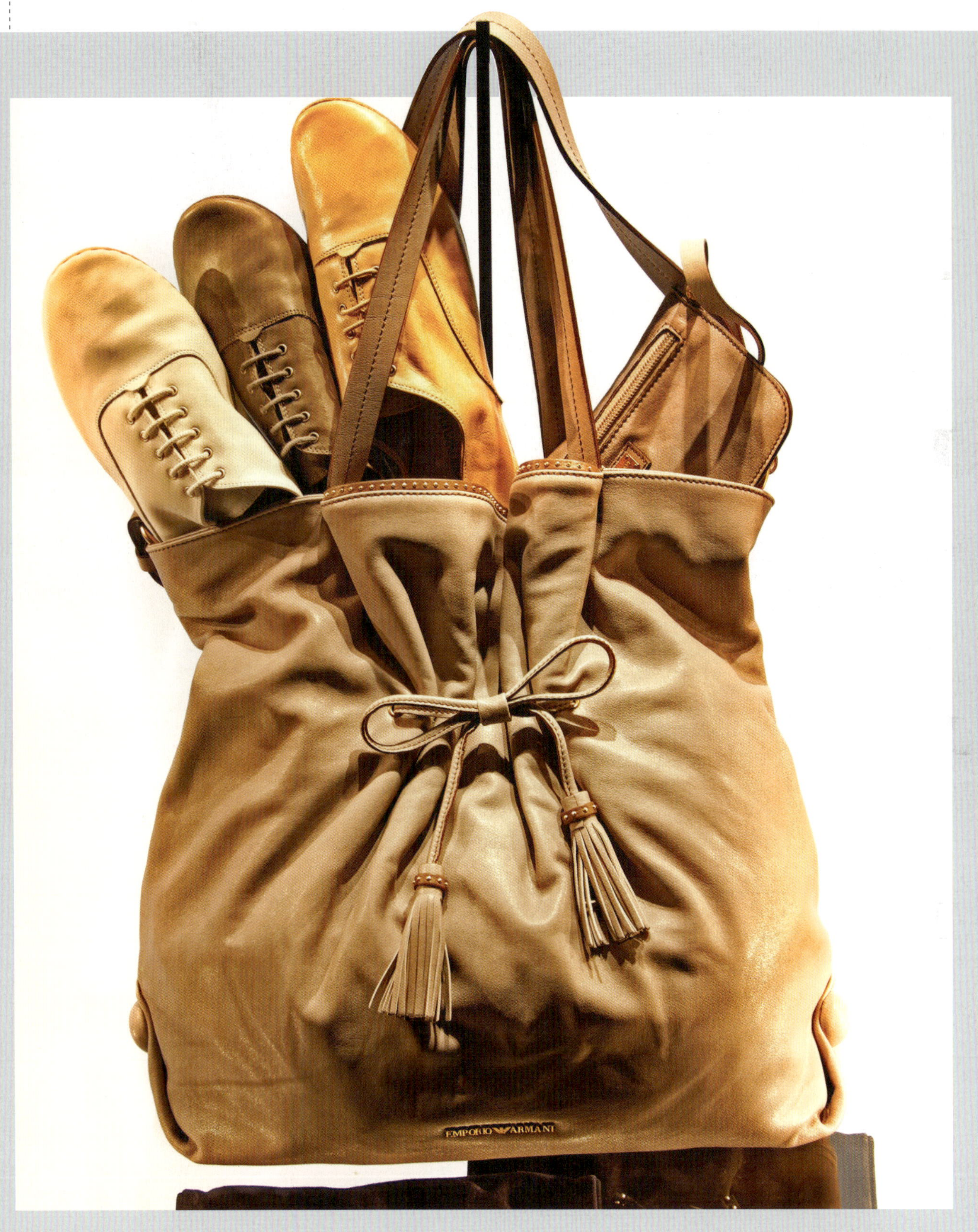

ABOBE: A window in the Emporio Armani store on Rue du Faubourg Saint-Honoré, Paris, 2012

OPP PAGE: Outfit from the Emporio Armani Autumn/ Winter 2025-26 show during Milan Fashion Week, 2025

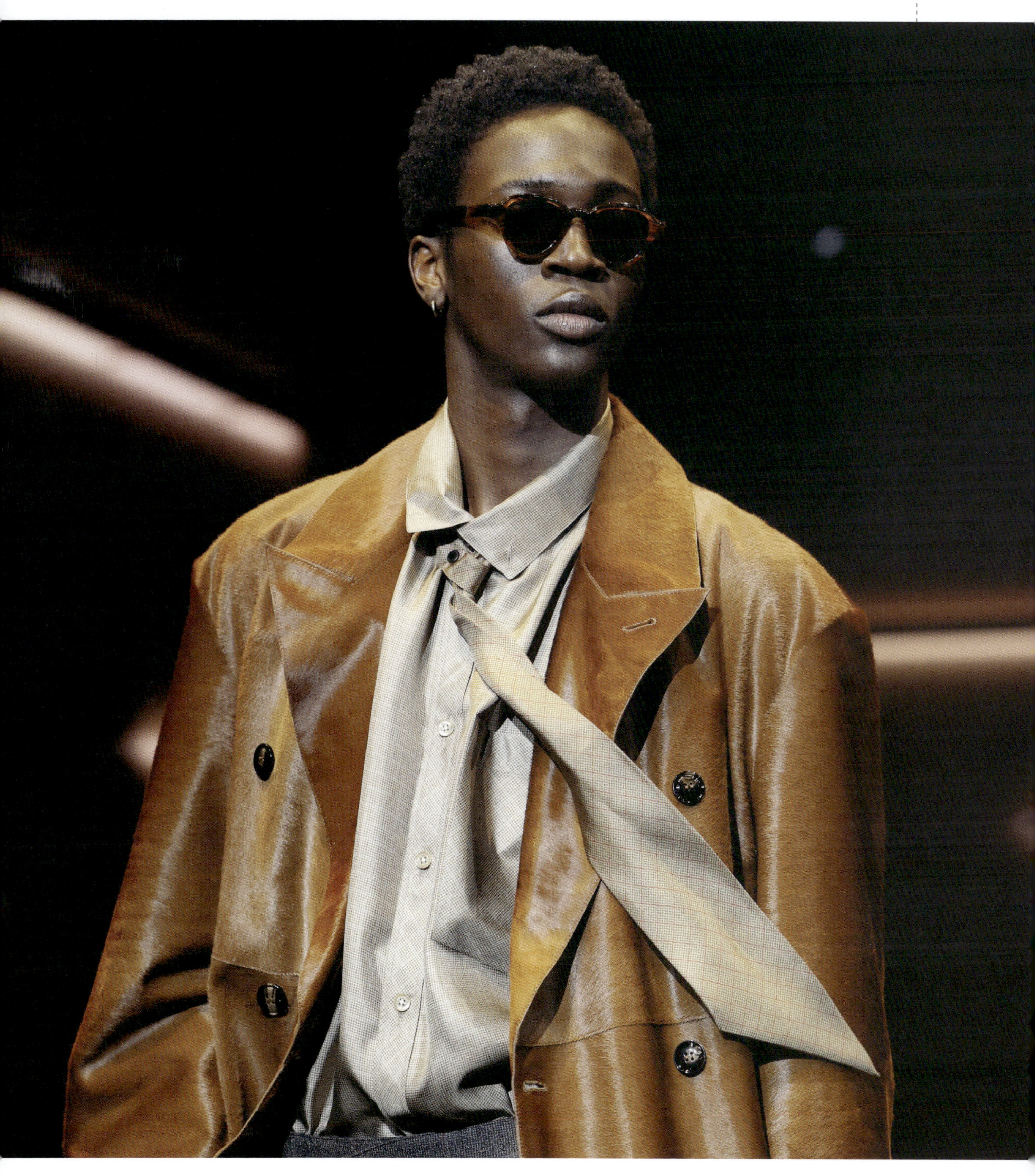

EMPORIO ARMANI CLASSICS

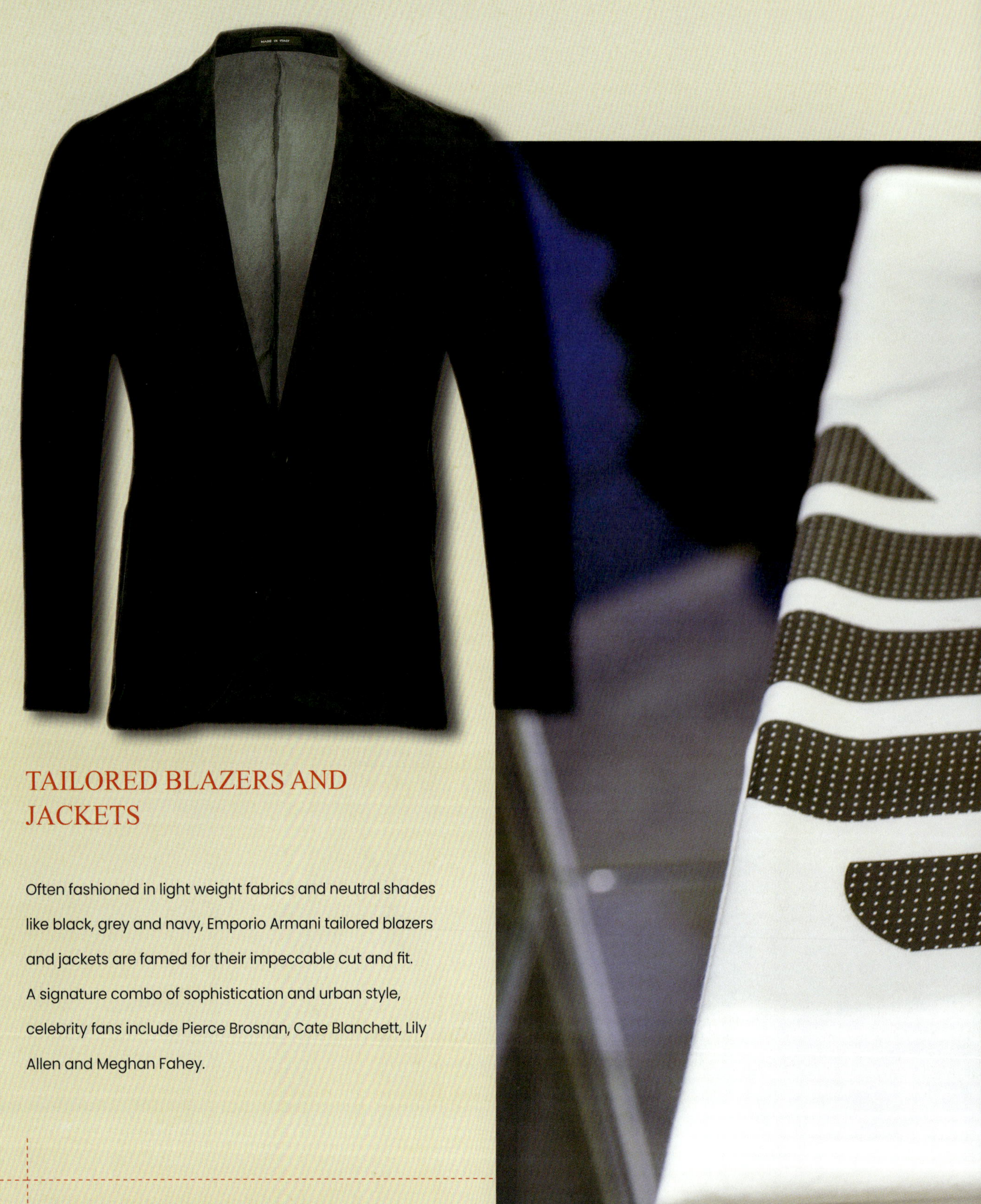

TAILORED BLAZERS AND JACKETS

Often fashioned in light weight fabrics and neutral shades like black, grey and navy, Emporio Armani tailored blazers and jackets are famed for their impeccable cut and fit. A signature combo of sophistication and urban style, celebrity fans include Pierce Brosnan, Cate Blanchett, Lily Allen and Meghan Fahey.

LOGO T-SHIRTS

The classic Emporio Armani 'Eagle' emblem features prominently on the brand's iconic T-shirts which blend luxury appeal with casual everyday wearability. Christiano Ronaldo is one of the many celebs who rocks an EA logo T-shirt.

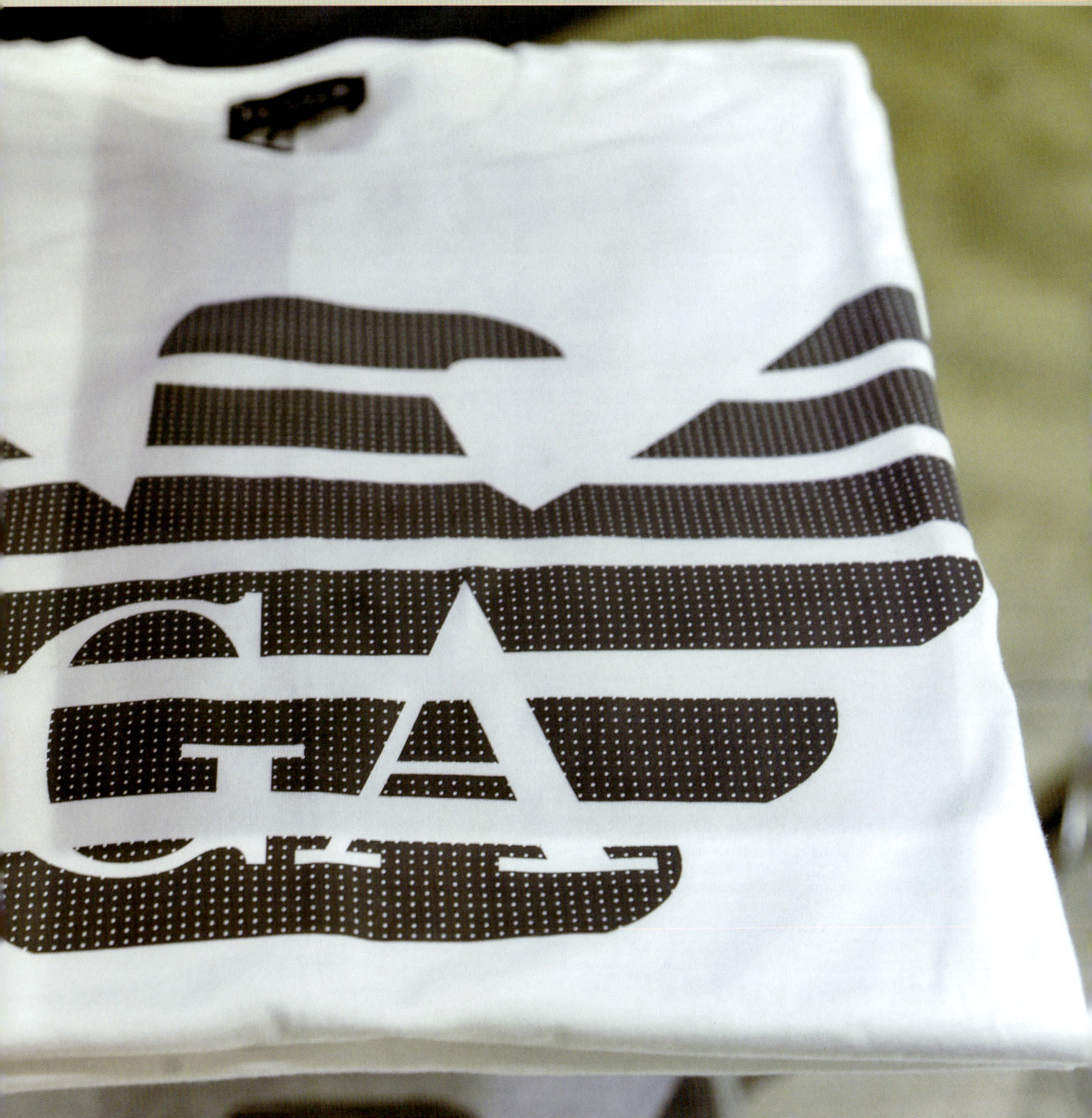

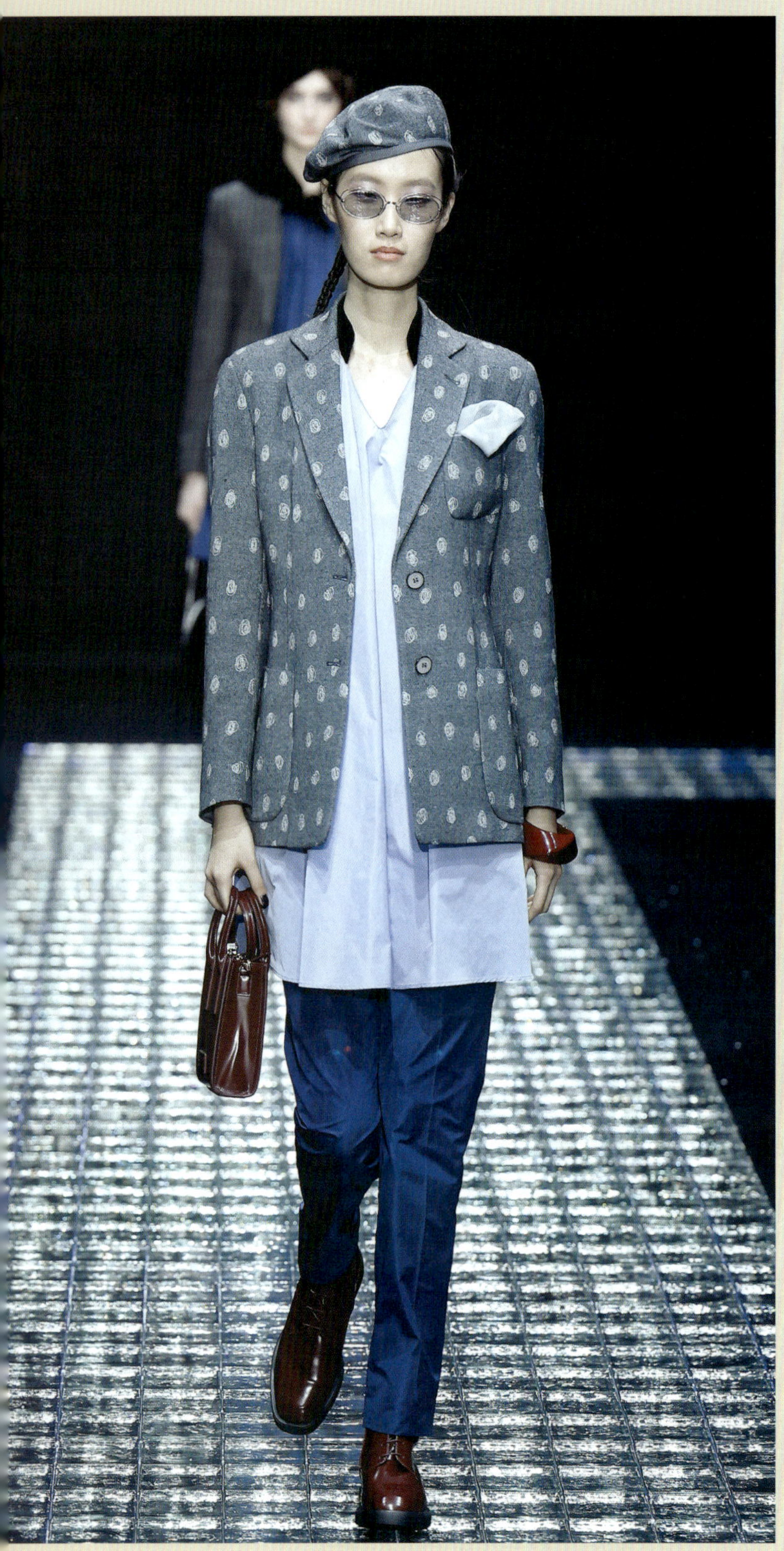

ABOVE: Emporio Armani Womenswear Autumn/Winter 2024-25 runway show during Milan Fashion Week, 2024

SLIM-FIT TROUSERS

Perfect for both formal and casual occasions, EA's classic slim-fit trousers and chinos—often designed with clean lines and fashioned in luxurious fabrics—are a brand staple. Emporio Armani's slim-fit trousers are a must-have in many a celebrity wardrobe, and are appreciated for their tailored elegance and on-trend appeal. In October 2024, Pamela Anderson showcased a chic velvet look at Giorgio Armani's star-studded show in New York, pairing a geometric sequined jacket with slim-fit velvet trousers.

EMPORIO ARMANI WATCHES

The brand's watches are a symbol of accessible luxury blending clean, modern design with precise craftsmanship. Typically, they feature minimalist dials, leather straps, or stainless steel bracelets, often emblazoned with the iconic eagle logo. Celebrity wearers include Calvin Harris, David Beckham and Shawn Mendes.

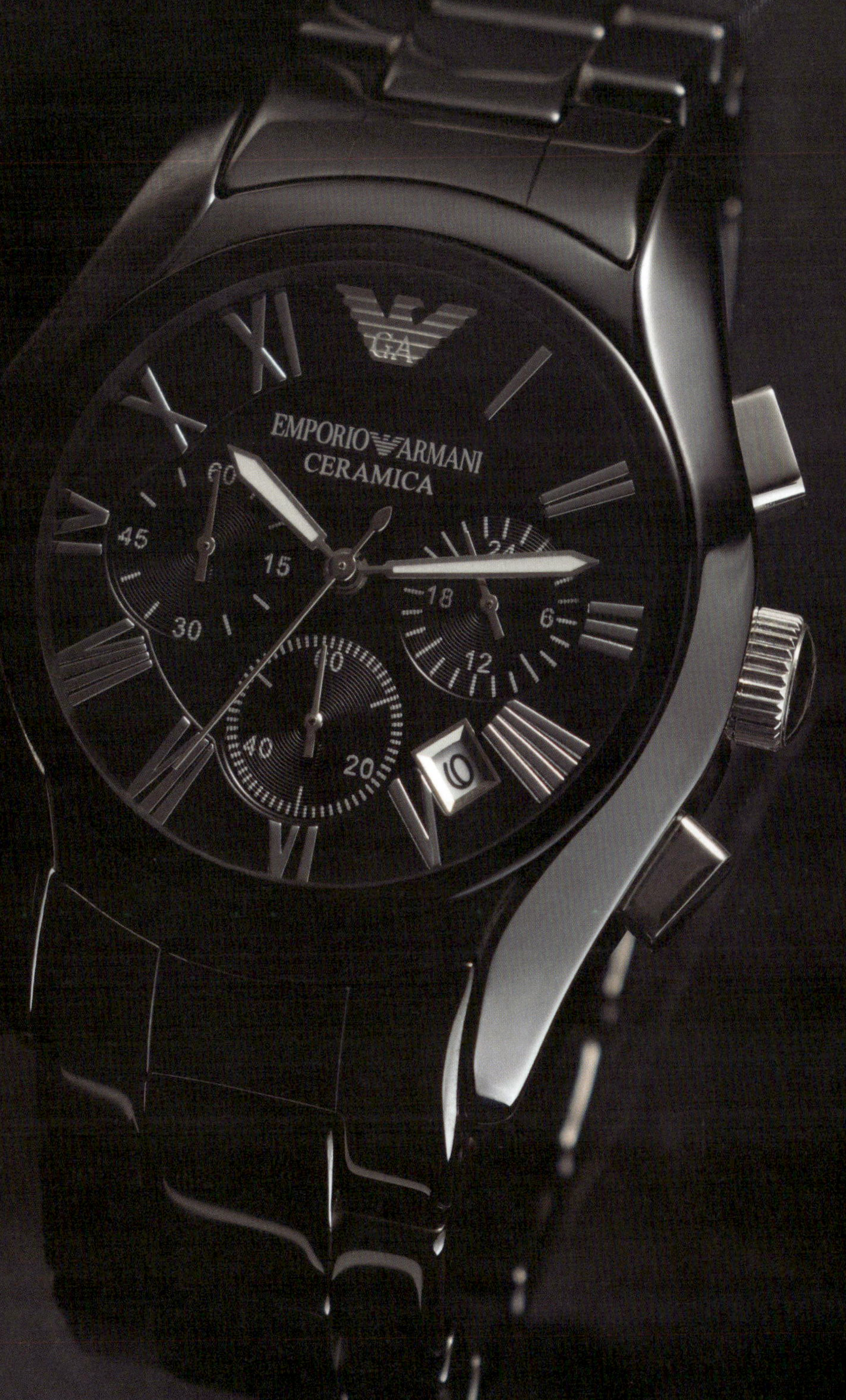
GA
EMPORIO ARMANI
CERAMICA

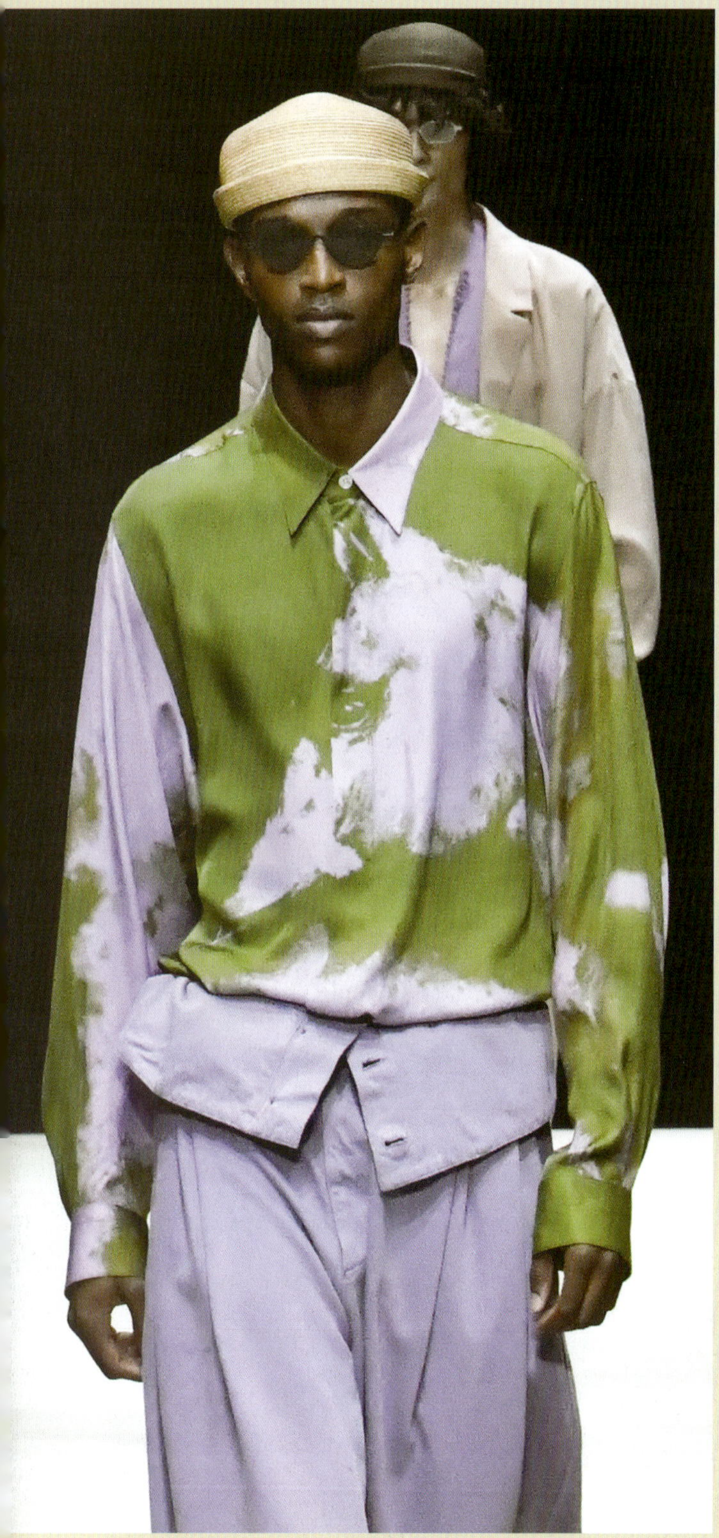

SILK AND SATIN SHIRTS

In muted prints and monochrome palettes, these button-up shirts in soft, flowing fabrics like silk or satin are a hallmark of the brand, reflecting a refined yet relaxed vibe. Favoured by A-listers such as actress Nina Dobrev.

LEATHER JACKETS

Timeless wardrobe pieces and the epitome of cool, Emporio Armani leather jackets, often in bomber or motor-inspired styles, are iconic for their understated elegance and high-quality craftsmanship. Robbie Williams, Trey Songz and Alexander Skarsgård have been pictured wearing one.

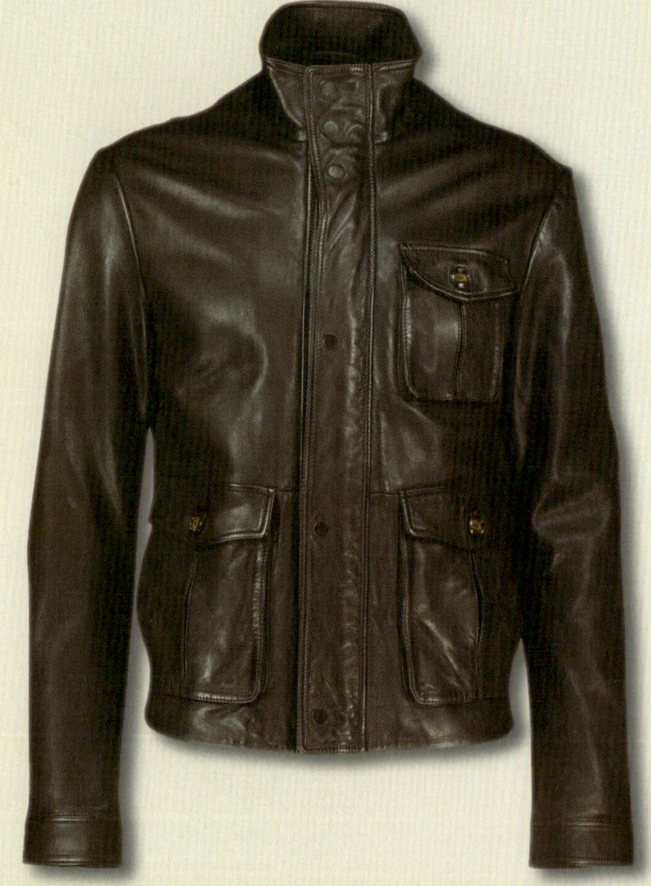

ABOVE: Emporio Armani Spring/Summer collection, Milan Fashion Week 2025
OPP PAGE: Pamela Anderson at the Emporio Armani Women's Spring 2025 fashion show in New York City, 2024

OUTERWEAR

Trench coats, pea coats, and puffers are classic Emporio Armani with their clean designs and modernist fabric. When football manager Mikel Arteta appeared at a game wearing four different jackets during the same one game in December 2019, fashionistas identified some of these outerwear items as being from the Emporio Armani menswear collection. Actress and activist Pamela Anderson attended the EA Women's Spring 2025 fashion show in New York City in October 2024 wearing an EA satin patterned jacket.

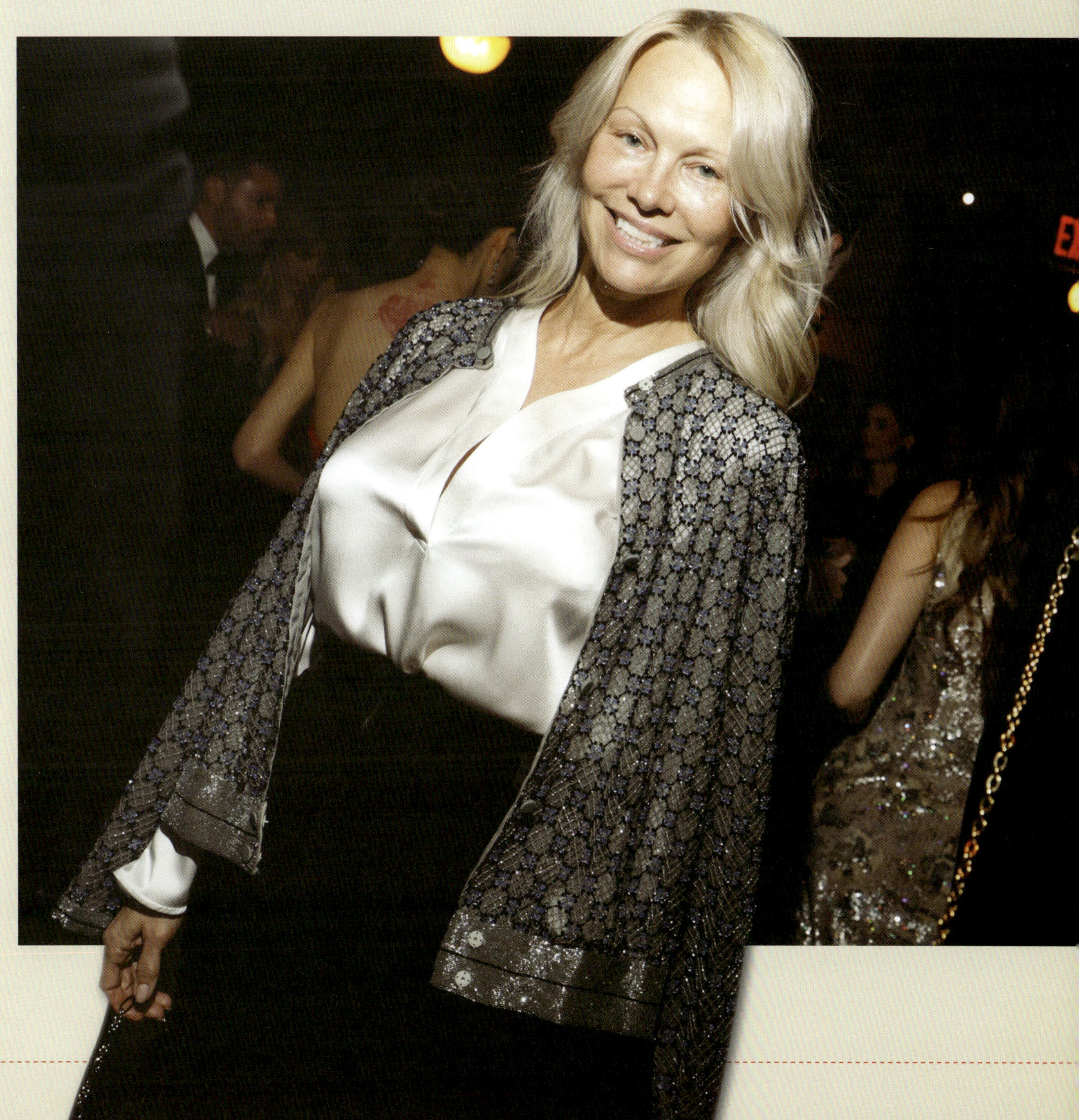

ACCESSORIES

Leather belts, wallets, and bags are classic Emporio Armani pieces. Often crafted in understated designs and decorated with the iconic eagle logo.

UNDERWEAR

One of the brand's most iconic product lines—indeed the cornerstone of the EA identity—these pieces are known for comfort, fit and the recognisable waistband featuring the Emporio Armani logo. Made famous by David Beckham, Cristiano Ronaldo and Calvin Harris.

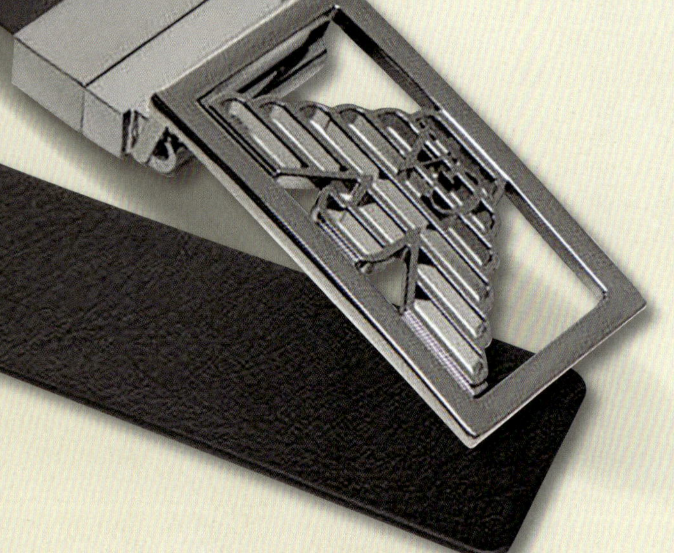

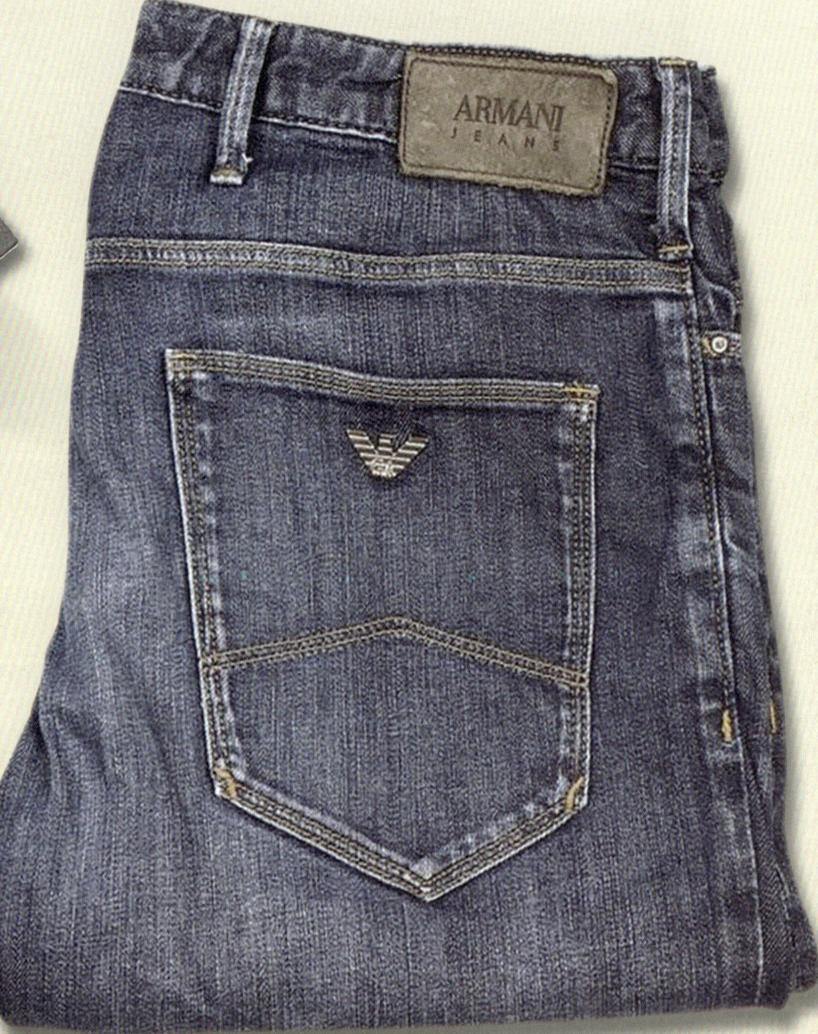

DENIM

Emporio Armani jeans are often dark-washed or slightly distressed to align with the label's urban look. Made from premium denim, they offer a sleek, on-trend fit. Rihanna is a fan.

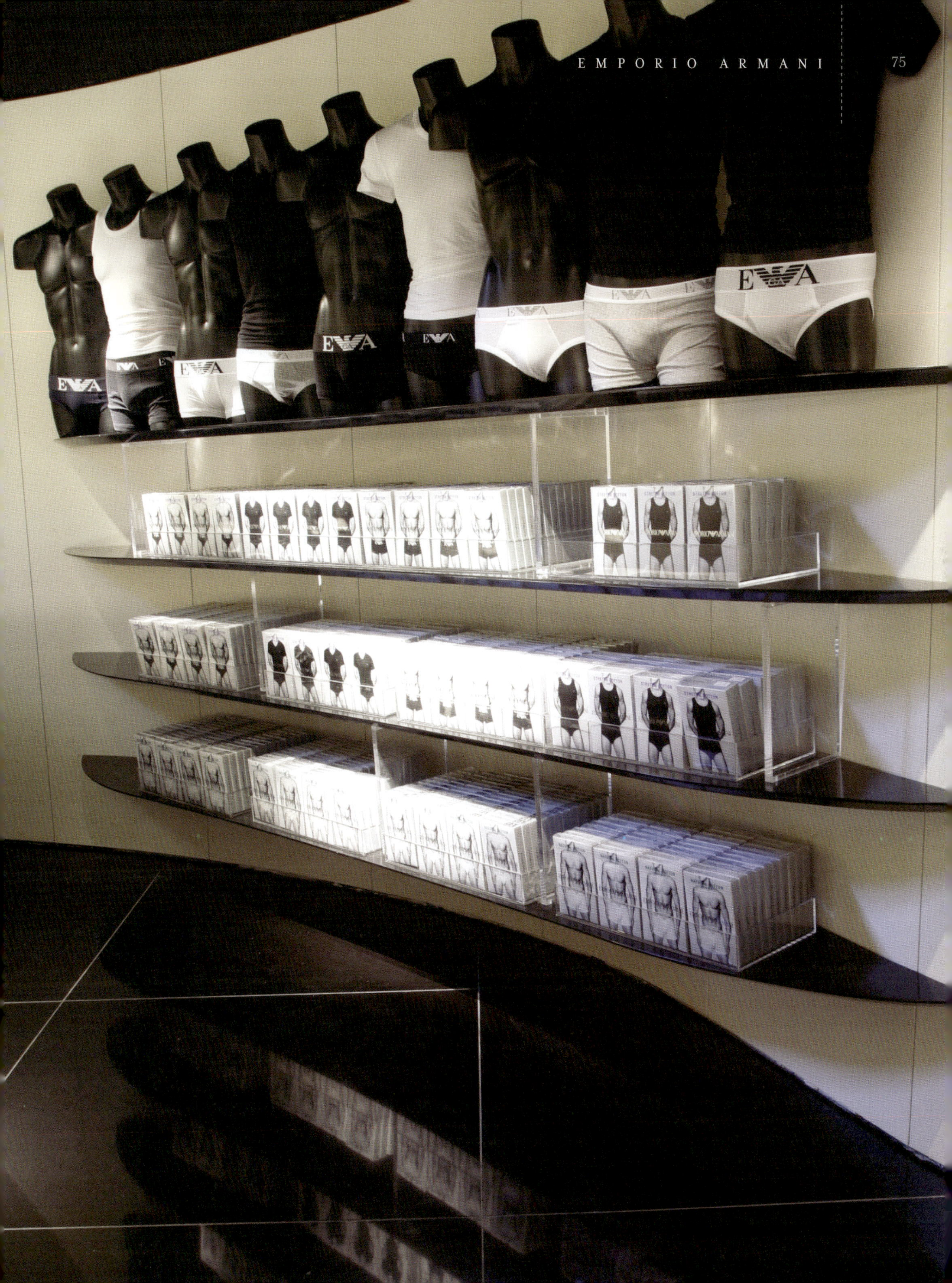

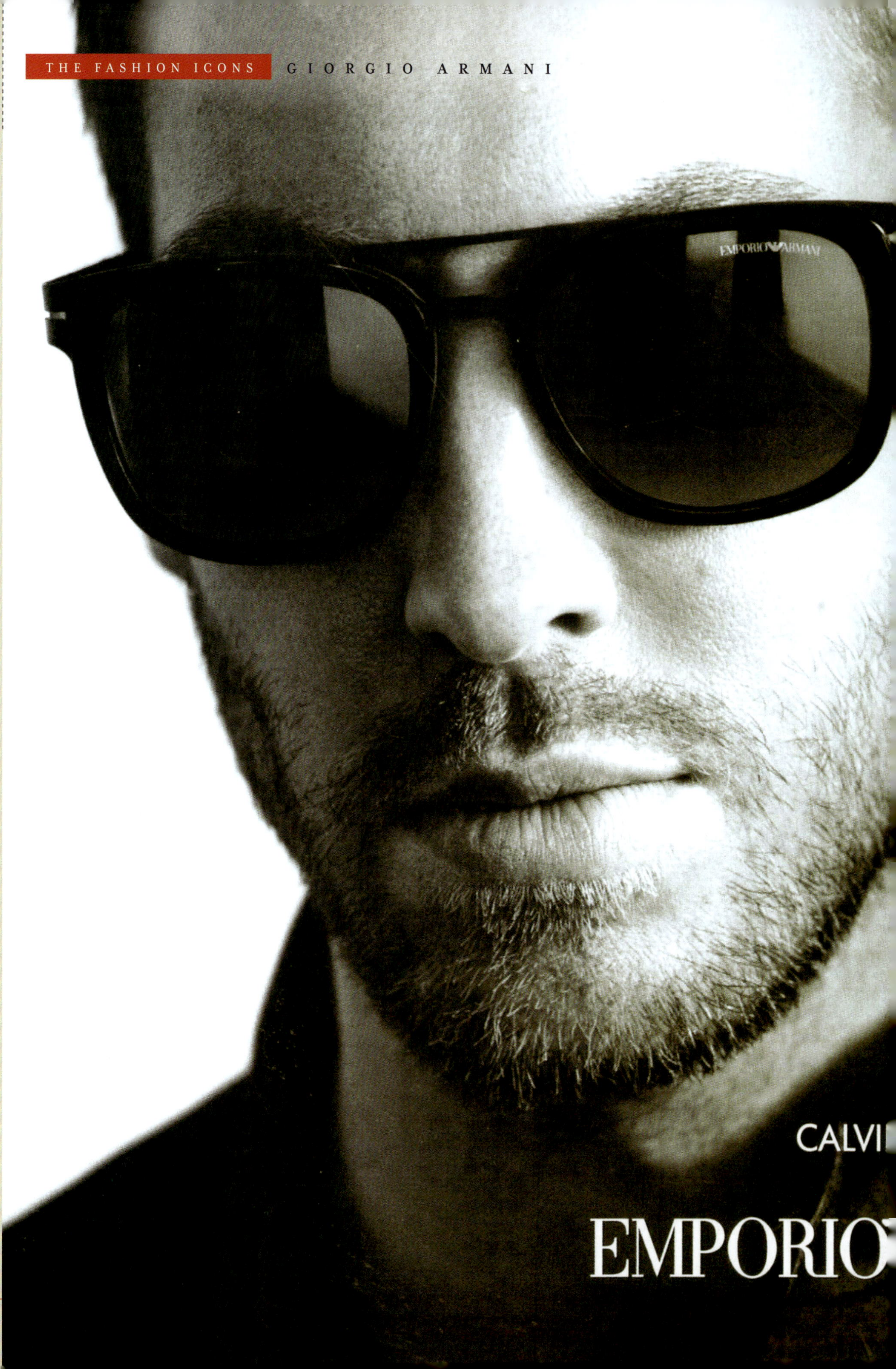

EMPORIO ARMANI
CALVI
EMPORIO

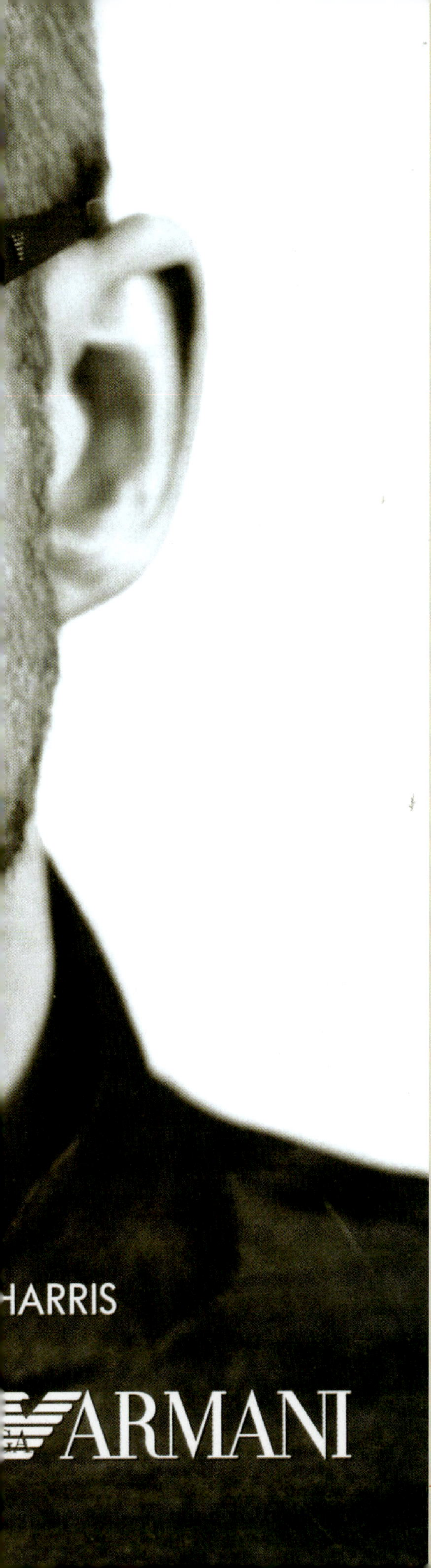

SUNGLASSES

Emporio Armani sunglasses are renowned for their sleek, modern frames and sophisticated design. Aviators and wayfarer styles are particularly popular. Celebrity aficionados include actress Eva Green, rock star Bono and actor Matthew McConaughey.

FRAGRANCE

Emporio Armani offers a distinctive collection of fragrances that blend contemporary style with timeless elegance. Best-selling men's cologne includes the warm and spicy 'Stronger With You' and the citrusy yet woody 'Emporio Armani He'. Female favourites include the uber feminine 'Because It's You' and the seductively floral 'In Love With You'.

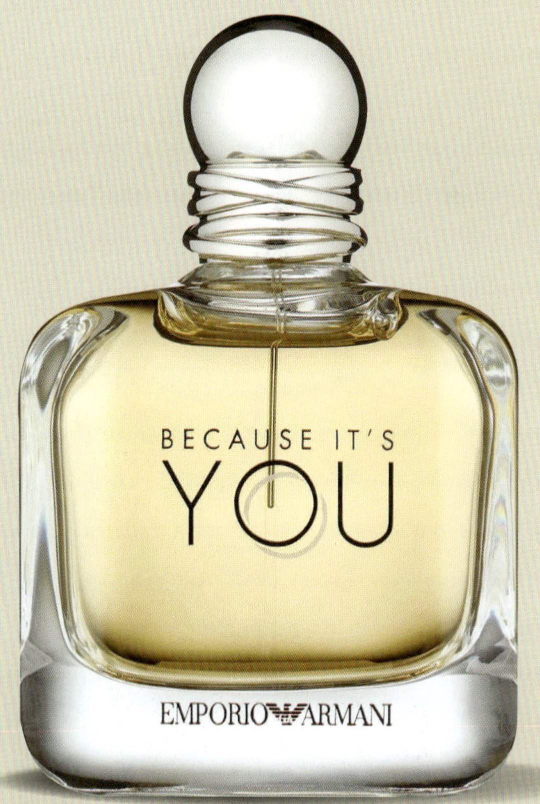

LEFT: Giorgio Armani Eyewear Campaign featuring Calvin Harris

ARMANI EXCHANGE (A|X)

"A fast fashion brand"

Giorgio Armani describing A|X

Giorgio Armani launched Armani Exchange (A|X) in 1991 as a way to expand his brand's reach to a younger, more fashion-forward audience. While his main brand, Giorgio Armani, was known for luxury, sophisticated and high-end tailoring, and Emporio Armani for contemporary, semi-luxury urban elegance, A|X would encapsulate youthful and casual, street-style fashion—stylish and high-quality everyday wear. Armani wanted to connect with younger consumers who loved fashion but couldn't afford his high-end collections. The aim was to create trend-driven bold designs and sporty silhouettes at a lower price point to compete with the likes of Diesel, Calvin Klein and Guess, while maintaining Armani's signature sophisticated yet modern aesthetic. By the 1990s, fast fashion and casual streetwear were growing trends. Armani recognised this shift and created A|X as his response to the changing fashion industry. The brand was initially launched in the US, targeting American street fashion trends, but its appeal swiftly spread across the globe. It remains one of Armani's most recognisable labels, sitting below Emporio Armani and Giorgio Armani. This allows Armani to cater to different levels of luxury without compromising his core identity and USP.

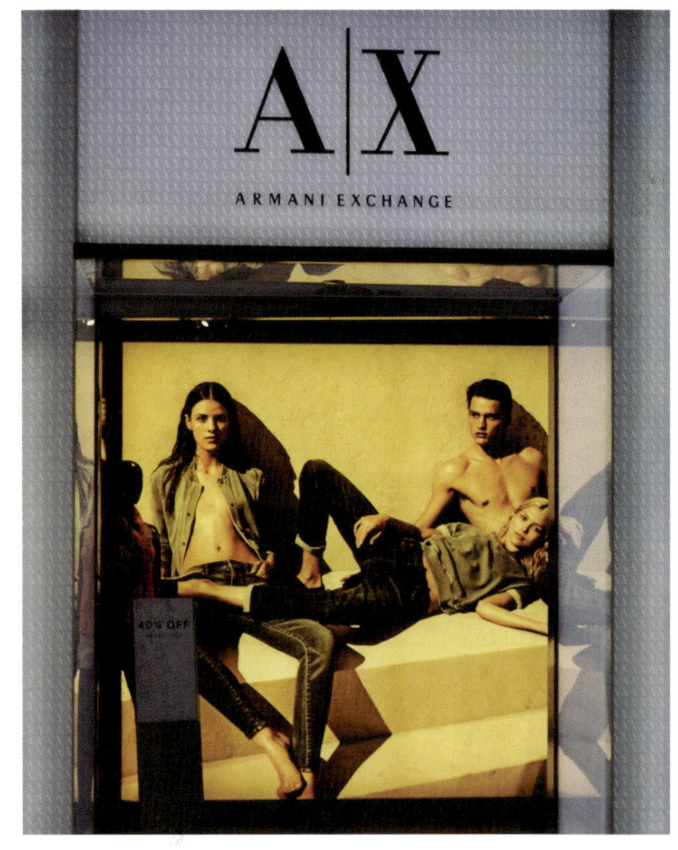

ABOVE RIGHT: Armani Exchange store in Toronto
OPP PAGE: AX Armani Exchange photoshoot during the Spring/Summer fashion show in Shanghai, China, 2005

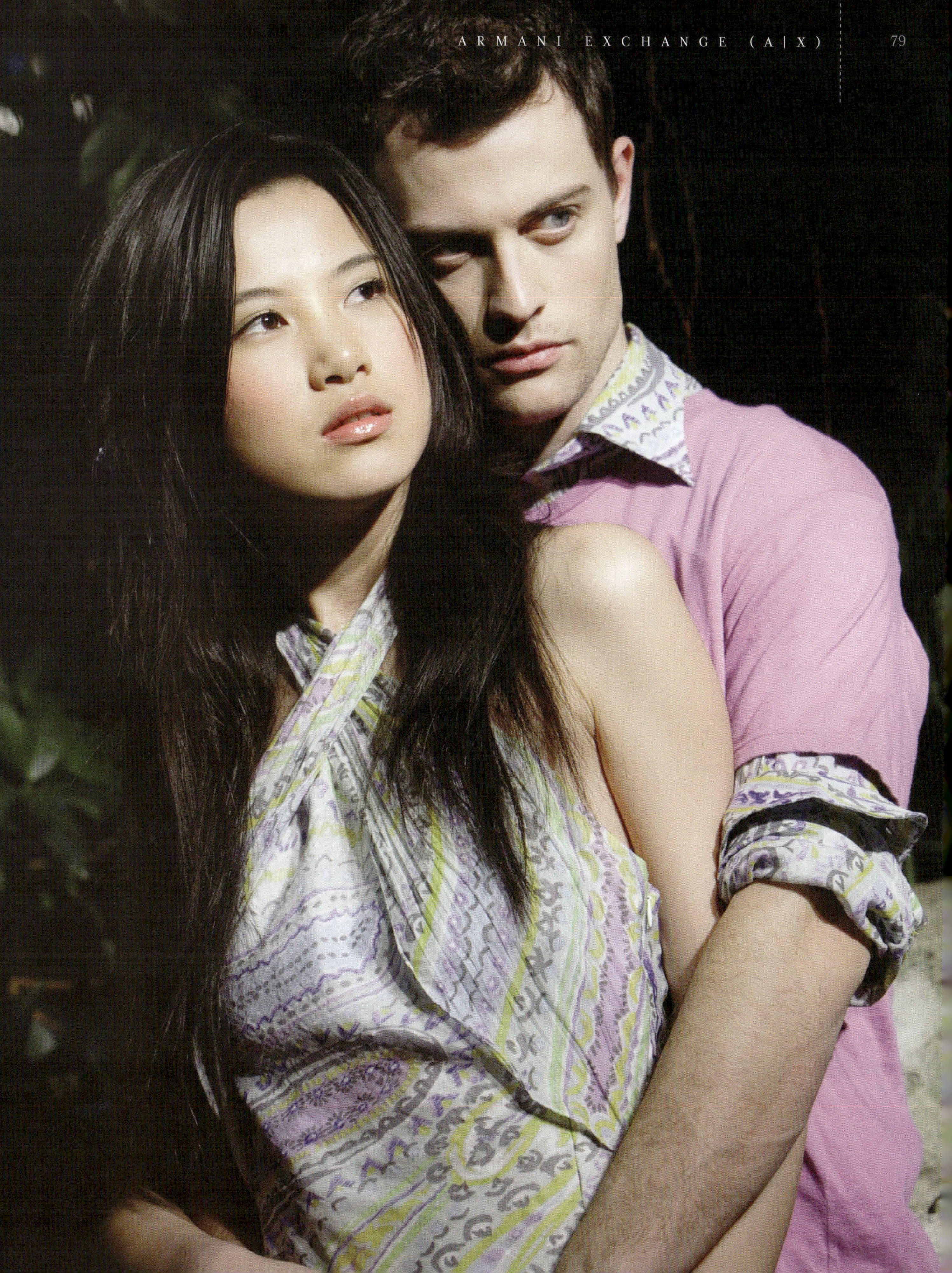

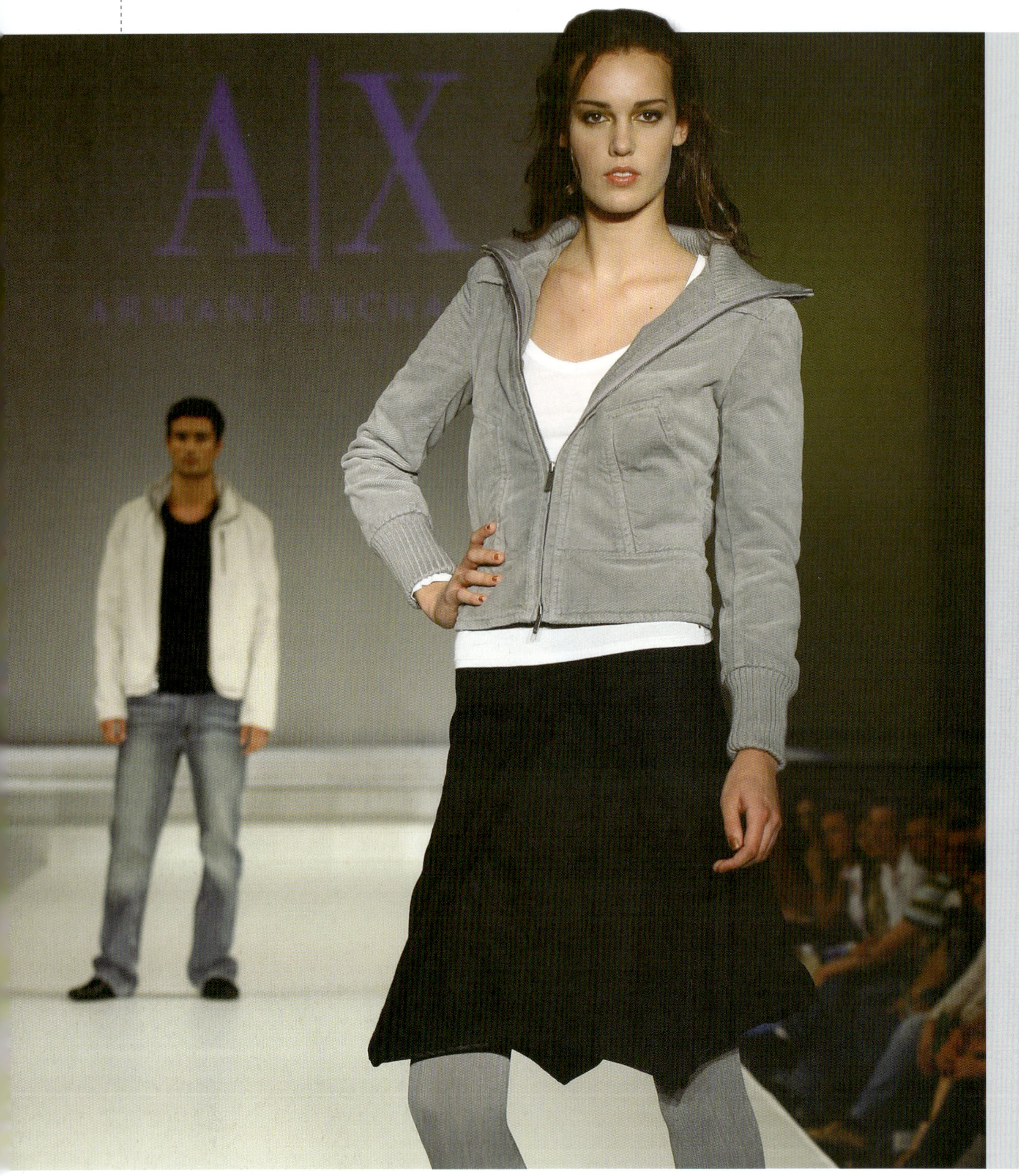

ABOVE: Armani Exchange designs featured in the Salon Show at the L'Oréal Melbourne Fashion Festival, 2007
OPP PAGE: Armani Exchange store

Almost immediately after its launch, A|X became popular with stylish and trend-conscious celebrities and sports stars. Rihanna, Justin Timberlake, Drake, Cristiano Ronaldo, Gigi and Bella Hadid, Hailey Bieber and David Beckham are just a handful of well-known figures who have worn A|X when 'off duty'. Versatile and comfortable, the line is perfect for casual luxury and aligns with contemporary fashion trends. Over the years, the likes of Cara Delevigne, Dutch DJ Martin Garrix and French/American actor and model Luka Sabbat have become Armani Exchange Brand Ambassadors & Campaign Models. Key A|X products include graphic T-shirts, sweatshirts and hoodies with the A|X logo; distressed, slim-fit, and classic jeans; lightweight bomber jackets, puffer jackets and stylish leather jackets; baseball caps, sunglasses, backpacks and trainers, and modern wristwatches.

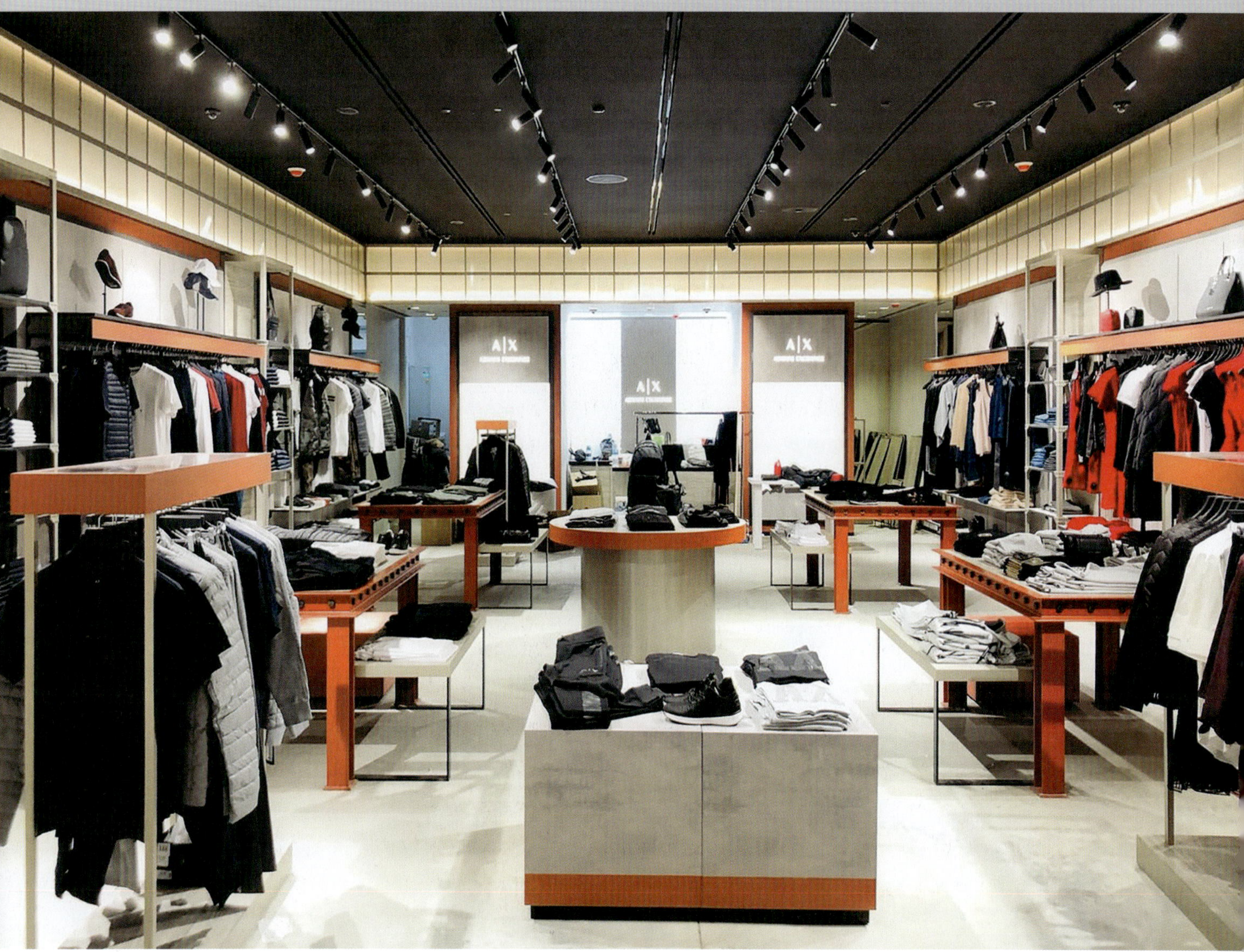

CLASSIC A|X

Over the years, several items have become emblems of the brand's aesthetic.

DENIM JACKETS

A|X's denim jackets combine classic cuts with modern detailing, making them versatile pieces suitable for many occasions.

LOGO T-SHIRTS

A|X's logo tees are iconic, featuring the bold 'A|X' emblem. These shirts have become a staple in casual fashion, offering a minimalist yet stylish look.

LEATHER JACKETS

A|X's leather jackets are known for their sleek design and quality craftsmanship, embodying the Armani ethos and timeless appeal.

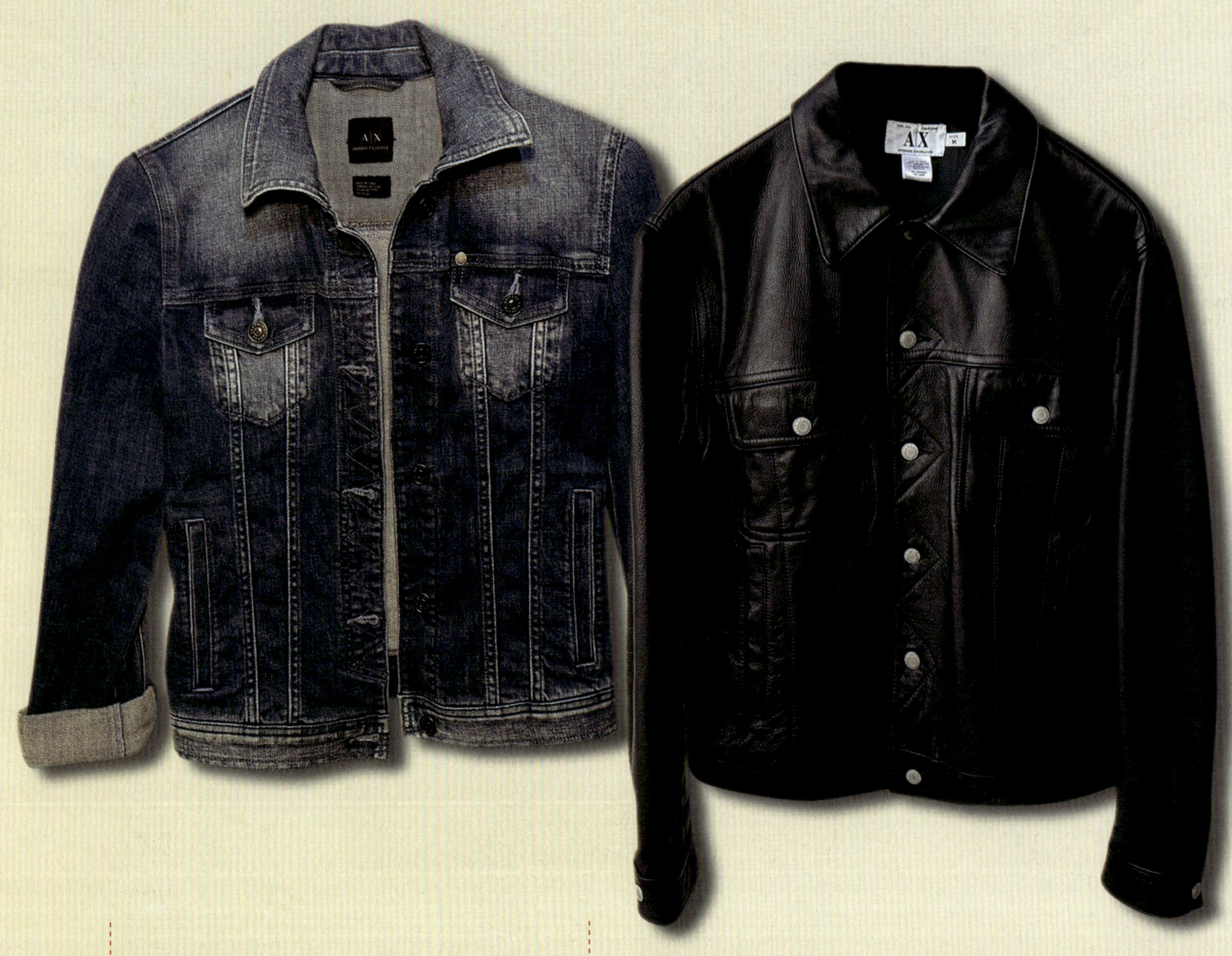

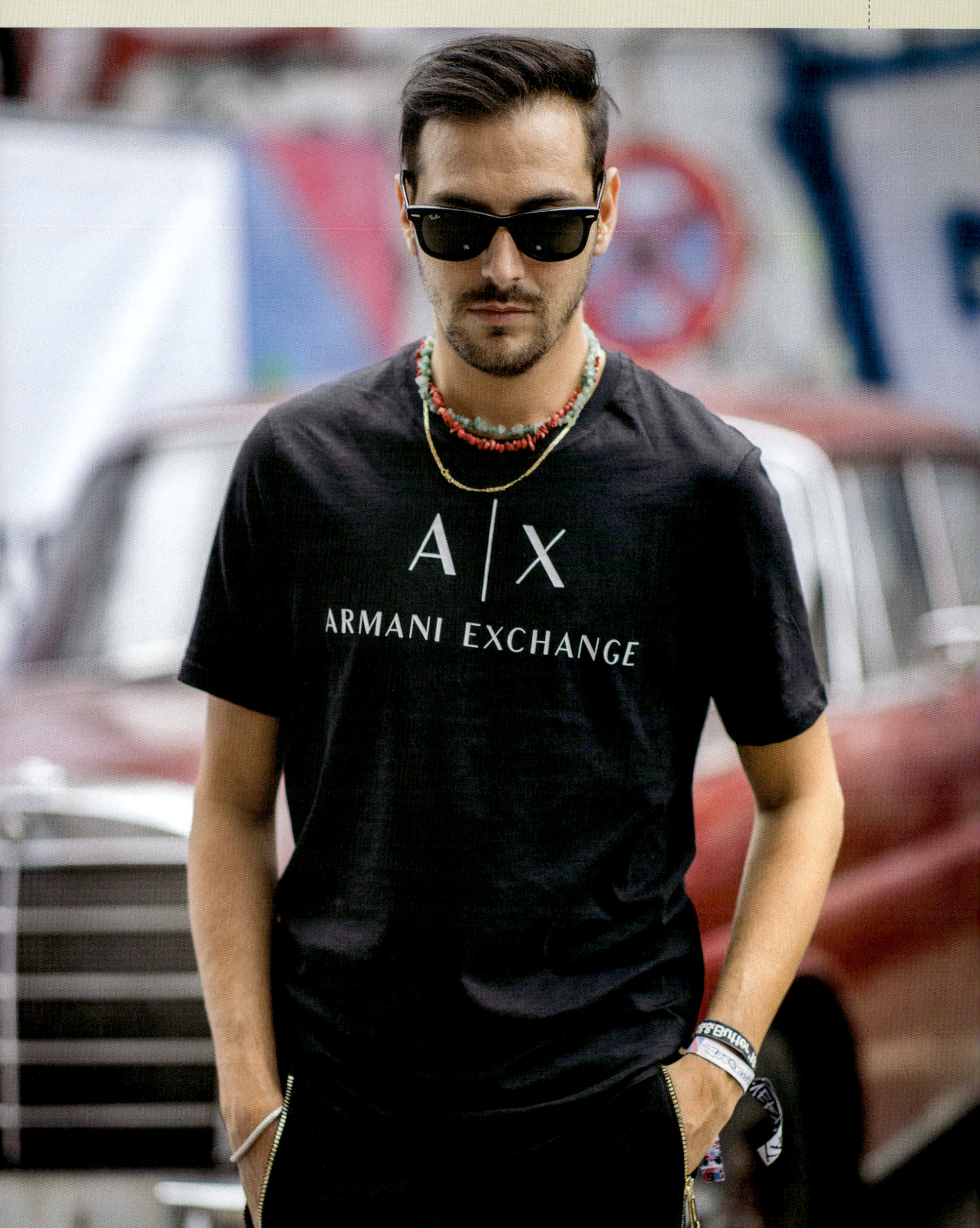

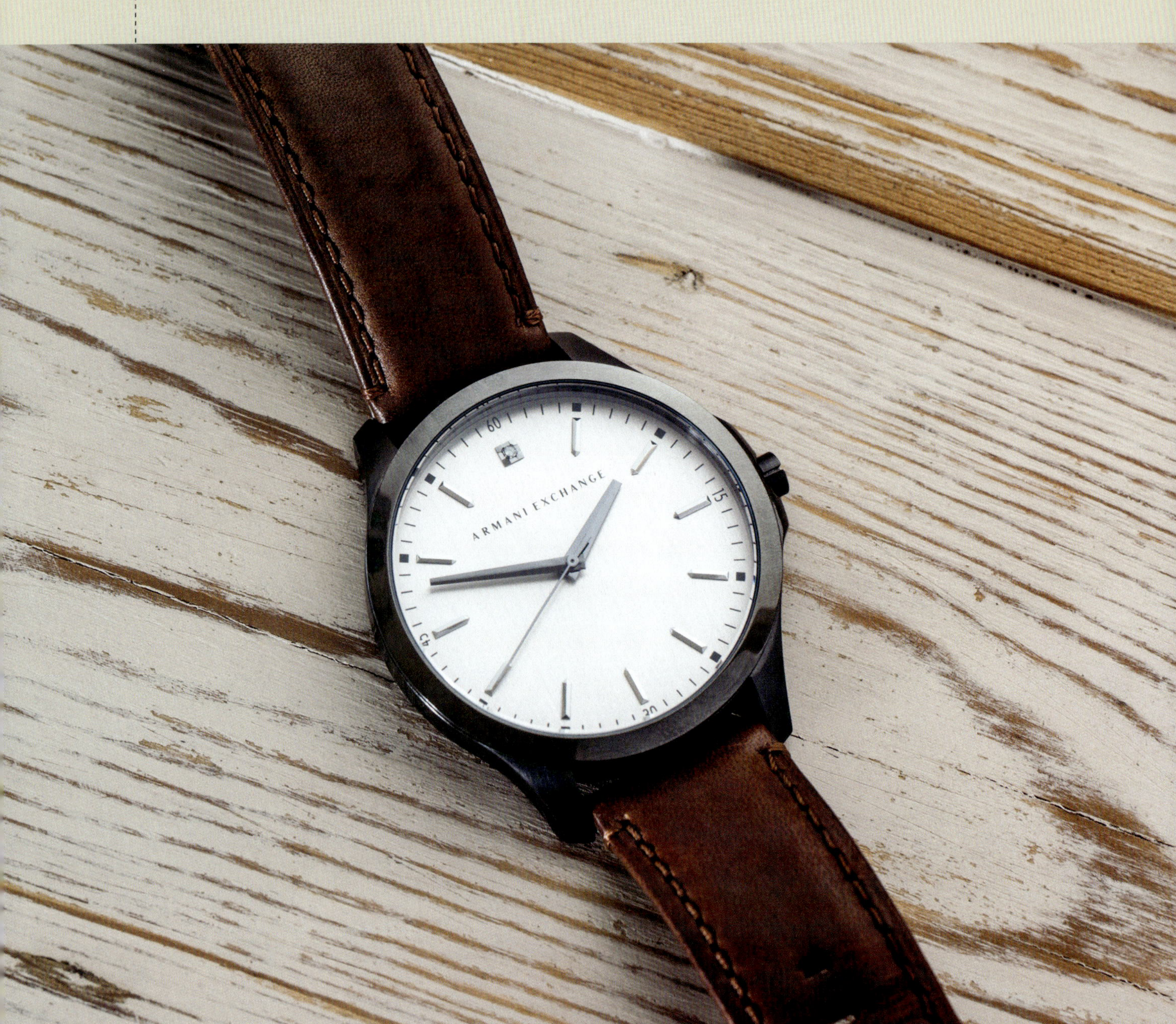

WATCHES

A|X time-pieces are known for their versatility, durability, and timeless style—making them suitable for many an occasion. The brand offers a diverse collection of wristwatches that blend contemporary design with functionality, and cater to both men and women.

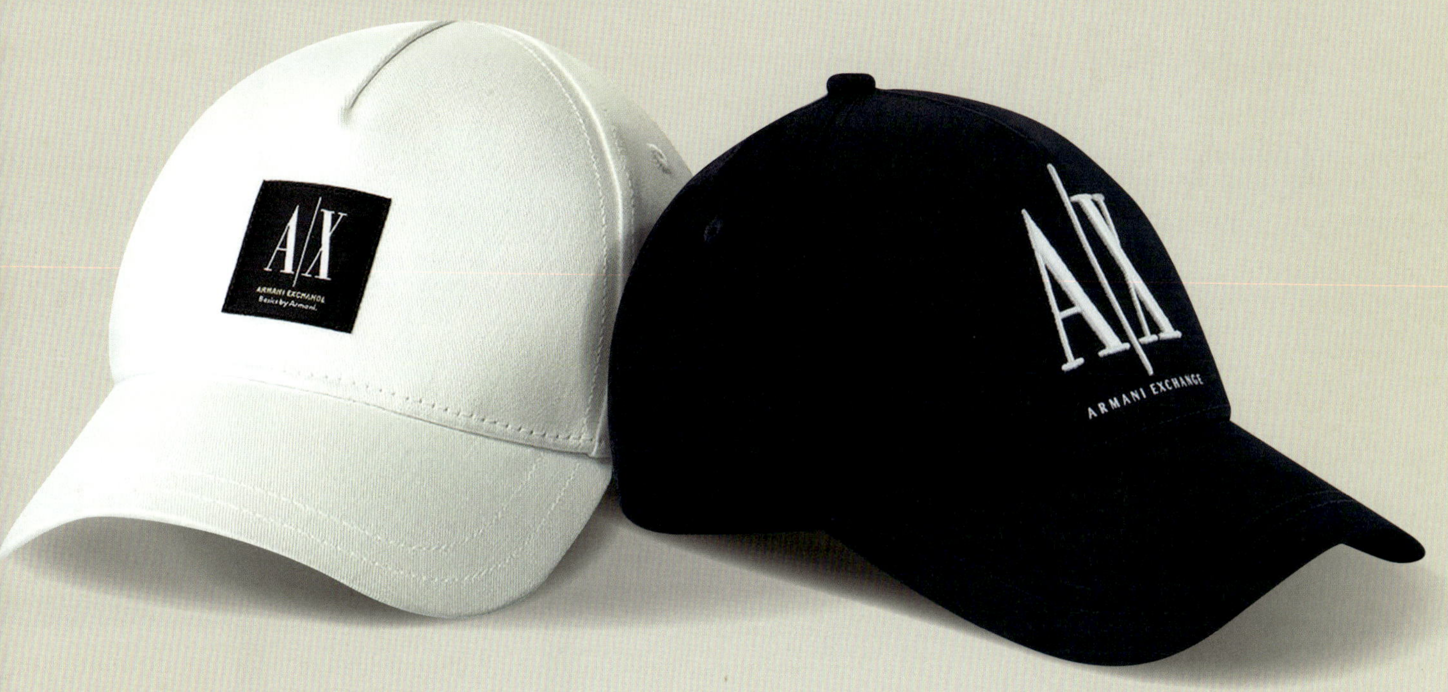

HATS

The Vintage Armani Patch Hat and the Classic Embroidered Logo Baseball Cap showcase the brand's attention to detail and commitment to quality.

SUNGLASSES

Armani Exchange offers a wide range of sunglasses for men and women that blend contemporary design with functionality. Their collection features various styles, including aviators, cat-eye frames, and rectangular designs, crafted from high-quality materials to ensure durability and comfort.

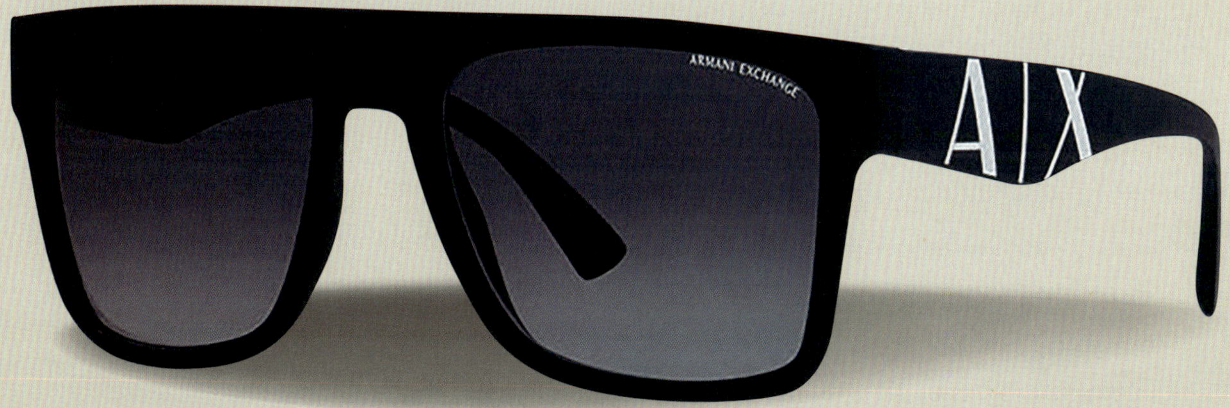

ARMANI CASA

"To create something exceptional, your mindset must be relentlessly focused on the smallest detail"
Giorgio Armani

Armani Casa was founded in 2000 as the luxury home furnishing and interior design division of Giorgio Armani. Famed for its understated elegance, refined minimalism and sophisticated luxury, it has grown into a global symbol of high-end home decor.

The concept of Armani Casa stemmed from Giorgio Armani's personal passion for interior design. He envisioned a home collection that reflected his distinctive fashion philosophy—timeless, sleek and luxurious. Inspired by his travels and love for the Art Deco movement, Armani wanted to extend his signature aesthetic beyond clothing and into interior spaces. Initially offering luxury furniture, lighting and textiles, in 2004 the designer established the Armani Casa Interior Design Studio to provide bespoke luxury interiors for residences, hotels, yachts, and private jets. He showcased these interiors to sublime

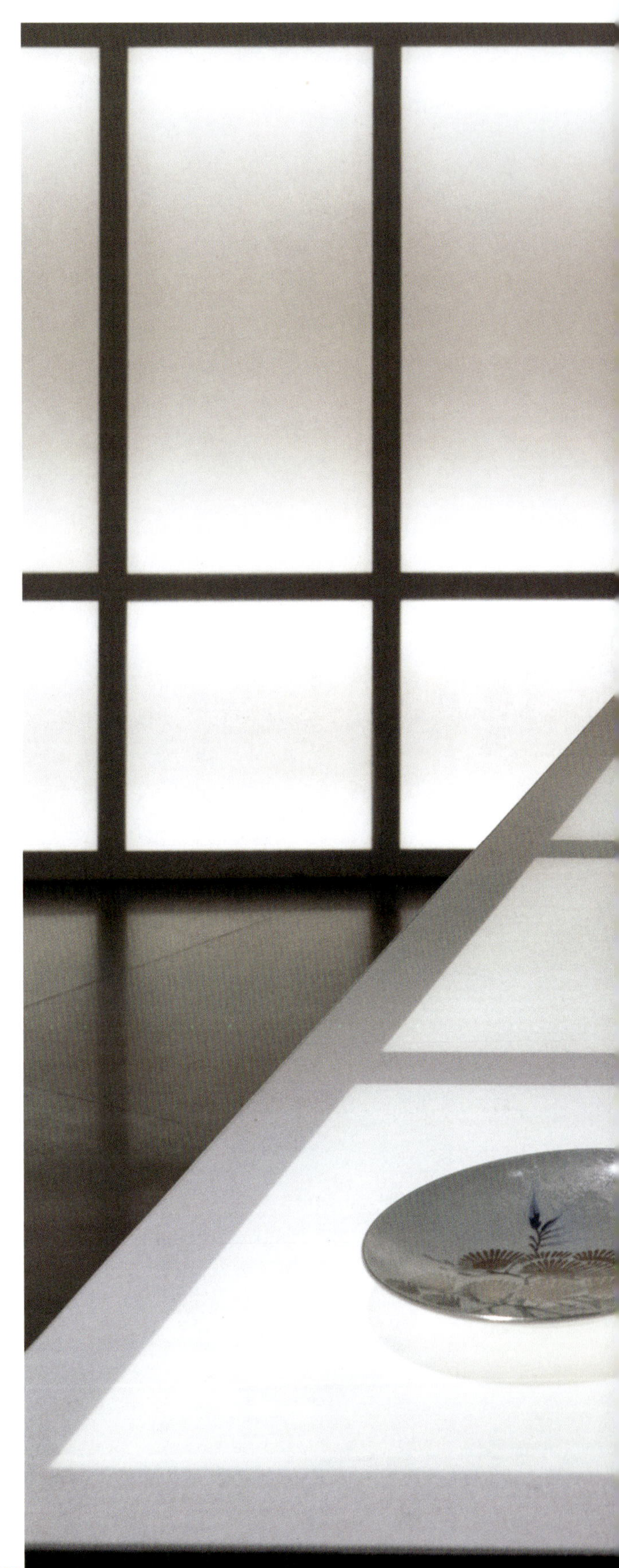

RIGHT: Armani Casa exhibition during Milan Design Week in Italy, 2025

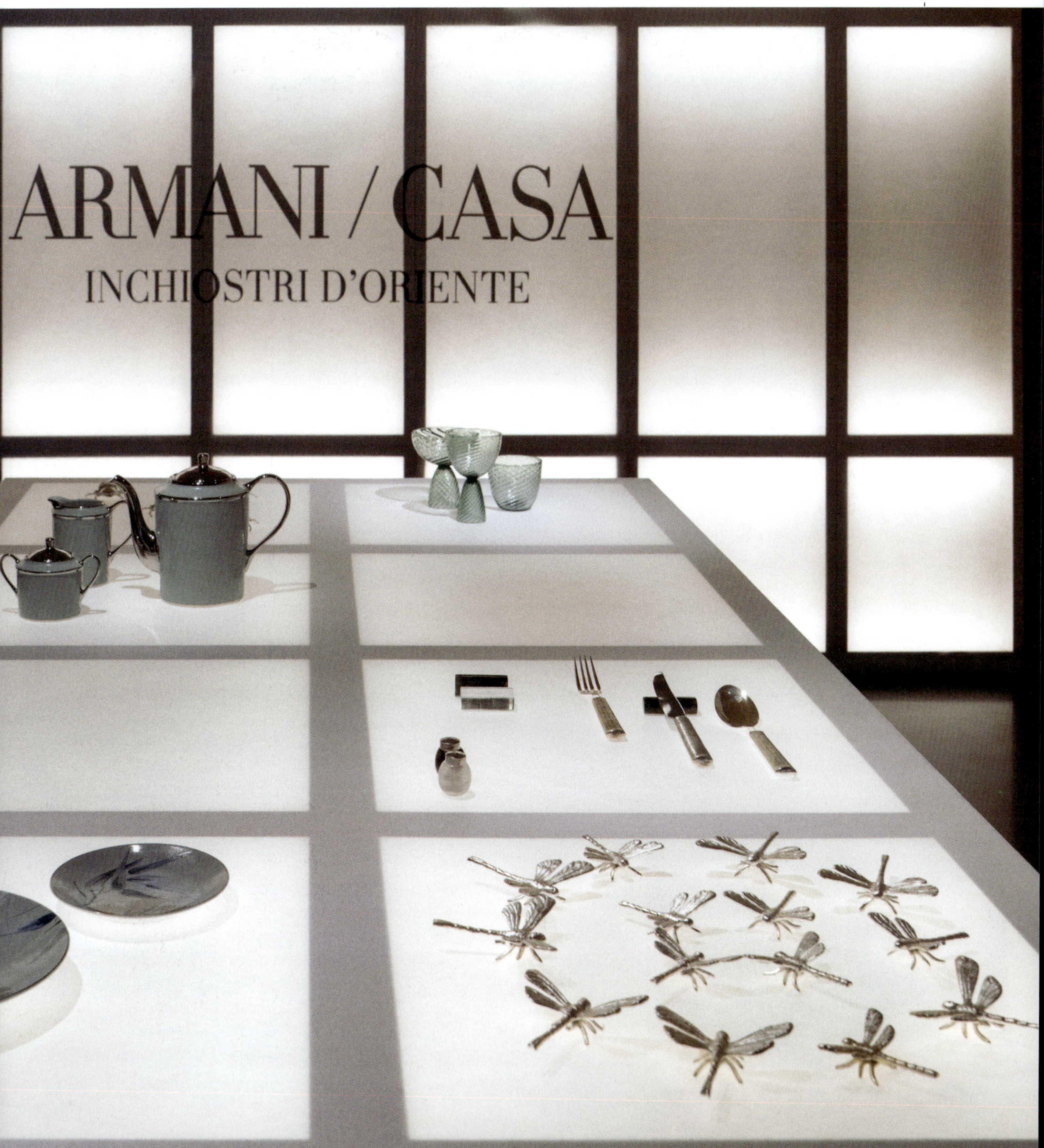

ARMANI / CASA
INCHIOSTRI D'ORIENTE

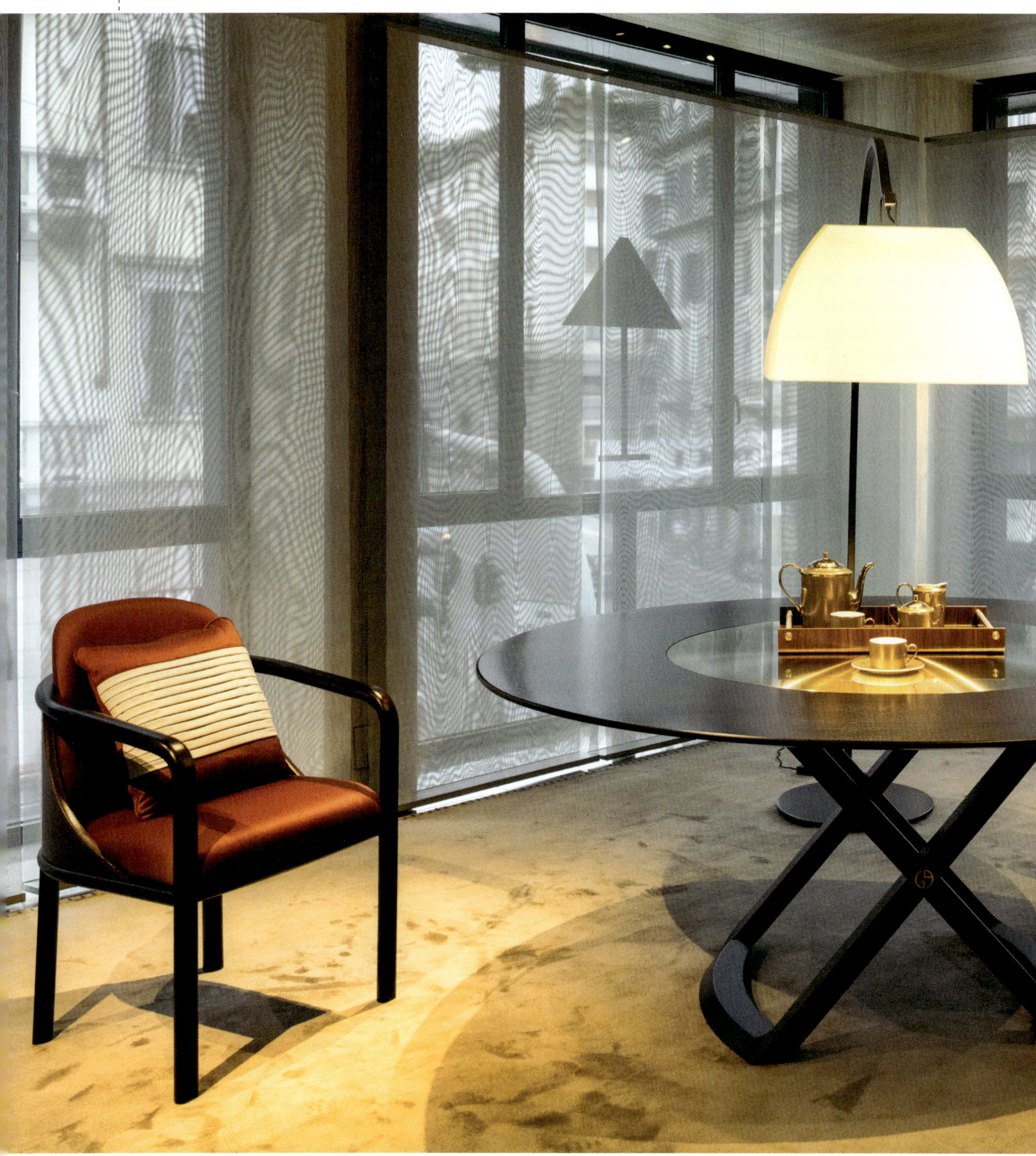

ABOVE: Armani Casa exhibition during Milan Design Week in Italy, 2025

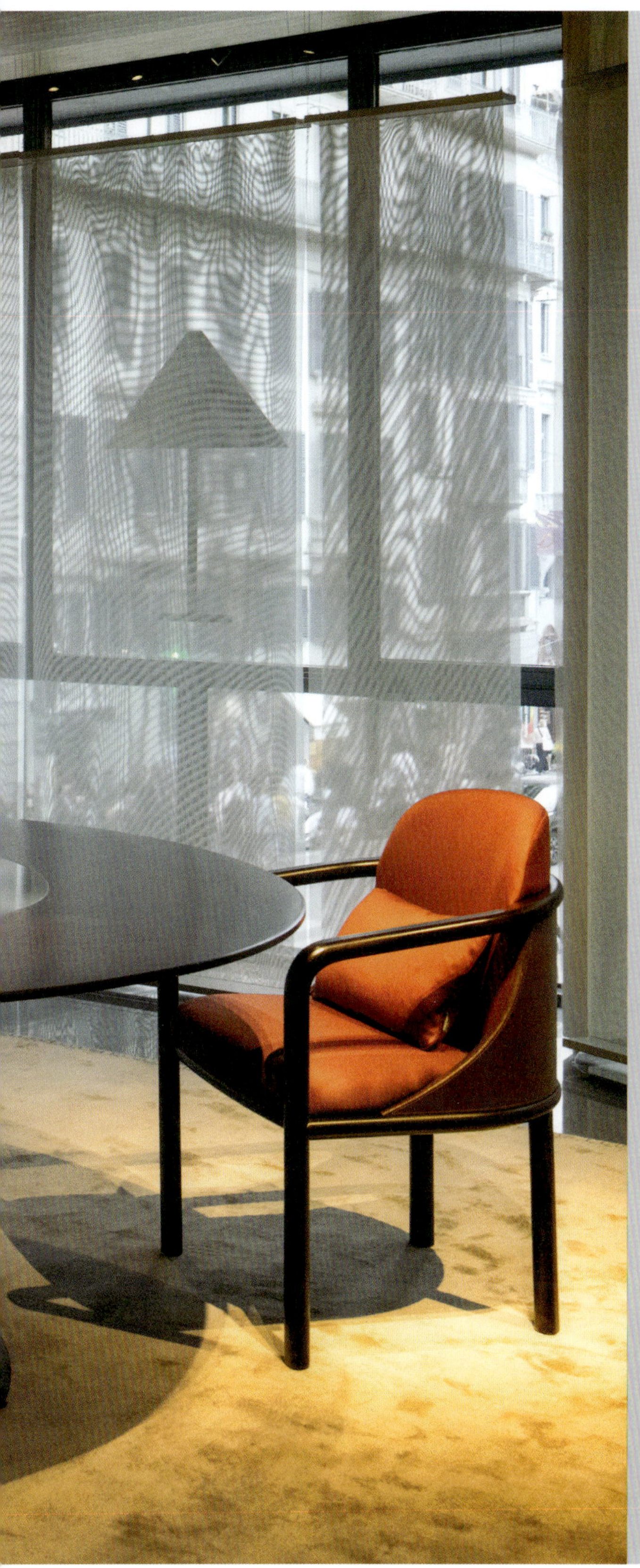

effect in 2010 when he opened the first Armani Hotel in Dubai, designed entirely by the Armani Casa team, setting a new benchmark for luxury hospitality. A year later the Armani Hotel Milan opened, blending minimalist elegance with Italian craftsmanship. From 2015, the company expanded into real estate partnerships, collaborating on luxury residential projects worldwide. Now a leader in high-end home decor, Armani Casa offers custom interior design services while continuing to release exclusive furniture, lighting, textiles and decor collections. It remains a preferred choice for luxury residences, hotels, and high-net-worth clients worldwide.

Armani Casa reflects Giorgio Armani's love for balance, subtle elegance and refined simplicity—in neutral tones, of course. He uses natural materials such as exquisite marbles, exotic woods, silk and metals—and is inspired by Japanese and Art Deco influences. The AC range of furniture features investment pieces for your home—encapsulating sofas, tables, chairs, beds, and storage pieces with sleek silhouettes and refined finishes. Lighting pieces include statement chandeliers, table lamps, and wall sconces—all blending function with the classic GA aesthetic. For textiles, think luxurious bedding, cushions and upholstery fabrics featuring subtle patterns; while Armani Casa accessories feature vases, trays, mirrors, and tableware that reflect the brand's timeless elegance. Armani Casa pieces are investment items -designed with timeless elegance, quality craftsmanship and subtle luxury.

CLASSIC ARMANI CASA LUXURY PIECES

TROCADERO TABLE

Merging modernism and Art Deco, this stylish dining table made from finest wood and marble, featuring sleek geometric legs, is both timeless and contemporary.

CLUB BAR CABINET

Inspired by vintage Art Deco designs, this is a sophisticated bar cabinet incorporating lacquered wood, glass shelving and metallic detailing. A signature piece for luxury interiors.

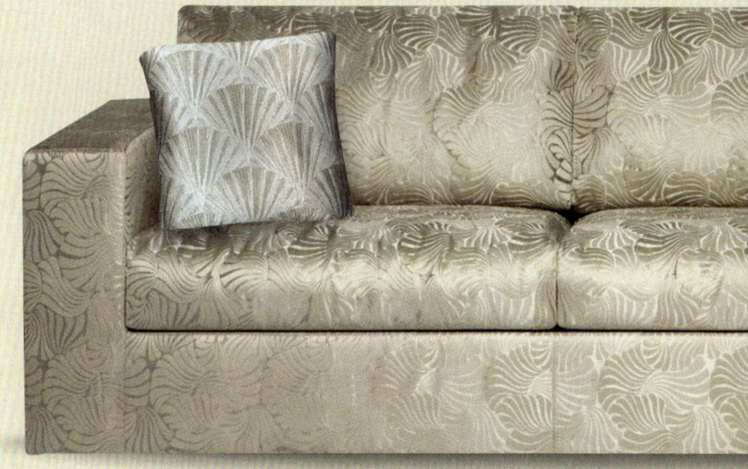

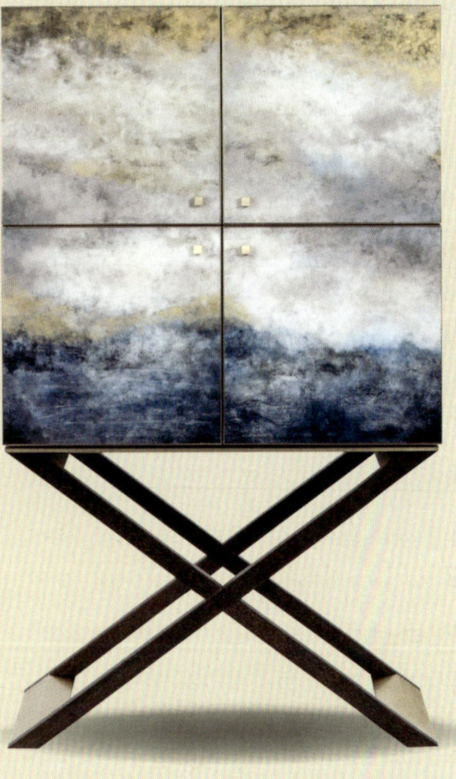

CANALETTO SOFA

Considered the most iconic sofa in the Casa collection, the Canaletto features clean lines, deep seats and luxurious proportions which reflect Giorgio

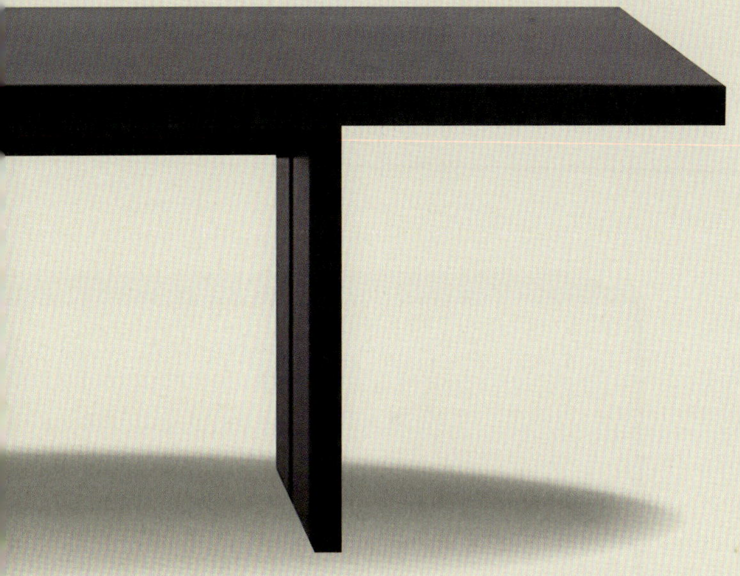

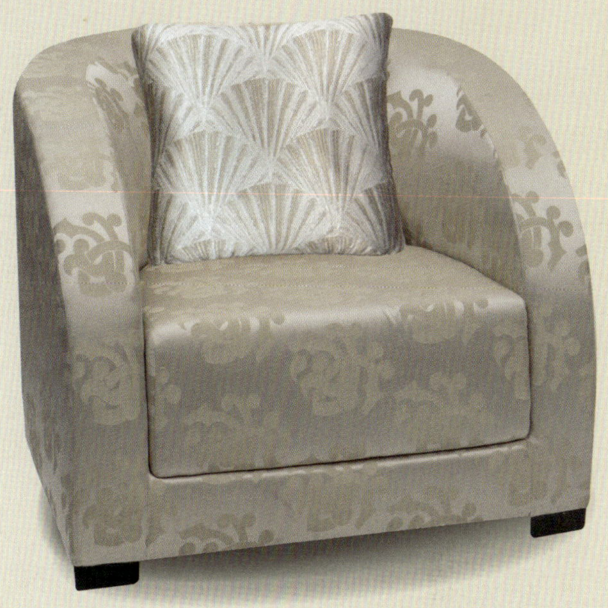

CLUB ARMCHAIR

A modern interpretation of the classic lounge chair, upholstered in leather, velvet or premium fabrics. Comfortable yet stylish, the Armani Casa club armchair is at home in both traditional and contemporary settings.

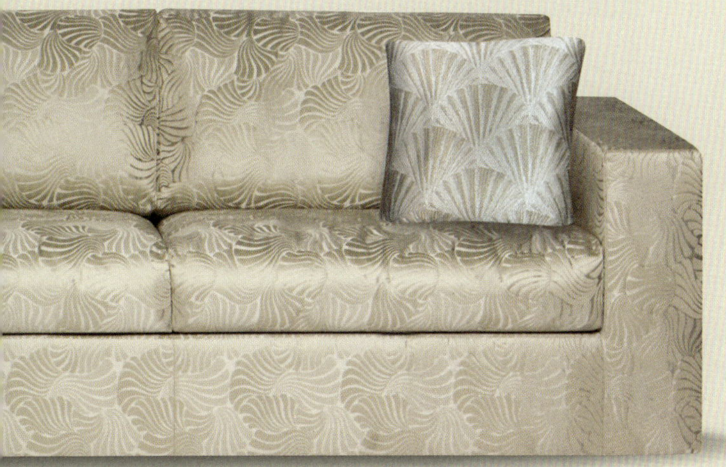

Armani's minimalist elegance and understated glamour. It is one of the few luxury sofas that adapts to both formal sitting areas and casual lounging.

LOGO LAMP

A subtle, statement lighting piece that fits effortlessly into any luxury interior, this classic table lamp is available in matte metal or glossy lacquer finishes.

ARMANI CASA TABLEWARE COLLECTION

The range incorporating uber-elegant glassware, plates and cutlery with signature Armani textures, minimalist design and often featuring gold accents, neutral tones, or fine crystal is perfect for luxury dining.

VENEER & LACQUERED WOOD CABINETS

The AC sleek storage cabinets and sideboards—featuring glossy finishes, wood veneers or metallic trims—combine functionality with Armani's signature minimalism. Timeless elegance.

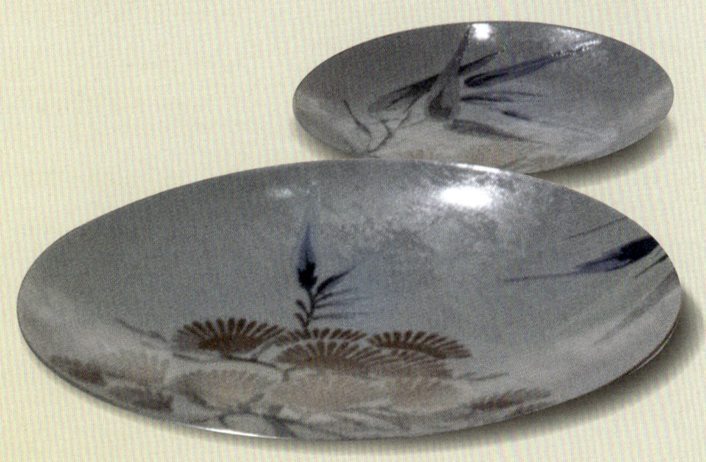

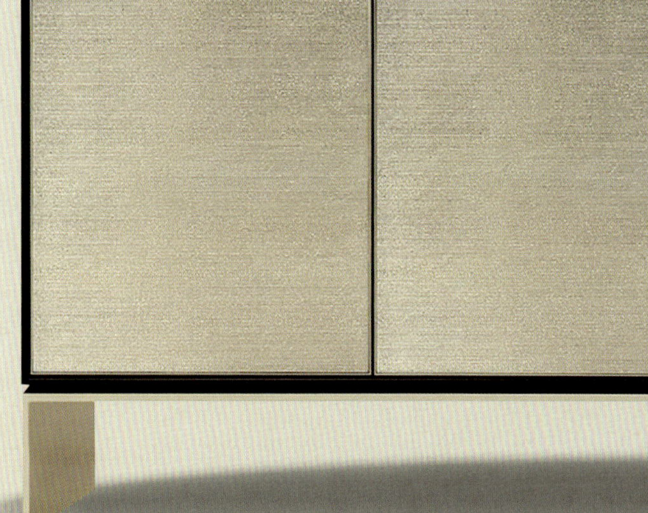

DANDY BED

Uber comfortable and stylish bed with a completely padded high headboard which is designed in the shape of an arch so that the most external parts are detached from the wall. This unique feature endows the bedroom interior with lightness and motion and allows the bed to be located centrally in a room.

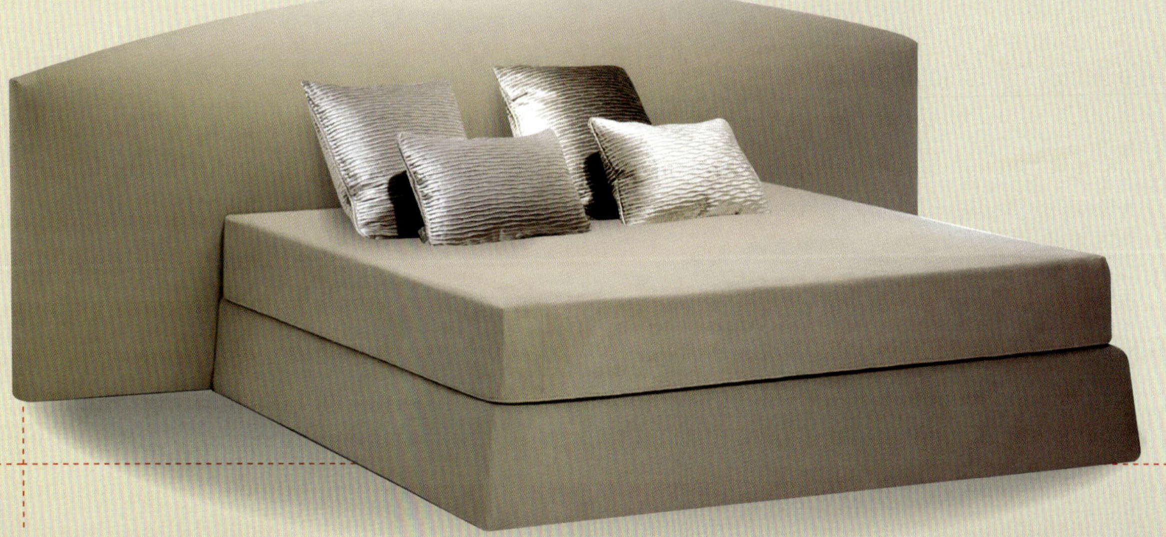

ARMANI CASA HOME FRAGRANCES & ACCESSORIES

Signature candles, diffusers and trays that bring the Armani aesthetic to everyday spaces, adding a touch of elegance and sensory luxury to any room.

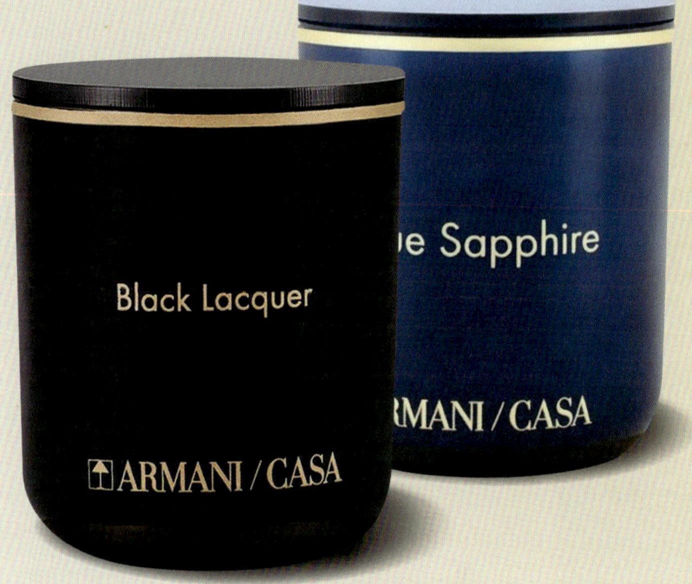

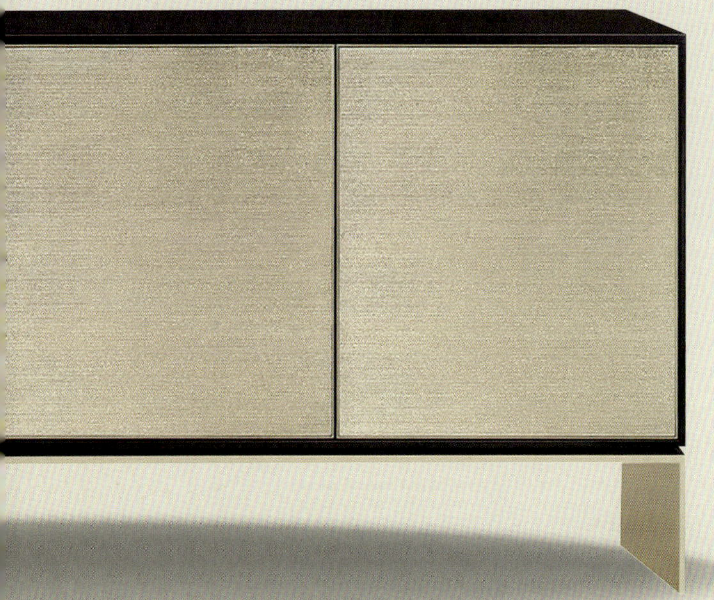

ARMANI CASA SIGNATURE RUGS

A blend of artisanal craftsmanship and modern luxury, these AC handwoven silk and wool rugs feature subtle geometric patterns or nature-inspired motifs.

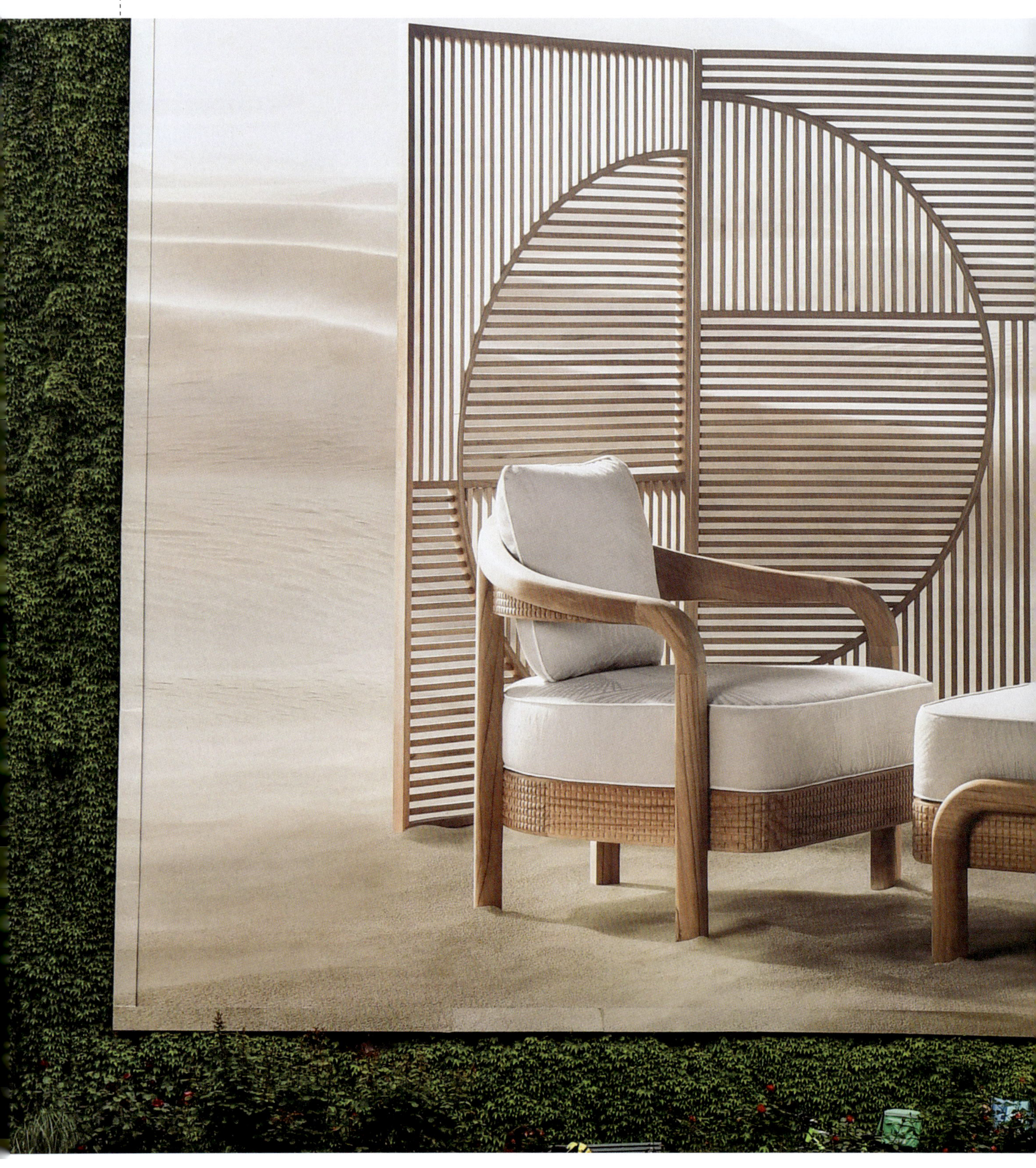

ABOVE: Armani Casa advertisement on a billboard along Via Broletto in Milan's Brera district, Italy

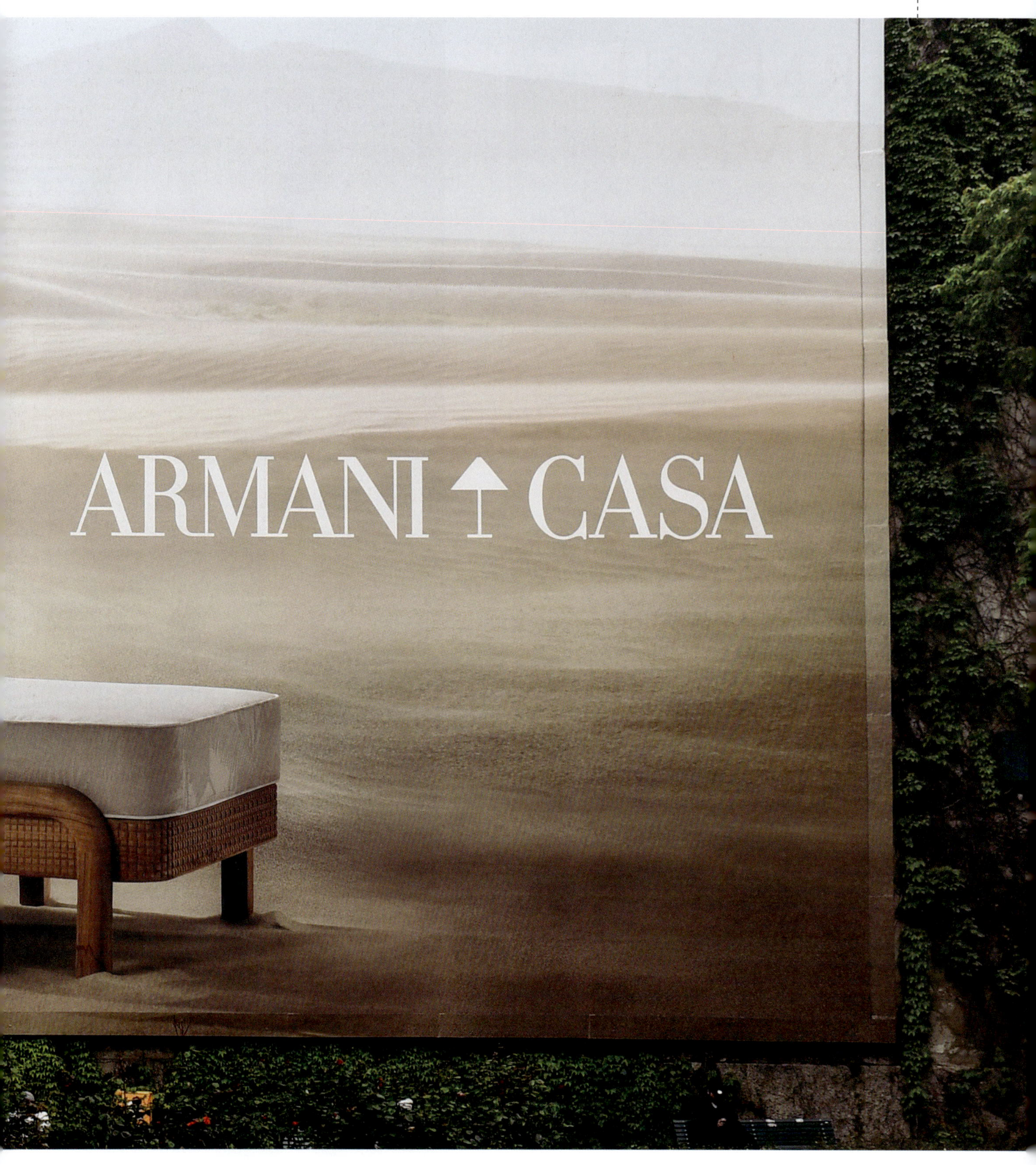

ARMANI CASA

ARMANI PRIVÉ

"Elegance is not about being noticed, it's about being remembered"
Giorgio Armani

Launched in 2005 to create the House of Armani's most exclusive Haute Couture, Armani Privé was originated for A-plus listers—high-profile clients, red carpet appearances, and couture enthusiasts. From the get-go, Armani Privé's remit has been to exemplify timeless elegance and sophistication, meticulous craftsmanship and innovative design. The label has succeeded—and then some.

When Giorgio Armani unveiled Armani Privé during Paris Haute Couture week in January 2005, he did so with a clear intention—to bring his philosophy of *'less is more'* to the echelons of haute couture. Already an icon of ready-to-wear fashion, Armani wanted to explore the boundaries of craftsmanship and creativity, offering a bespoke experience that catered to the most discerning clientele. This look set the tone for the collection, emphasising Armani's signature minimalist elegance combined with luxurious detailing. The inaugural collection opened with a

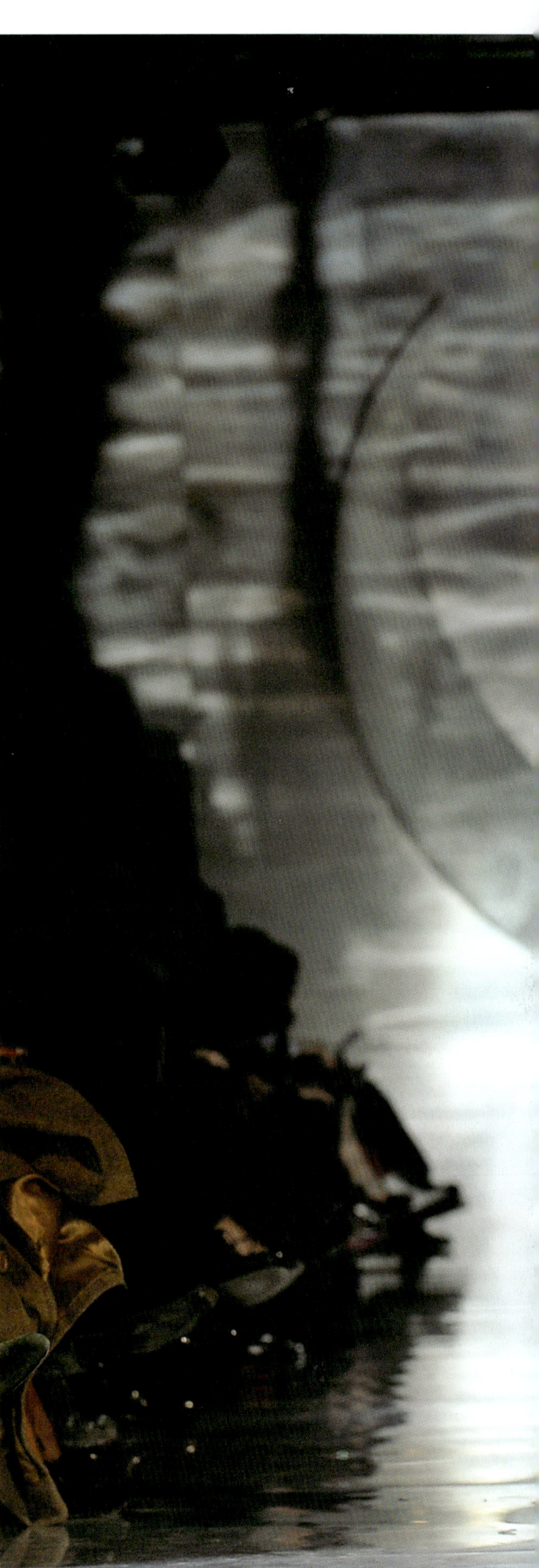

RIGHT: Models walking the runway at the Giorgio Armani Privé Haute Couture Spring/Summer 2010 show during Paris Fashion Week, January, 2010

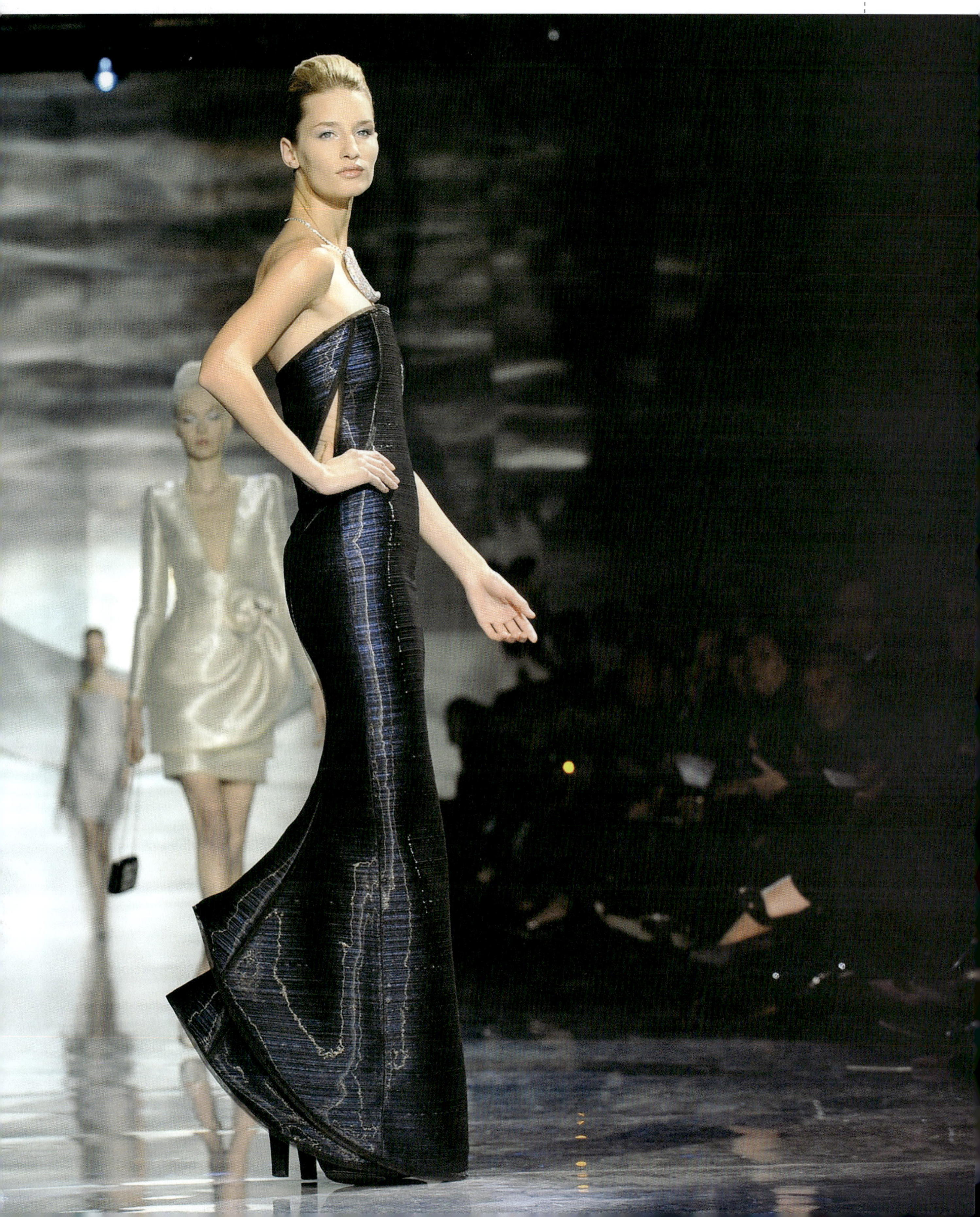

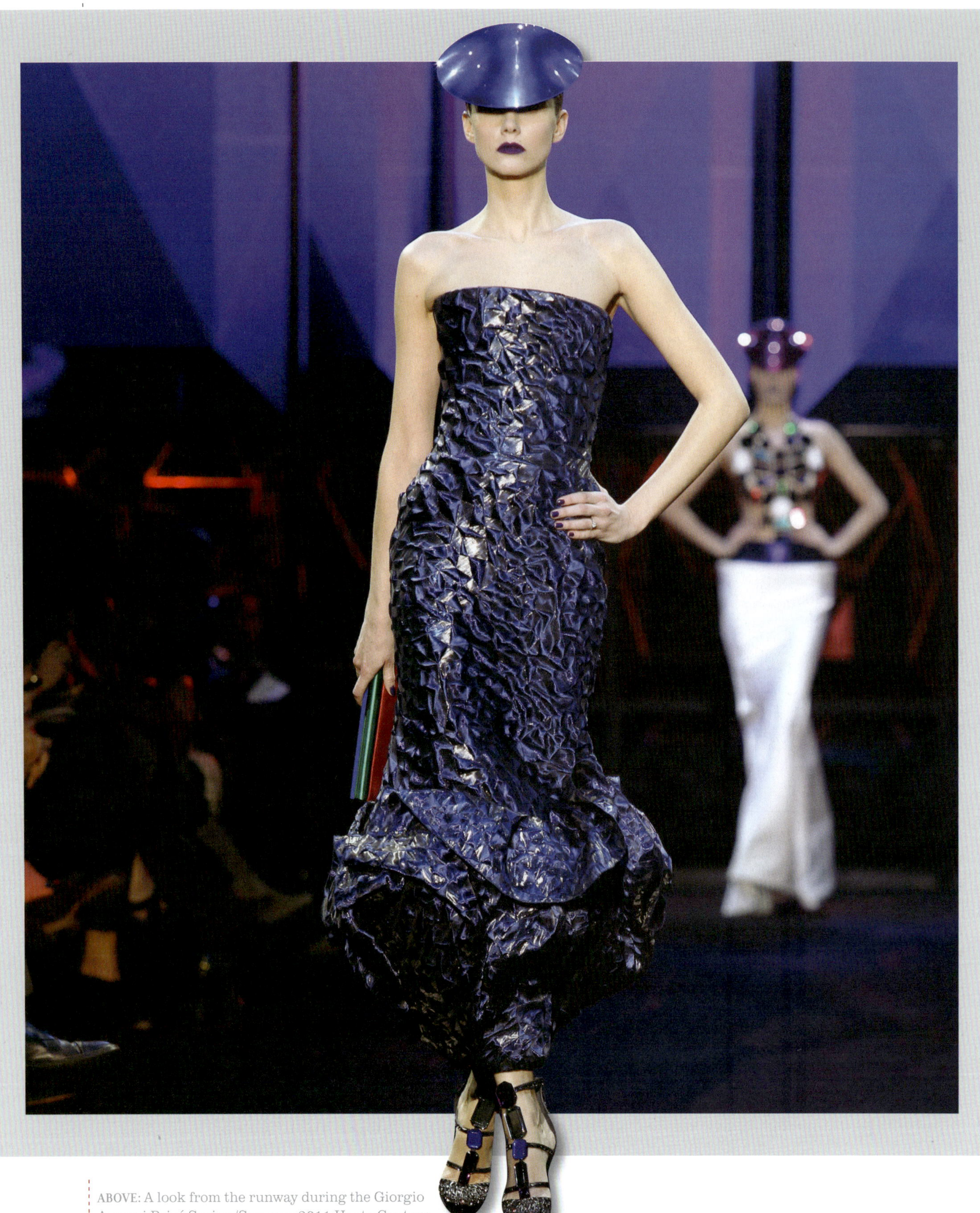

ABOVE: A look from the runway during the Giorgio Armani Privé Spring/Summer 2011 Haute Couture show at Espace Vendôme, as part of Paris Fashion Week, January, 2011

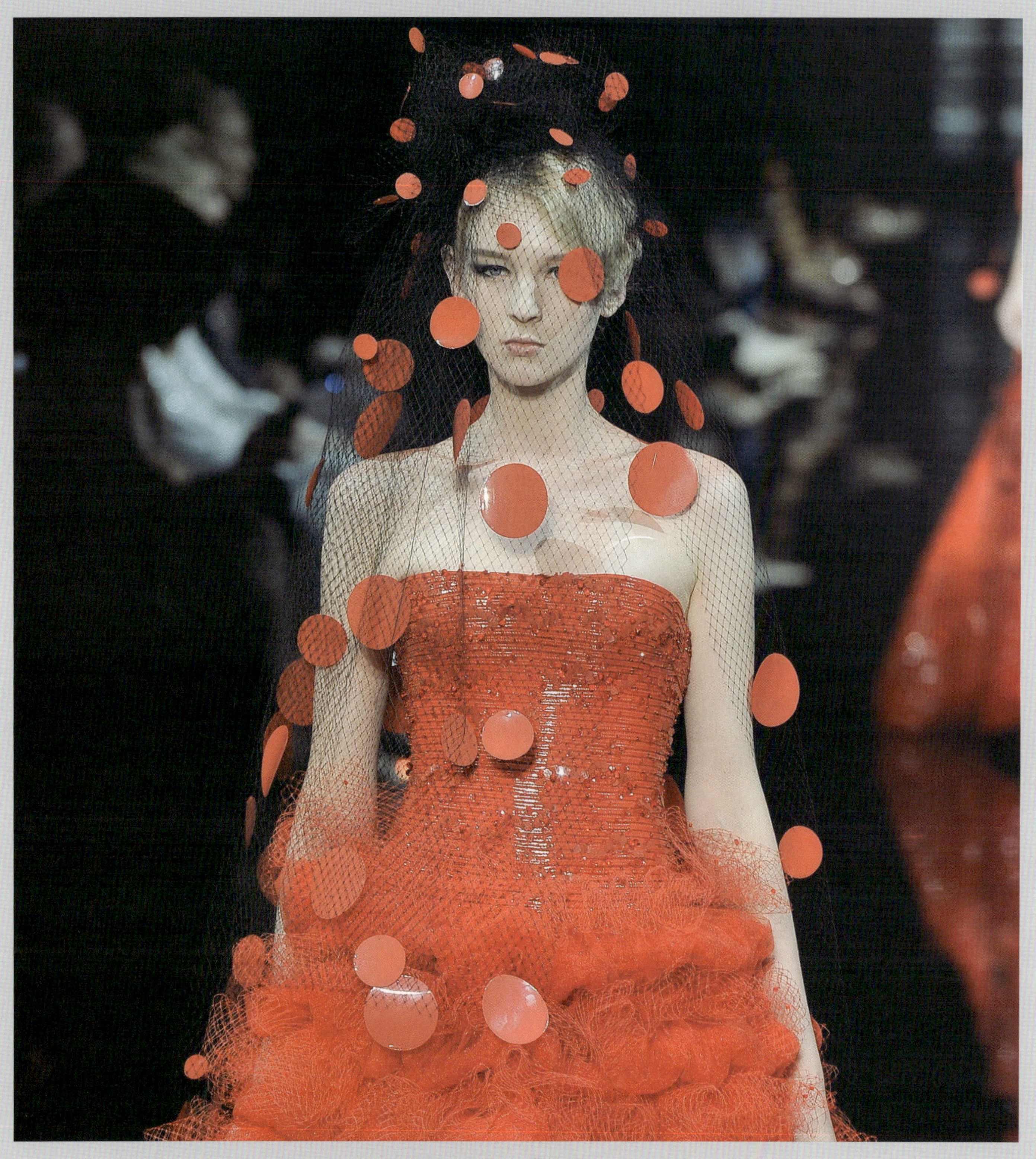

ABOVE: Giorgio Armani Privé Autumn/Winter 2014–2015 Haute Couture runway show at Paris Fashion Week, 2014

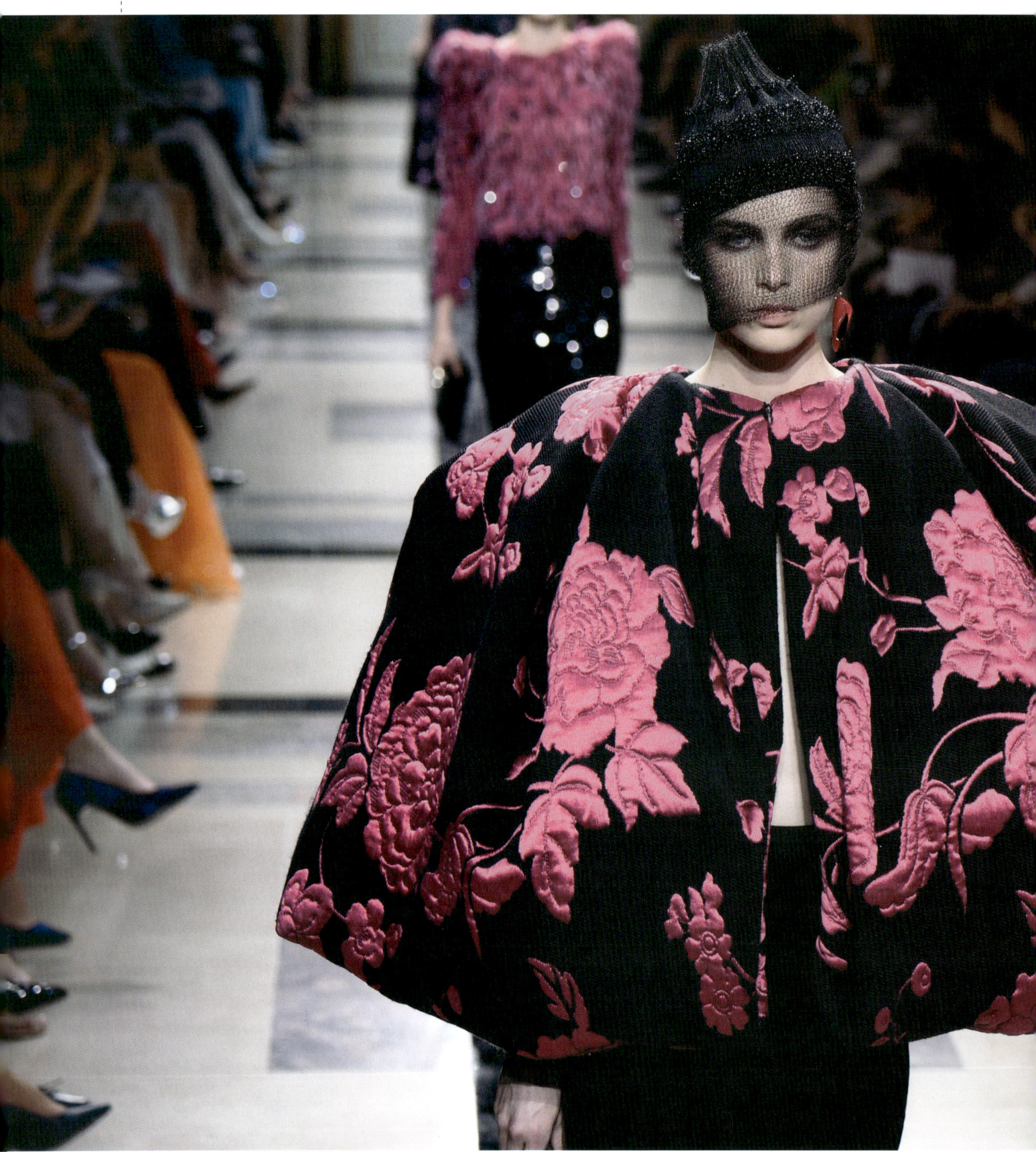

ABOVE: Giorgio Armani Privé Haute Couture Autumn/ Winter 2017–2018 collection on the runway at Paris Fashion Week, 2017

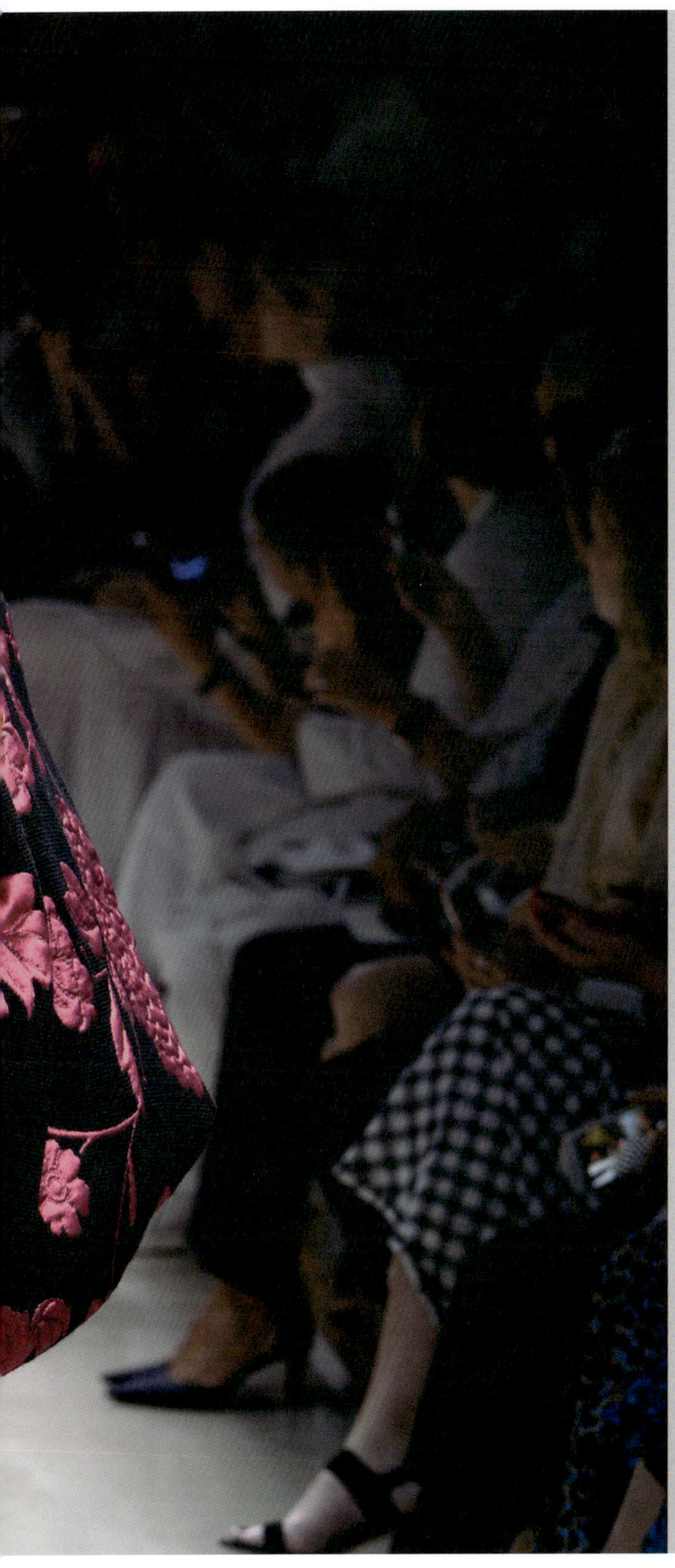

truly striking ensemble which included a black tulle jacket embroidered with crystals, paired with a narrow champagne duchesse satin skirt featuring a stiff, petal-like hemline. This inaugural collection was an immediate hit, lauded and admired for its minimalist aesthetic and extraordinary tailoring. In a fashion landscape often characterised by excess, Armani Privé offered a breath of fresh air, proving that simplicity could be as captivating as extravagance. The debut collection—a truly celestial combination of clean lines, luxurious fabrics and muted tones—set the tone for what would go on to become the Armani Privé template.

At the heart of Armani Privé lies an unwavering dedication to craftsmanship. Each AP design is testament to the skill and artistry of the ateliers behind it. From hand-sewn embellishments to precisely tailored silhouettes, every detail is meticulously considered. The process of creating an Armani Privé garment begins with a conversation between designer and client, ensuring that each piece reflects the wearer's personality and desires. The fabrics used are of unparalleled quality, often custom-made for the collection. Silk, organza, velvet, and chiffon are transformed into heavenly creations. The embellishments used—whether they be crystals, beads, or embroidery—are applied with an almost surgical precision, ensuring that every design achieves the perfect balance of subtlety and sophistication.

One of the most visible stages for Armani Privé is the red carpet. Celebrities and style icons frequently

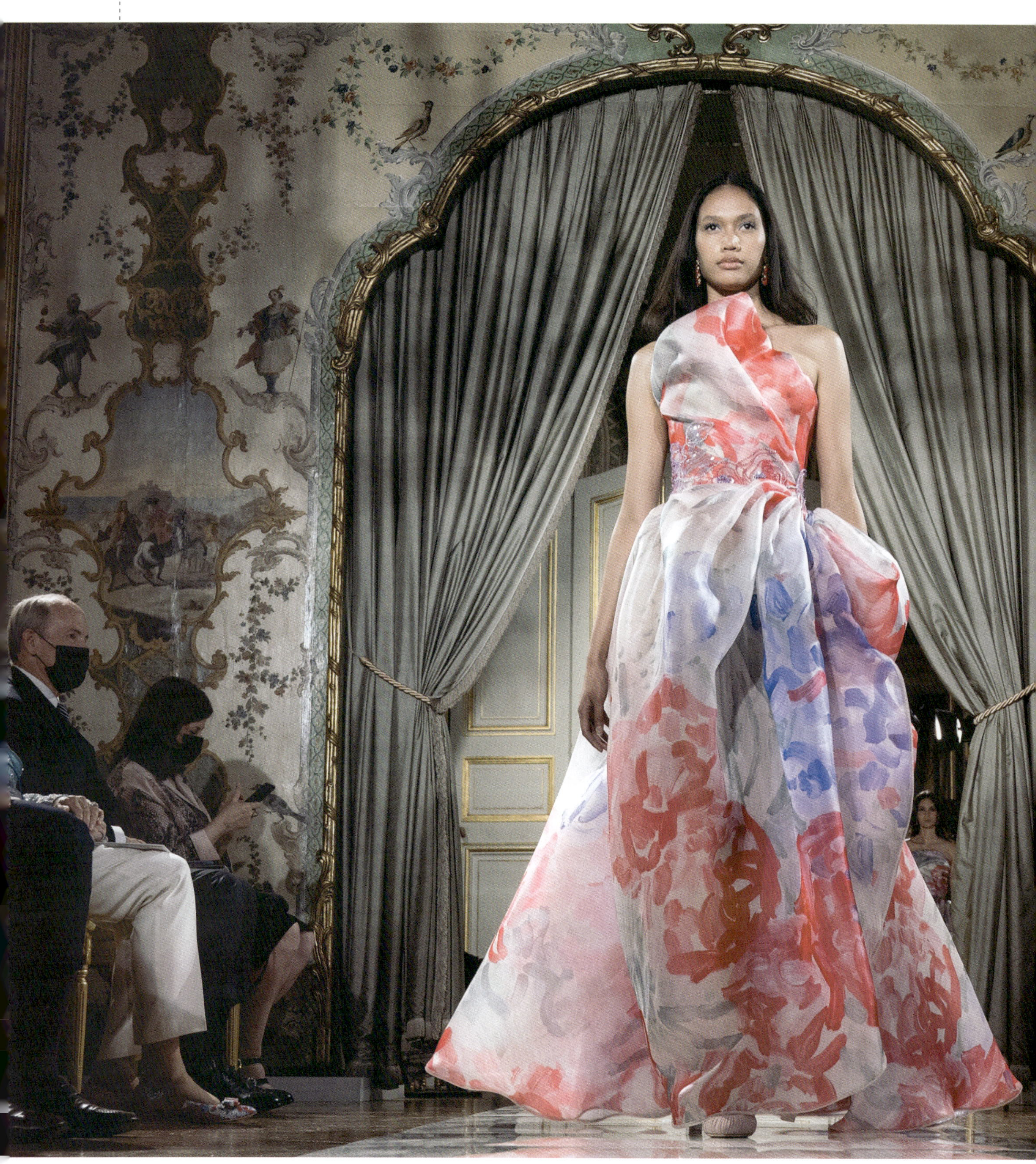

ABOVE: Tia Wan walks the runway during the Giorgio Armani Privé Haute Couture Autumn/Winter 2021–2022 show, as part of Paris Fashion Week, 2021

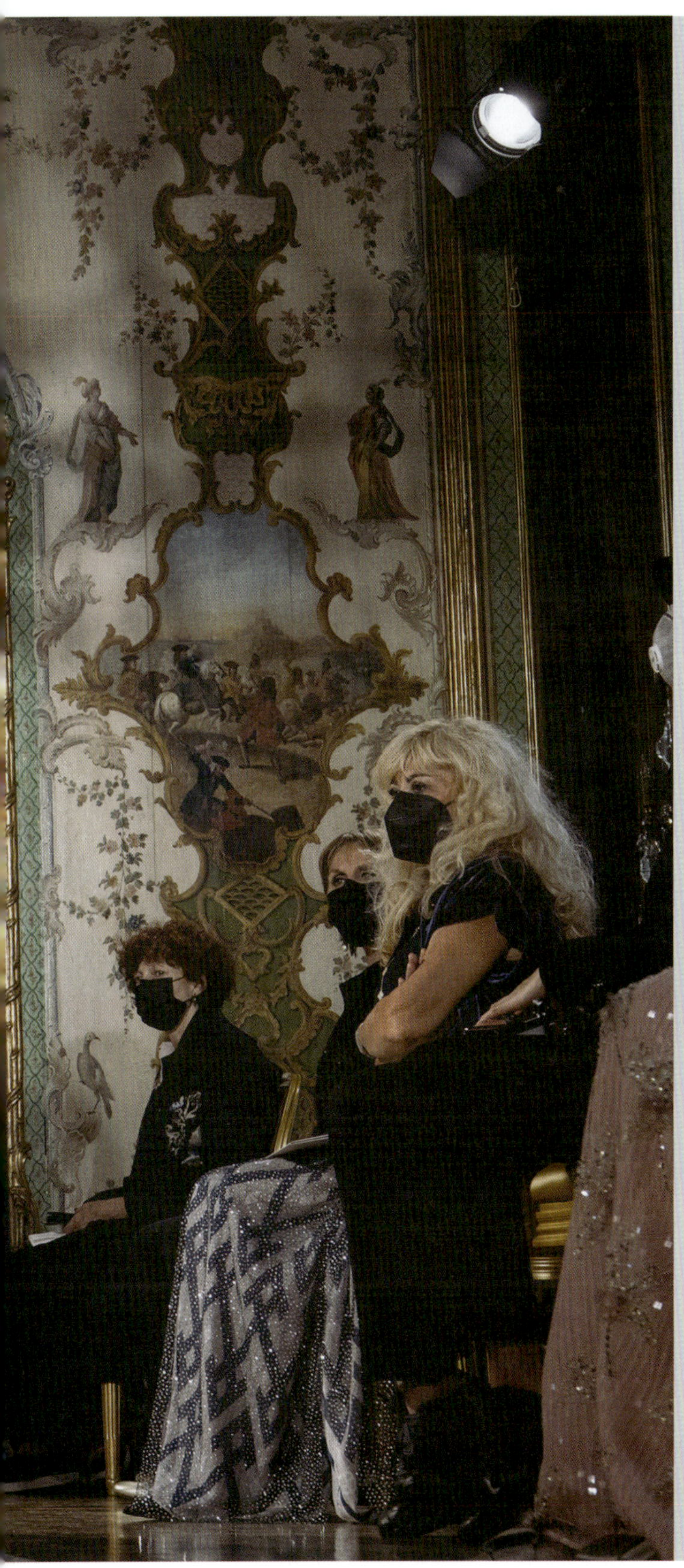

choose the label for its unparalleled elegance and ability to command attention without overwhelming. The likes of Cate Blanchett, Zendaya, and Penélope Cruz have all graced major events in Armani Privé creations, often making best-dressed lists all over the world. These moments transcend fashion—they are of artistic and cultural significance as they showcase the very best of visual glamour. Each red carpet appearance is a skilful collaboration, with the atelier crafting bespoke designs that complement the individuality of the wearer while maintaining the brand's signature style.

While rooted in the classic Armani aesthetic, Privé has evolved over the years, drawing inspiration from art, architecture and global cultures. Each collection tells a story, whether it's a tribute to the glimmering canals of Venice or to the modernist lines of urban skylines. Armani's ability to meld these influences with his minimalist philosophy ensures that Privé remains relevant and revolutionary.

Owning an Armani Privé piece is about more than just the garment—it is about the experience. Clients are invited into a world of exclusivity, where every detail—from the initial sketch to the final fitting—is tailored to their desires. This personalised approach is the essence of haute couture, and Armani Privé excels in making each client feel like the sole focus of the designer's attention. The Privé collections are typically showcased in intimate settings, reflecting the exclusivity of the line. At the Fall/Winter 2024-2025 Armani Privé show at Paris Fashion

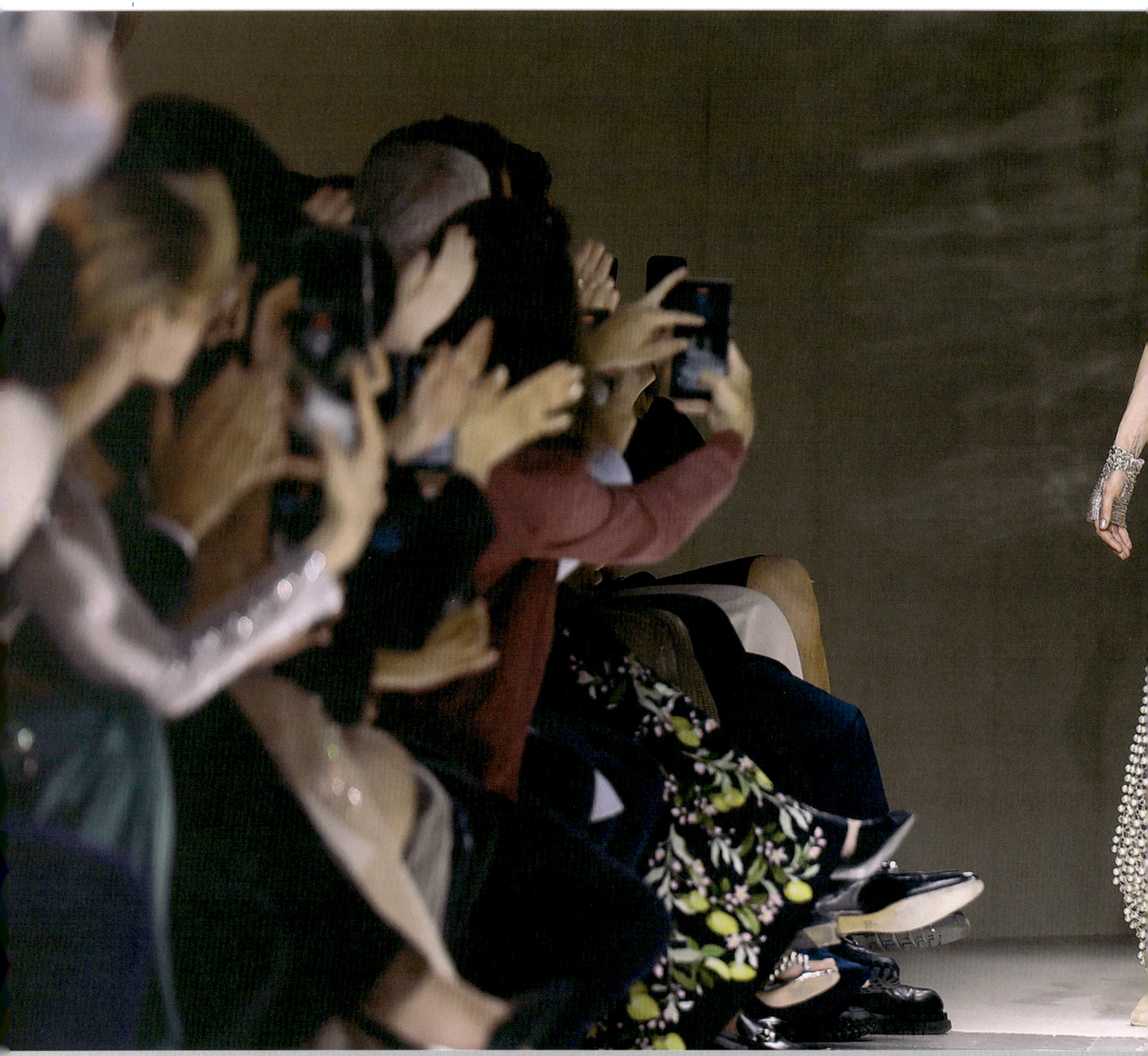

Week in June 2024, TikTok beauty influencer Meredith Duxbury expressed her admiration for the collection. She highlighted a stunning sheer, long-sleeved black lace dress with black pearls draping from the neck to the waist, describing it as *'so elegant and chic—and it was something original I haven't seen before on a runway!'*

Armani Privé is more than a fashion label—it is a

ABOVE: Giorgio Armani walks the runway during the Giorgio Armani Privé Haute Couture Autumn/Winter 2024–2025 show at Paris Fashion Week, 2024

testament to the enduring power of elegance and glamour. The fashion world often prioritises immediacy over longevity but Armani Prive reminds us that true luxury lies in the details. Through its exquisite craftsmanship, innovative designs, and commitment to timeless beauty, Armani Privé continues to define what it means to be at the very pinnacle of luxurious bespoke high fashion. It is not merely a brand but a legacy.

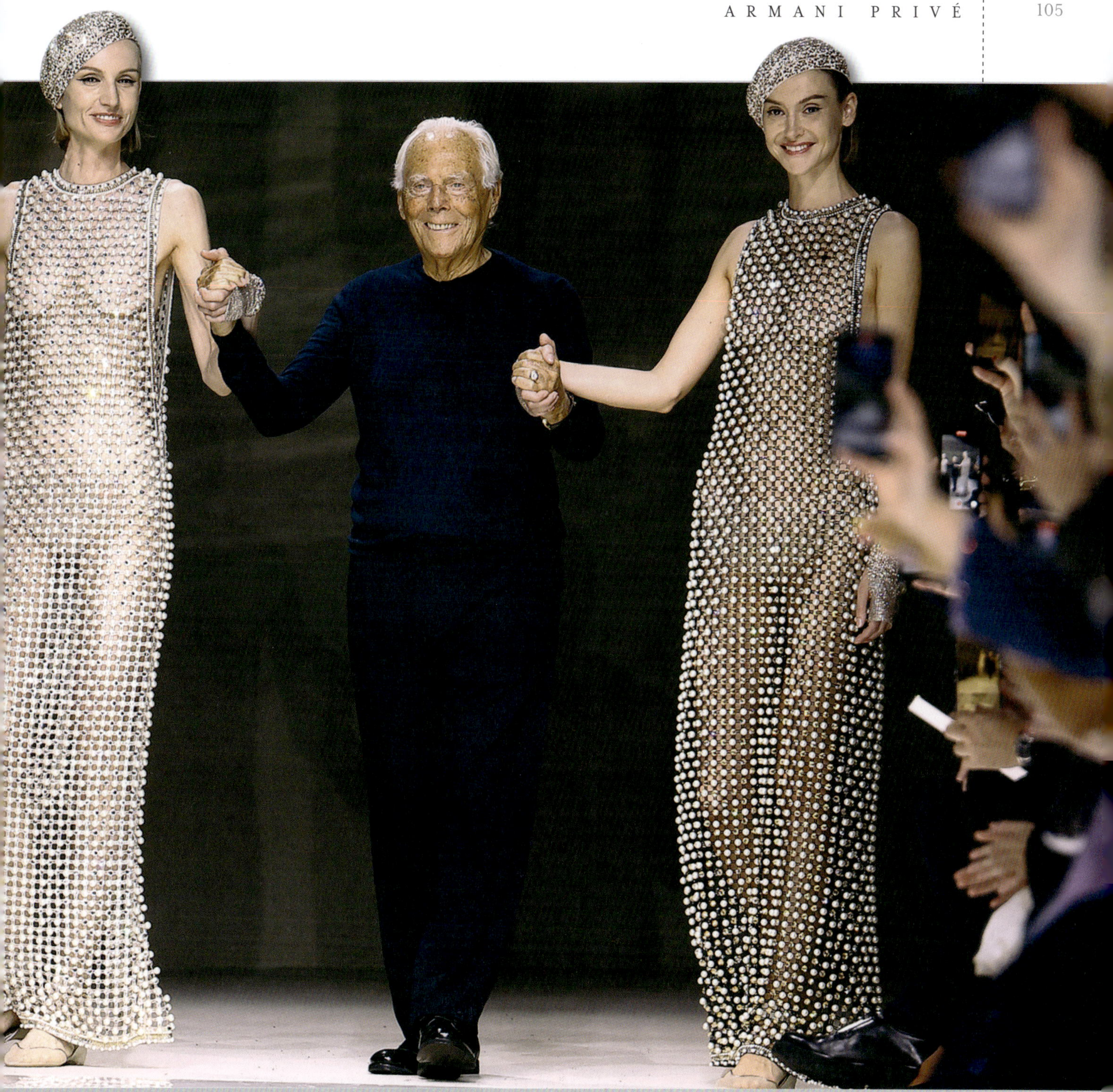

ARMANI BY NUMBERS

Armani figures to blow the mind!

7

Armani's major lines of Georgio Armani (Haute Couture, Luxury Ready-to-Wear), Emporio Armani (Contemporary Fashion), Armani Exchange (Youth-Oriented, Affordable), Armani Privé (Couture), Armani Beauty (Cosmetics and Fragrances) Armani Casa (Home and Interior Design), Armani Hotels and Resorts

235 MILLION

The amount of Euros the brand generates globally in any one year

500 PLUS

The number of Armani stores, mono-brand boutiques and outlets around the world

10000

The amount of dollars raised by Armani in 1975 to start his business. Part of it was raised by selling his Volkswagen car

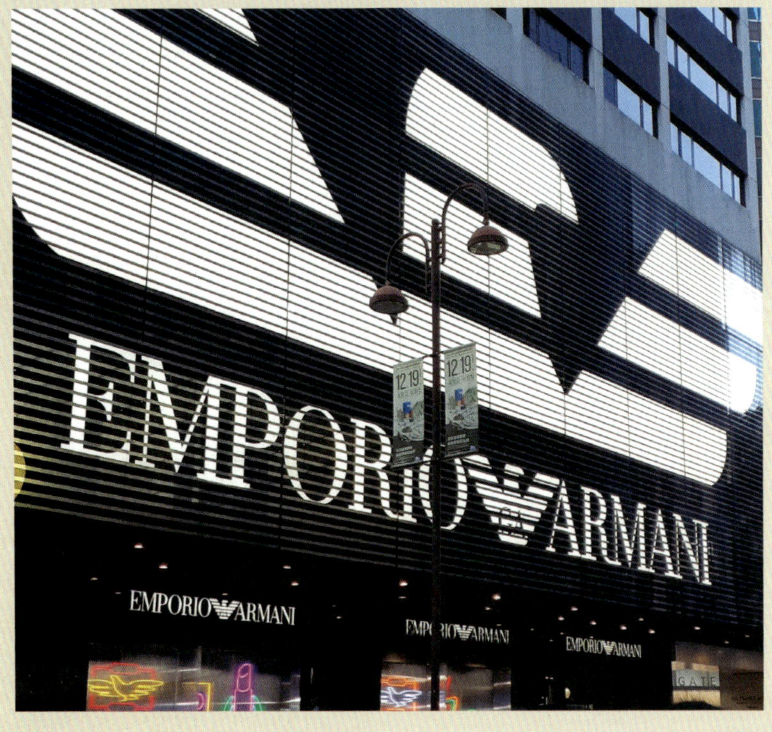

46

The number of countries in which Armani has stores

180-PLUS

The number of Armani fragrances including the iconic Acqua di Giò, Sì, and Code. Acqua di Giò is among the top-selling men's fragrances world-wide

2

The number of times a day Georgio Armani is said to think about a successor—*'When I wake up in the morning and when I go to sleep at night'*

3000

The hours it takes to create an Armani haute couture gown

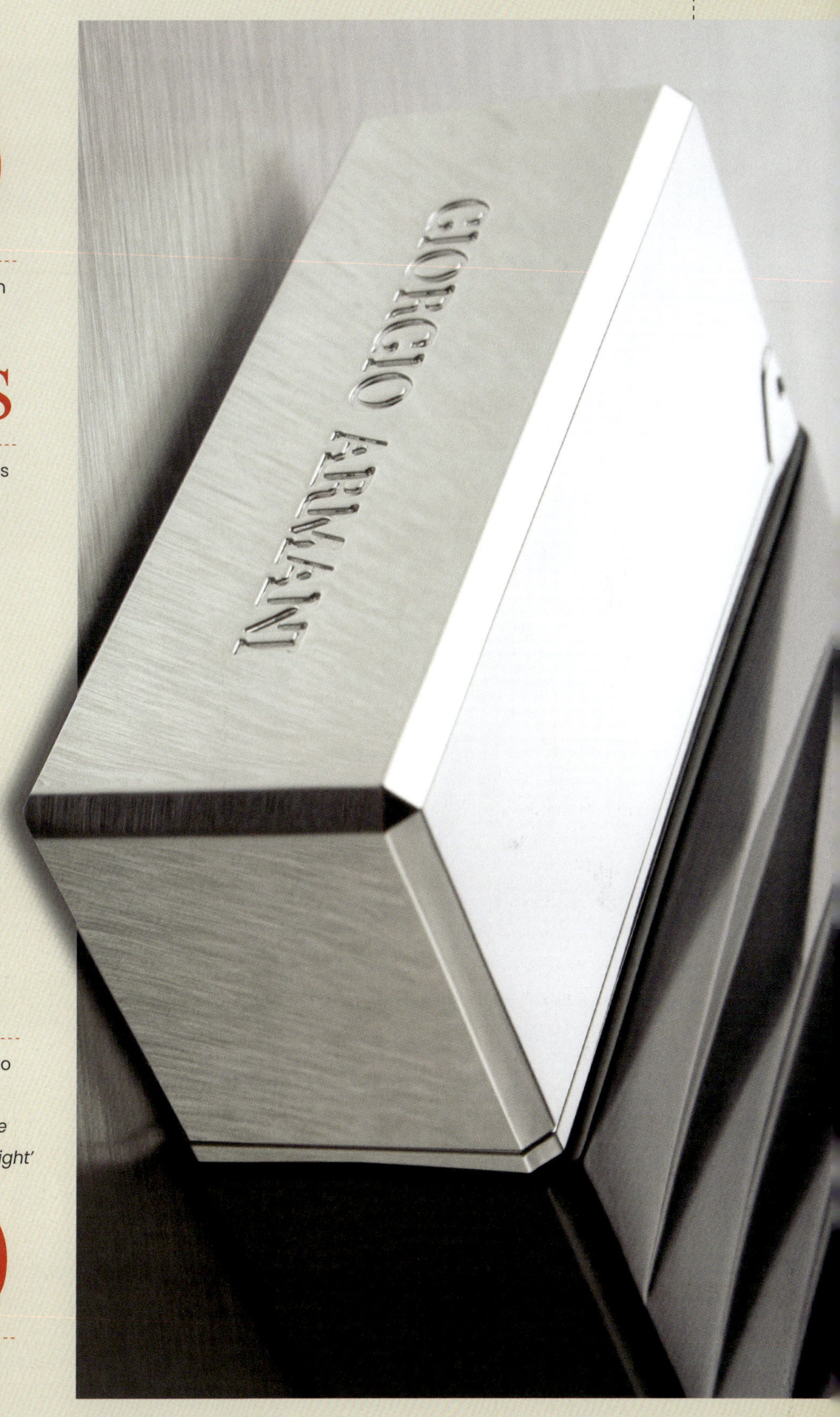

10
MILLION

The approximate amount of suits Armani has sold worldwide since 1980

7300

Armani employs this number of people

100

The percentage of the company Georgio Armani owns. He remains the sole owner of his fashion empire, a rarity among global luxury brands

250

The films Georgio Armani has designed for including *American Gigolo* (1980), *The Untouchables* (1987), *The Bodyguard* (1992), *The Dark Knight* (2008) and *The Wolf of Wall Street* (2013)

RIGHT: Christian Bale in a Giorgio Armani advertisement, created as part of *The Dark Knight* promotional campaign

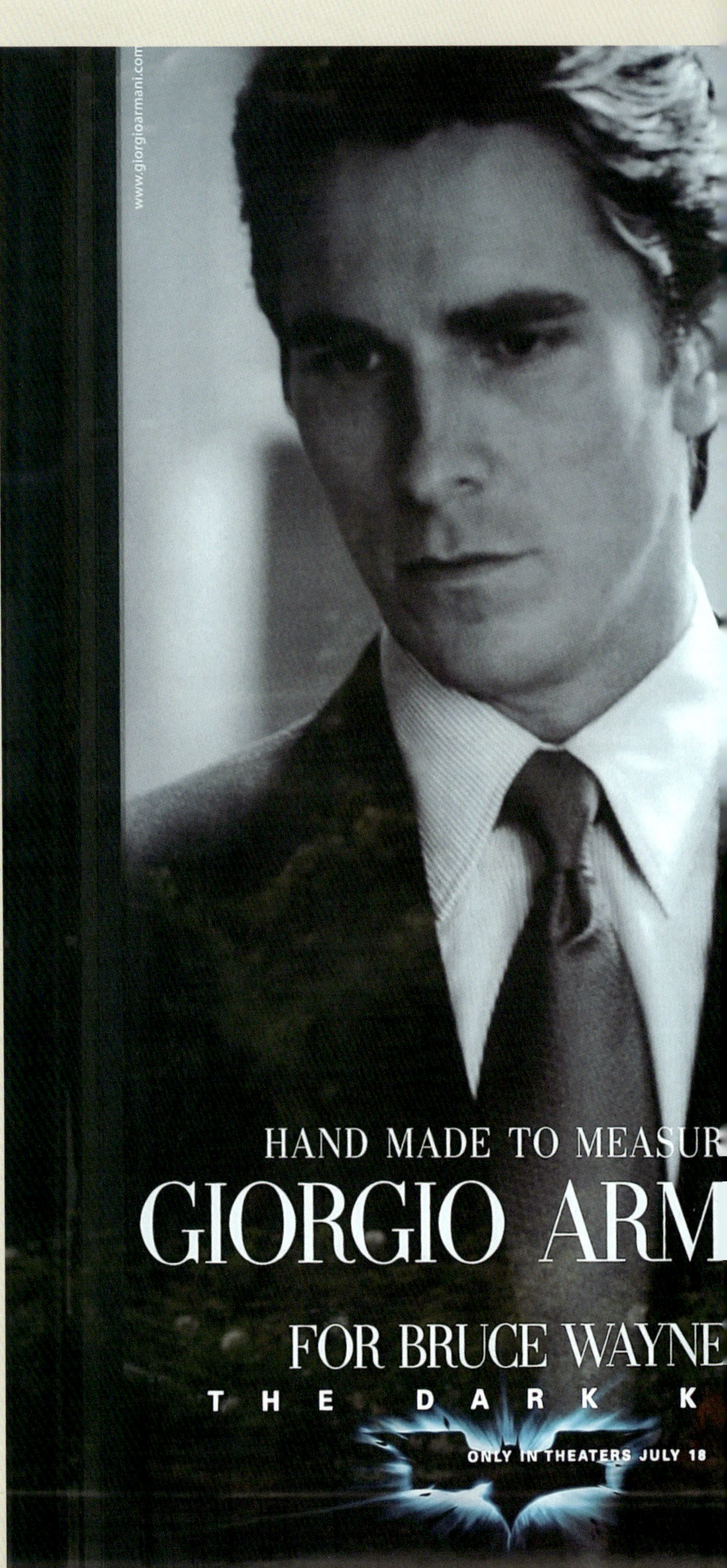

40

The number of shades the iconic Armani Luminous Silk Foundation comes in

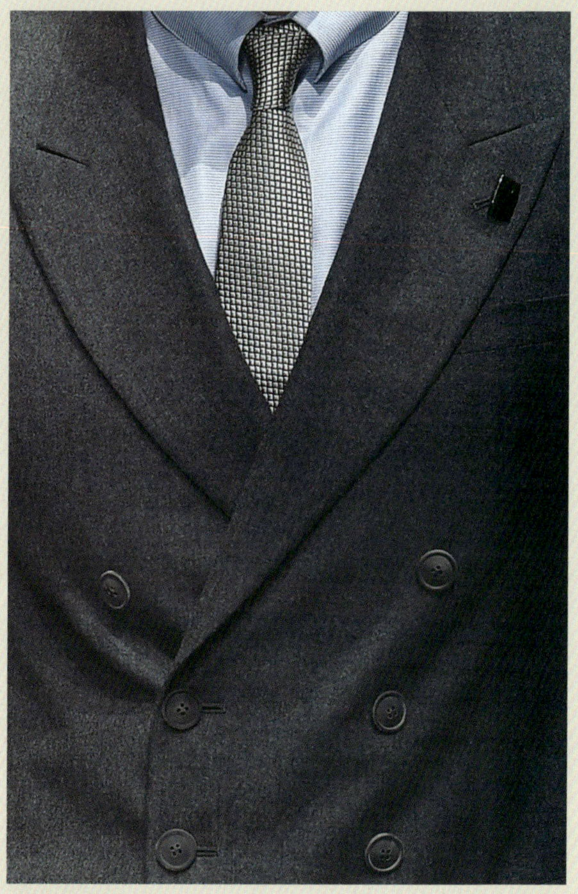

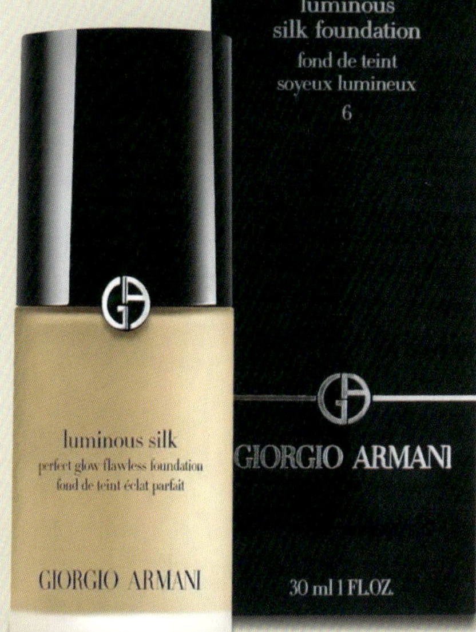

6

The number of times he's mentioned in the Pet Shop Boys' 1986 single "Paninaro"

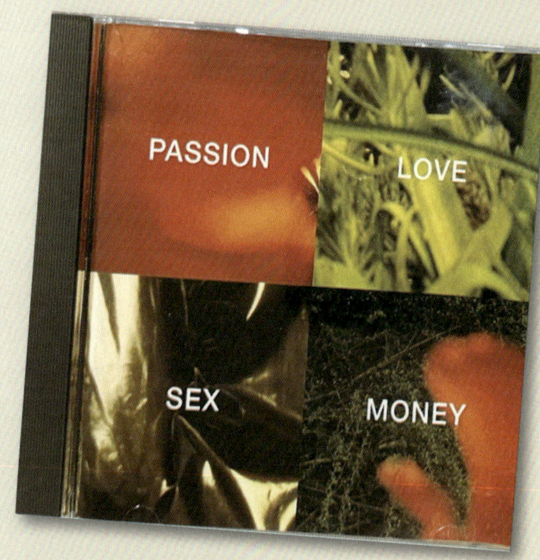

TOP LEFT: A classic Armani suit
TOP RIGHT: Armani Luminous Silk Foundation
ABOVE: Pet Shop Boys' 1986 single "Paninaro"

92

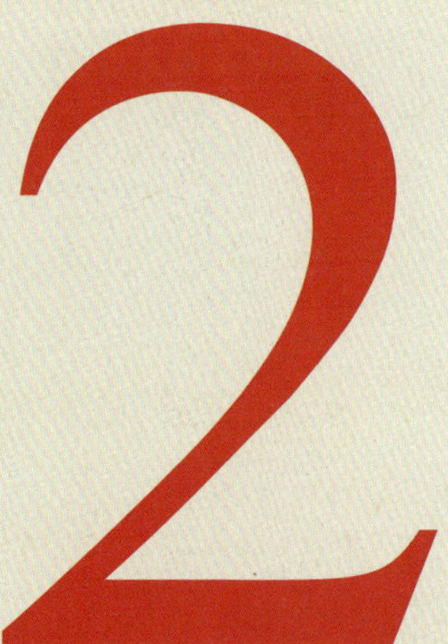

The number of houses Giorgio Armani calls home. There's his primary residence in Milan, Italy where he has lived since 1982; a property in Lombardy, Italy; a house in the seaside town of Forte dei Marmi on Tuscany's Versilia Coast; a house in the picturesque fishing village of Portofino; a compound on Pantelleria, an island between Sicily and Tunisia; a ski lodge in St Moritz in the Swiss Alps; a house in St Tropez on the French Riviera; a property on the Caribbean island of Antigua; and a penthouse in New York City

There are two operational Armani Hotels—the Armani Hotel Dubai and the Armani Hotel Milano. Opened on April 27, 2010, the Dubai hotel occupies the first 39 floors of the Burj Khalifa in Dubai, UAE. It features 160 guest rooms and suites, along with 144 residences. Launched in 2011, the Milan hotel is situated in the prestigious Manzoni 31 building in Milan, Italy—the world-famous fashion district known as the Quadrilatero della Moda

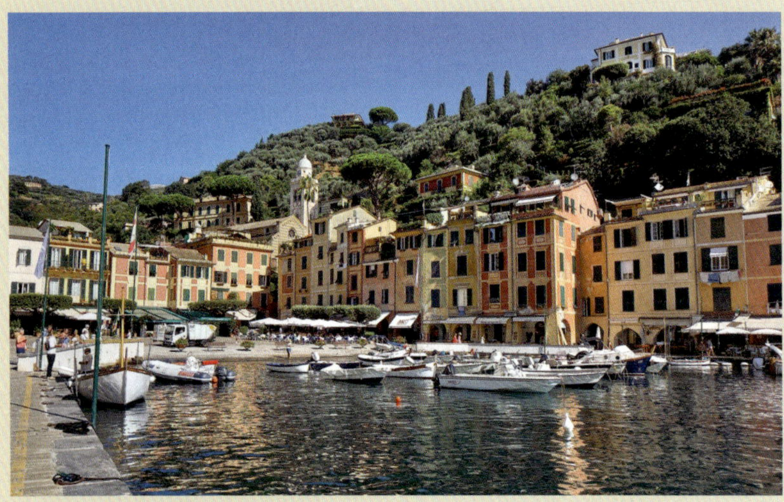

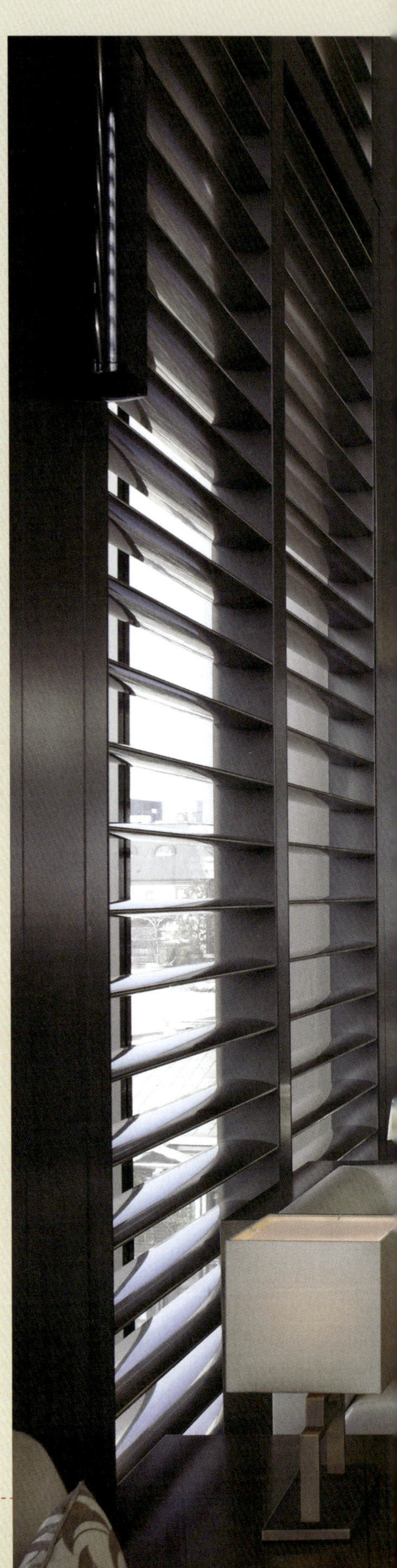

ABOVE: The stunning village of Portofino, Italy
RIGHT: Lounge bar at the Armani Hotel Milano, Italy
OPP PAGE: Dessert from Armani Ristorante at the Armani Hotel in the Burj Khalifa, Dubai

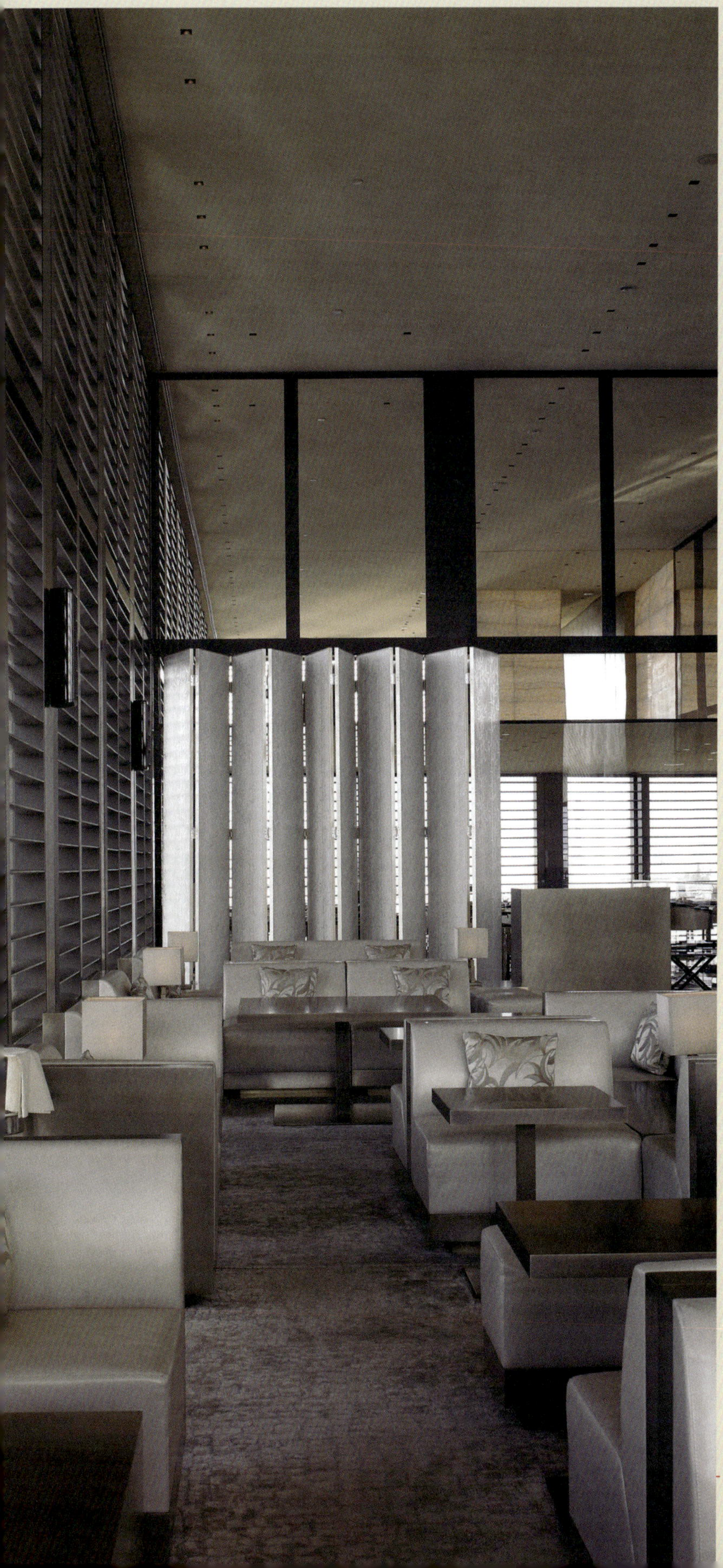

20
PLUS

Giorgio Armani has established a global presence in the culinary world with over 20 restaurants and cafés across four continents. These establishments offer a blend of traditional Italian cuisine and avant-garde culinary techniques, reflecting the brand's commitment to elegance and sophistication. Notable Armani dining venues include Armani/Ristorante New York: opened in late 2024, this restaurant is located on Madison Avenue and 65th Street and features a contemporary Italian menu crafted by executive chef Antonio D'Angelo, with signature dishes like Maine lobster with grapefruit and sabayon; Armani/Ristorante Paris: situated on the first floor of the Armani store in St-Germain-des-Prés, this Michelin-starred restaurant offers a refined dining experience with a menu curated by chef Massimo Tringali; and the Armani/Ristorante Dubai located within the Burj Khalifa

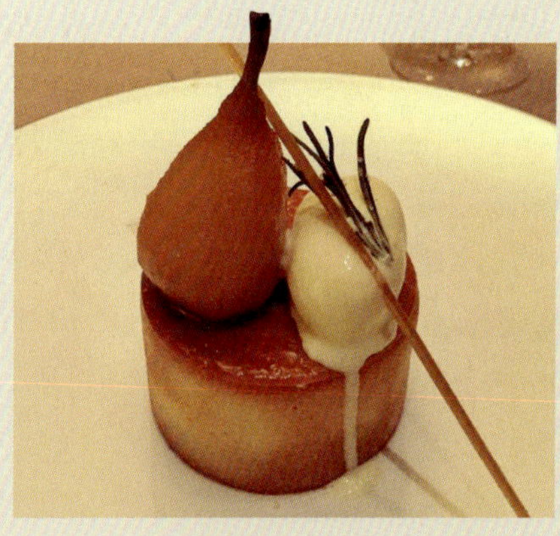

ARMANI MUSES

'Muse'—a person or personified force who is the source of inspiration for a creative artist.

For the luxury designer, a muse is far more than just a collaborator or model—they symbolise a designer's creative journey and cultural relevance. They help bridge the gap between the designer's artistic vision and the real world, making fashion about storytelling, culture and identity in addition to clothing. Giorgio Armani has worked with an array of muses and ambassadors over the decades, reflecting the brand's ethos of timeless elegance, sophistication and modernity. These individuals—from Hollywood icons and supermodels to international athletes—embody the Armani aesthetic and its commitment to understated luxury. Whether through haute couture gowns or contemporary campaigns, Armani's muses play a crucial role in maintaining the brand's relevance, prestige and sheer magic.

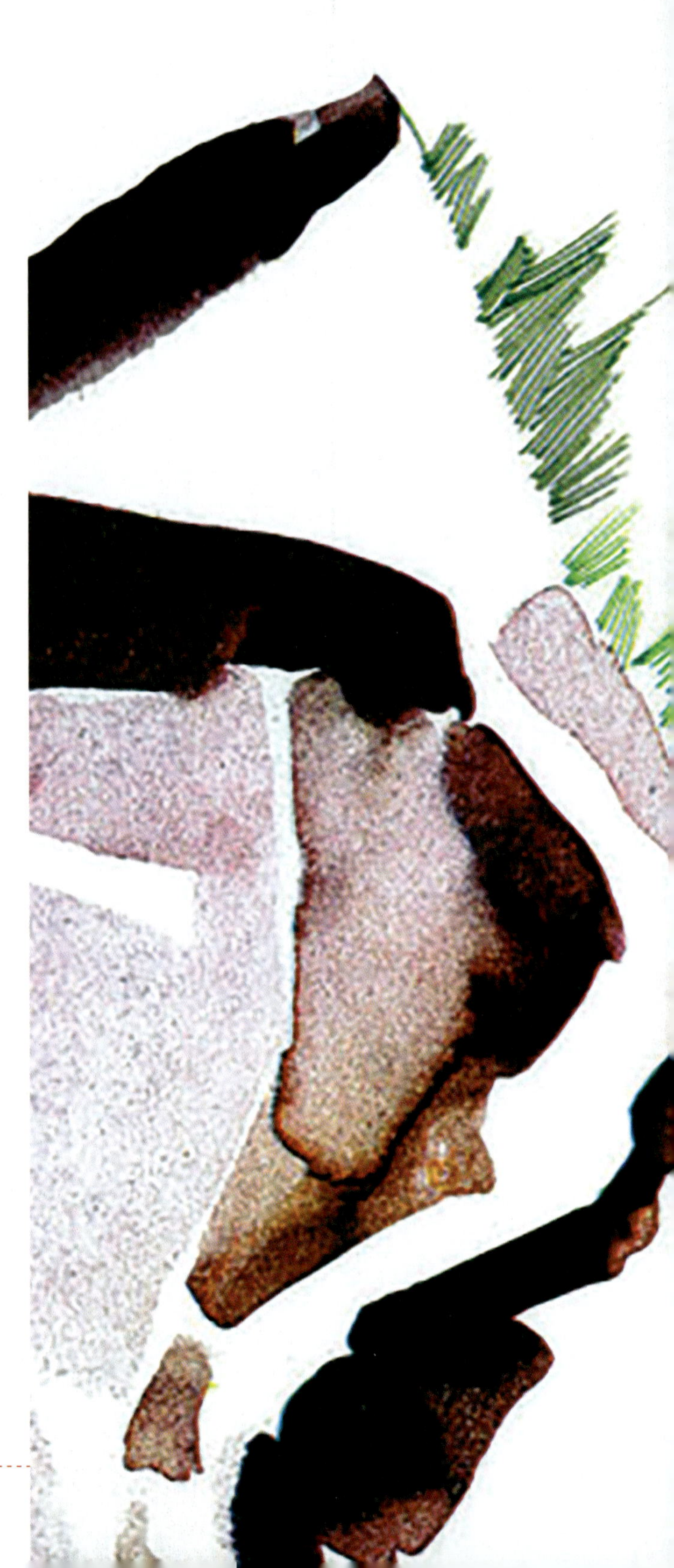

RIGHT: Giorgio Armani, portrait by Graziano Origa, 1979

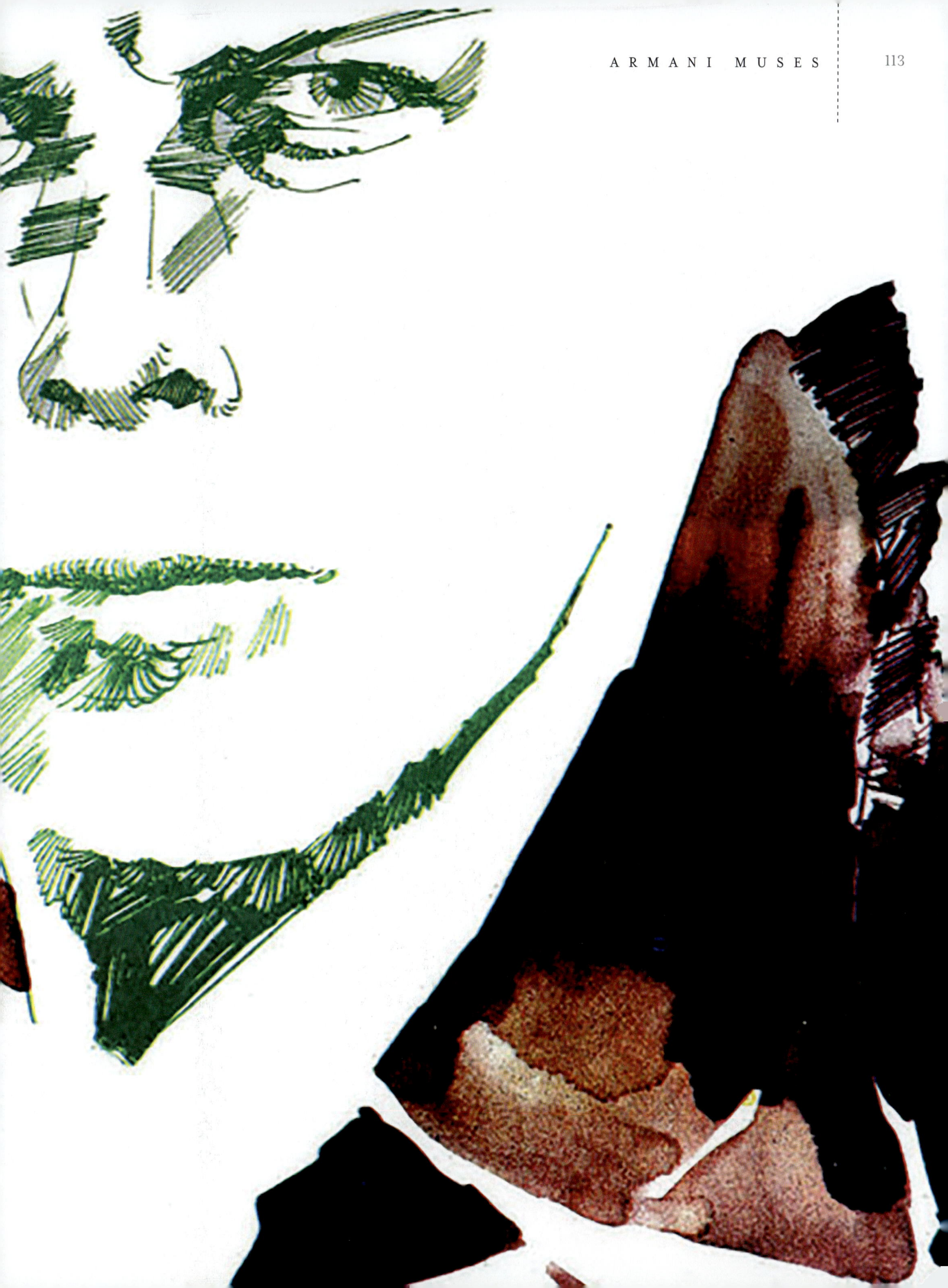

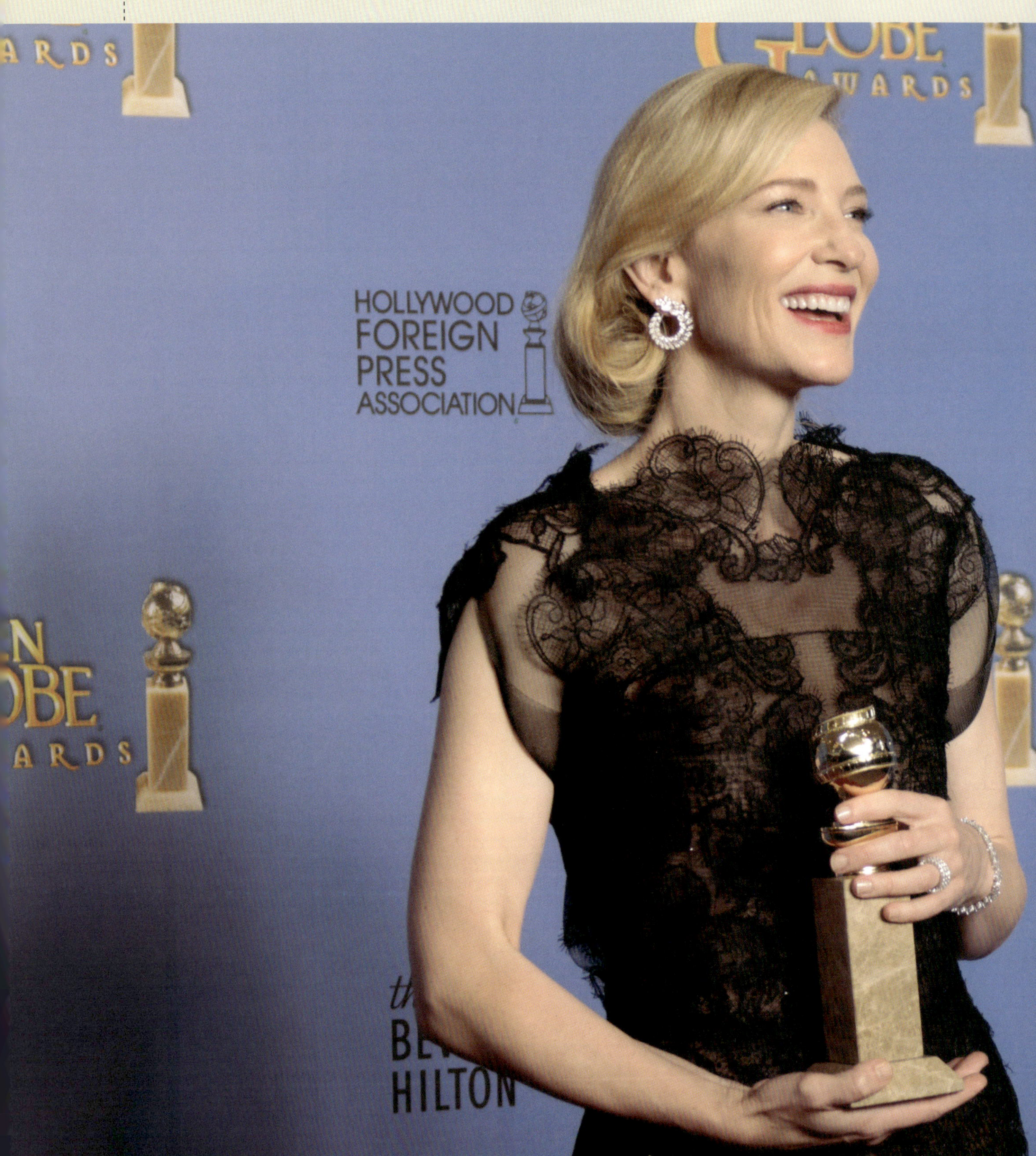

ABOVE: Cate Blanchett in a black lace Armani Privé gown at the 2014 Golden Globes, California

CATE BLANCHETT

Acting legend Blanchett personifies Armani's vision of sophistication, grace and intelligence. Her elegant, intellectual and versatile persona aligns seamlessly with Giorgio Armani's vision of refined sophistication. She embodies the brand's philosophy of understated glamour and has become one of its most enduring and celebrated ambassadors. Her association with the House began in the mid-noughties when she made frequent appearances in Armani Privé gowns on the red-carpet. At the 79th Academy Awards in 2007, Blanchett wore a shimmering silver one-shoulder gown by Armani Privé, adorned with Swarovski crystals. This dress was later recognised as one of the best Oscar dresses of all time. At the 2014 Golden Globes, she stunned in a black lace Armani Privé gown, exuding modern Old Hollywood glamour. She later recycled this dress for the 2018 Cannes Film Festival, showcasing her commitment to sustainable fashion. Her exquisite gold sequined Armani Privé gown at the 2014 Oscars solidified her status as a core Armani muse. Over the years, Blanchett has become more than just a red-carpet figure for Armani. She began representing the brand in campaigns, particularly as the face of the 'Si' fragrance line first launched in 2013. Her involvement in promoting 'Si' aligned her image with the brand's sophisticated and modern femininity.

ZENDAYA

Global star and fashion icon Zendaya has become one of the standout muses for Armani Privé. Her graceful yet confident style bridges the gap between youthful experimentation and timeless elegance and sophistication, making her an ideal name for Armani. Zendaya attended the Armani Privé Fall/Winter 2019–2020 show in a chic monochrome look, featuring a cropped white blouse and high-waisted black trousers, thus bringing contemporary flair to classic Armani tailoring. She subtly referenced Spider-Man's costume in the boldly designed custom red and black Armani Privé gown she wore at the 2019 *Spider-Man: Far from Home* Premiere. Five years later, she made another stand-out red-carpet appearance at the 2024 Academy Awards in a stunning antique rose Armani Privé gown featuring an embroidered palm motif and a paillette-embellished bodice. This look combined vintage inspiration with futuristic touches, embodying Armani's talent for blending eras. Zendaya's relationship with Armani isn't limited to red-carpet appearances. Her influence as a muse and ambassador extends into campaign work, exemplifying the brand's ethos across several areas.

RIGHT: Zendaya in a custom red and black Armani Privé gown at the premiere of *Spider-Man: Far From Home* in 2019
OPP PAGE: Lady Gaga in an Armani Privé statement piece at the Grammys in 2010

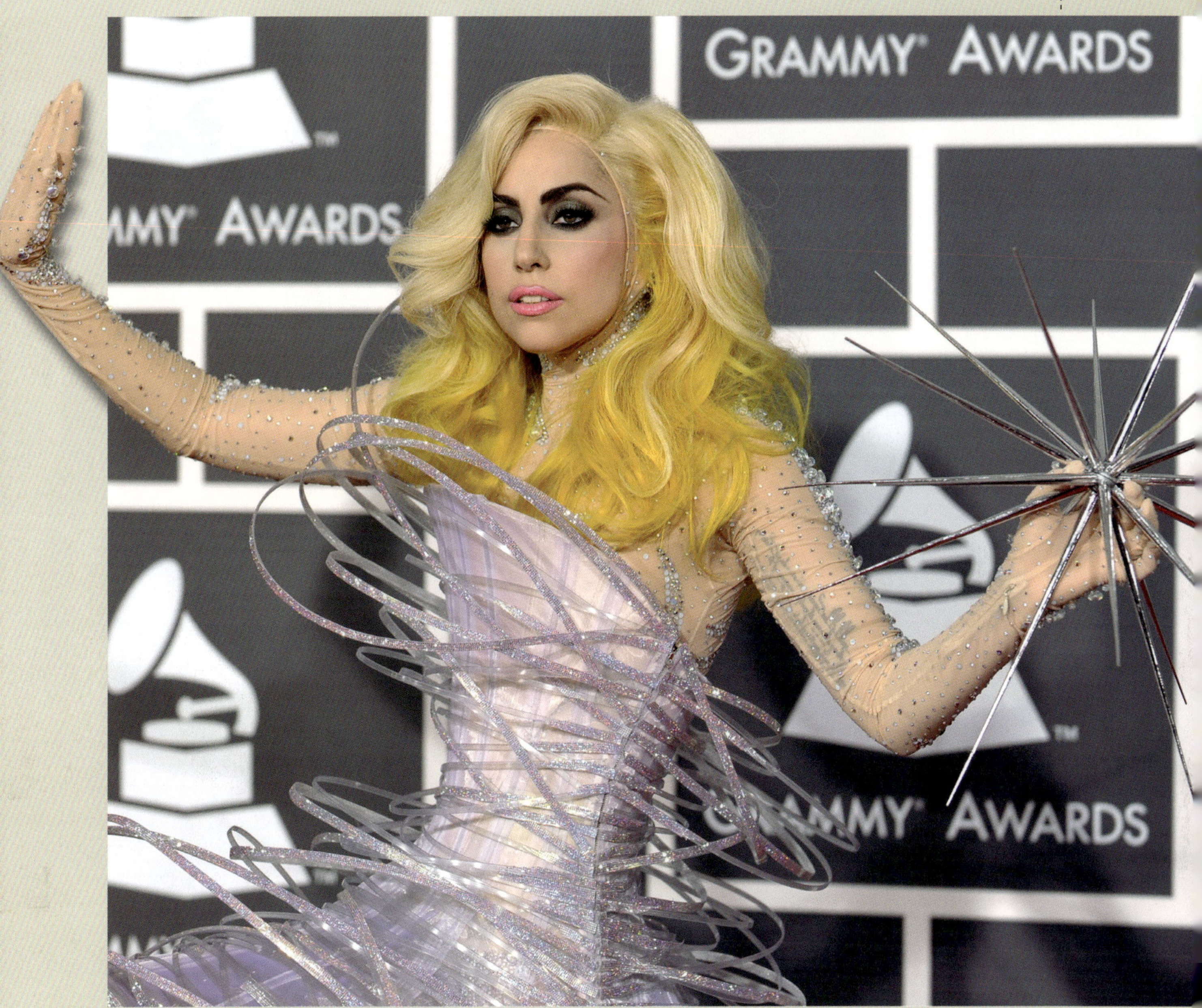

LADY GAGA

Flamboyant Gaga has embraced Armani's more avant-garde designs, especially from the Armani Privé line. Her bold yet elegant style resonates with Armani's ability to blend drama and sophistication.

Iconic appearances in Armani Privé include the intergalactic, sparkly gown she wore—accessorised with a metallic orb-like structure, for her first appearance at the Grammys in 2010. Also, the strikingly sleek black velvet gown with oversized sleeves worn at the 2019 Golden Globes.

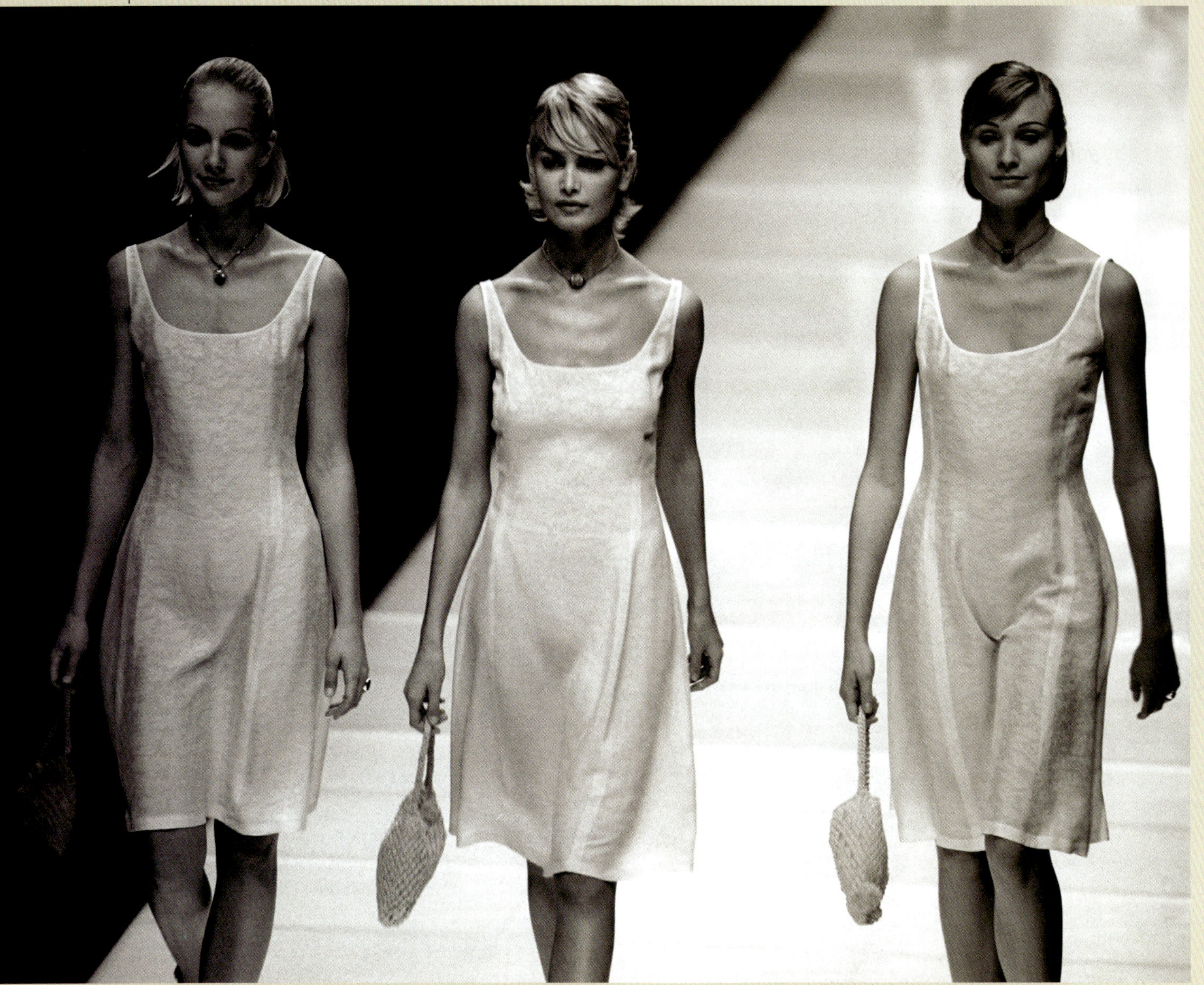

LINDA EVANGELISTA

One of the original supermodels, Linda Evangelista's collaborations with Giorgio Armani in the early 1990s are among her most memorable runway moments. Notably, during Milan Fashion Week in 1992, she graced the runway in a sophisticated grey suit, exemplifying Armani's signature elegance and simplicity. In the Spring/Summer 1991 Ready-to-Wear collection, Evangelista showcased a chic one-shouldered dress, highlighting Armani's minimalist aesthetic. Her appearances during this period were instrumental in defining the understated yet refined style that Armani is celebrated for.

ABOVE: Model Linda Evangelista (centre) at the Emporio Armani Spring 1996 Ready-to-Wear runway show
OPP PAGE: Kate Moss for Armani in magazine advertisements

KATE MOSS

Kate Moss became the face of Giorgio Armani's
Fall/Winter 2019-2020 campaign, marking her first
collaboration with the house. She rocked a series
of sophisticated looks, including tailored suits
and shimmering gowns, emphasising Armani's
signature minimalist elegance. For the campaign
Moss sported a short, choppy blonde hairstyle,
presenting a fresh and modern image. Armani
described the Croydon-born icon as *'a woman of
singular beauty, whose personality and energy
decisively set her apart from the fleeting fads of
the moment.'*

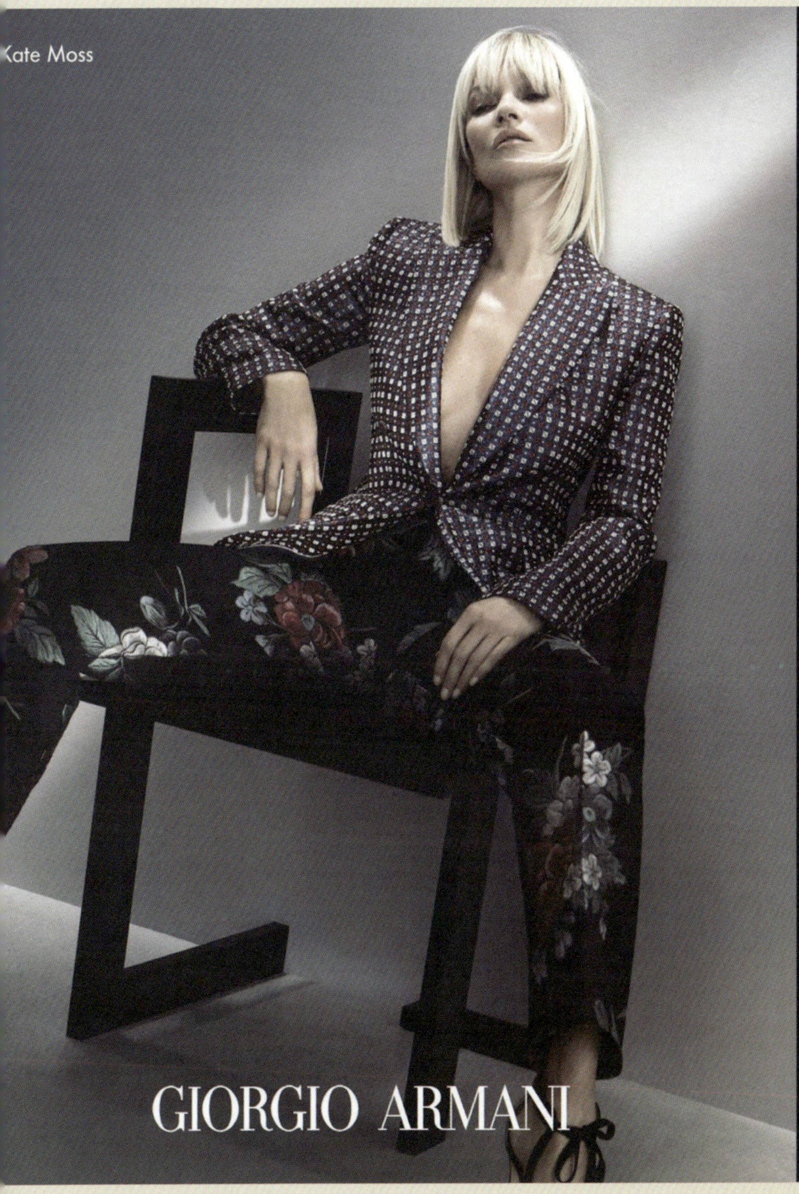

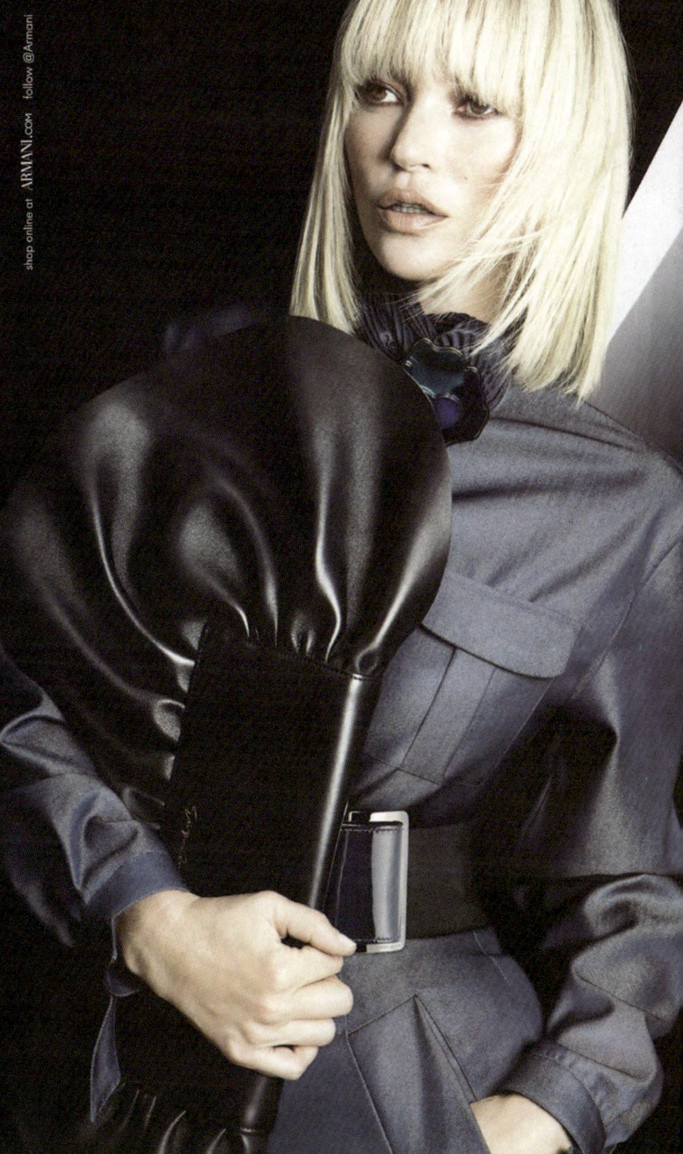

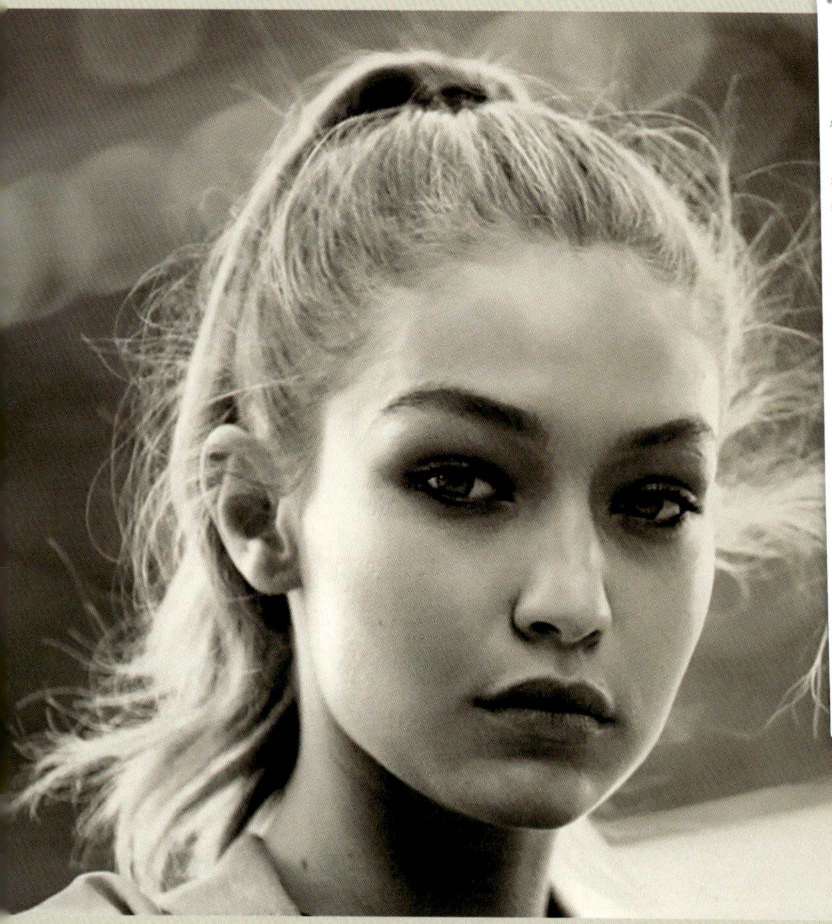

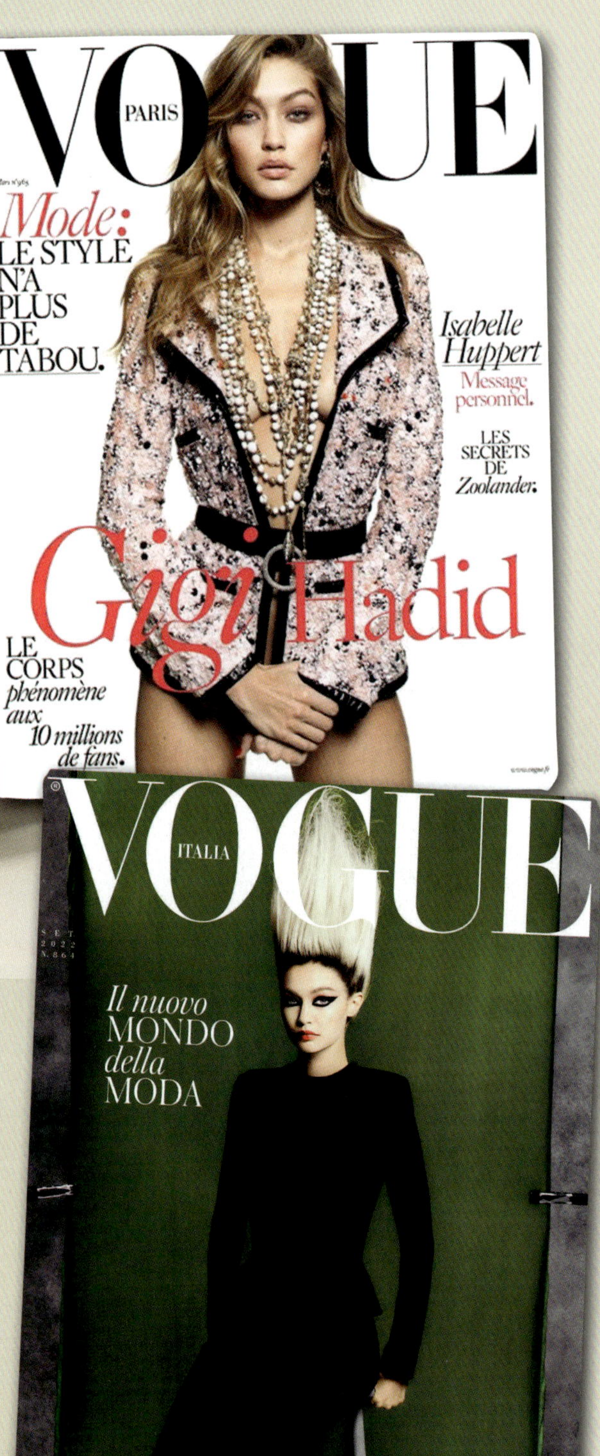

GIGI HADID

Gigi Hadid has collaborated with Giorgio Armani on several notable occasions. She graced the cover of *Vogue Paris* in November 2016 modelling a velvet, crystal-embellished ensemble from Armani Privé, complemented by a wide-brimmed hat. In September 2022, Gigi appeared on the cover of *Vogue Italia*, adorned in a Giorgio Armani Fall/Winter 2022–2023 long cady dress. Gigi is also said to love Giorgio Armani's Acqua Di Gioia fragrance.

ABOVE: Gigi Hadid
ABOVE RIGHT: Gigi Hadid Vogue covers
OPP PAGE: Penelope Cruz wearing a stunning Armani Privé gown at the 2012 Academy Awards

PENÉLOPE CRUZ

Spanish film star Cruz exudes sensuality and elegance, making her a perfect fit for Armani Privé's dramatic yet understated aesthetic. Standout appearances include 2012 Academy Awards where she paid homage to Hollywood's golden era in a custom Armani Privé gown. The ethereal dress featured a blend of blue and grey hues, reminiscent of a stormy sky, with off-the-shoulder straps and a fitted bodice. At the *On the Fringe* premiere in October 2022, Cruz modelled a sleek Giorgio Armani suit, highlighting the designer's timeless tailoring.

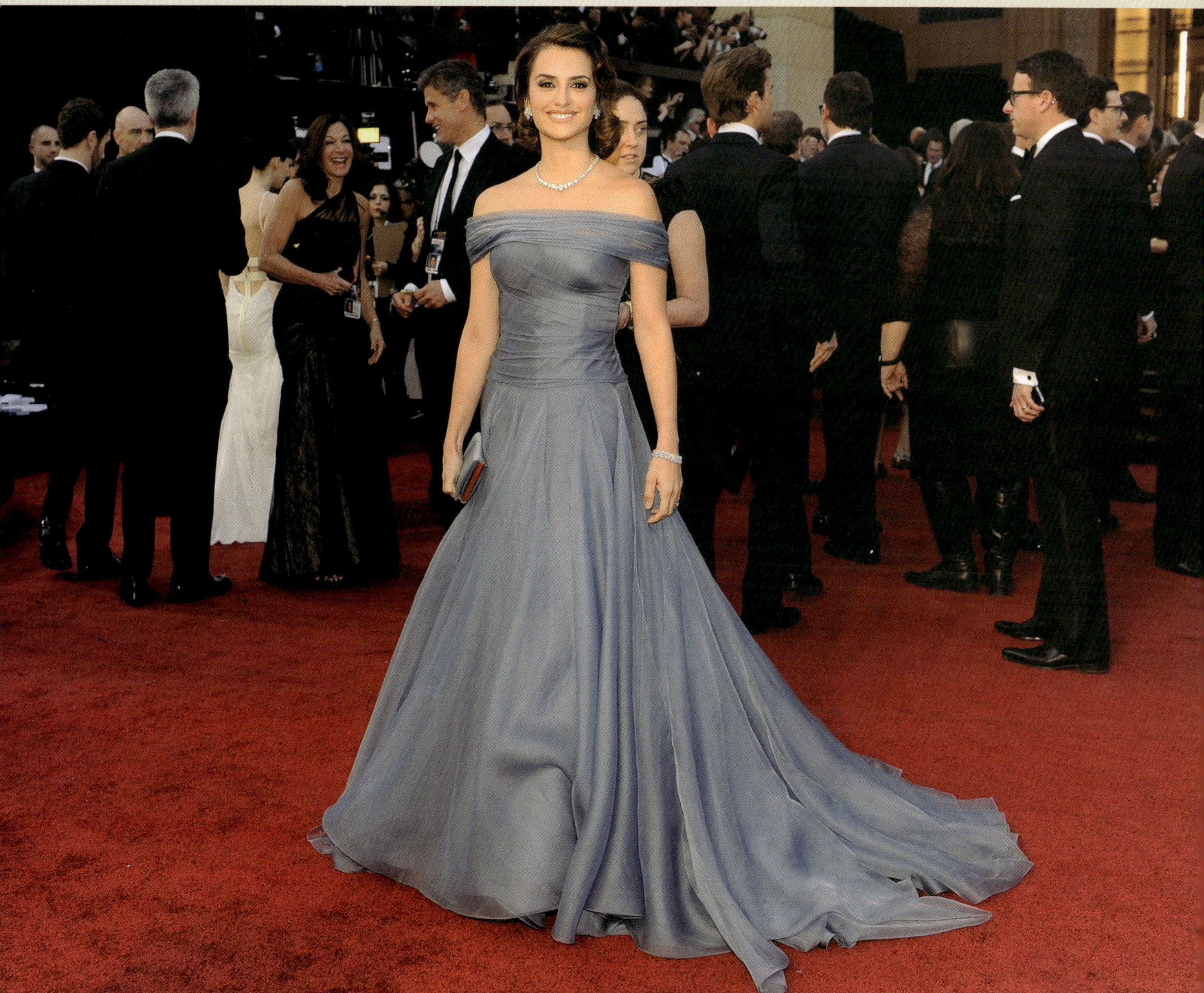

NATHALIE EMMANUEL

In November 2024, the British actress, renowned for her roles in *Game of Thrones* and *Fast & Furious* was appointed as a global make-up ambassador for the brand. She features in the Armani 2025 Luminous Silk Foundation campaign.

SYDNEY SWEENEY

In early 2023, the *Euphoria* star became an ambassador for Armani Beauty, showcasing the brand's products at various high-profile events, including the Venice Film Festival.

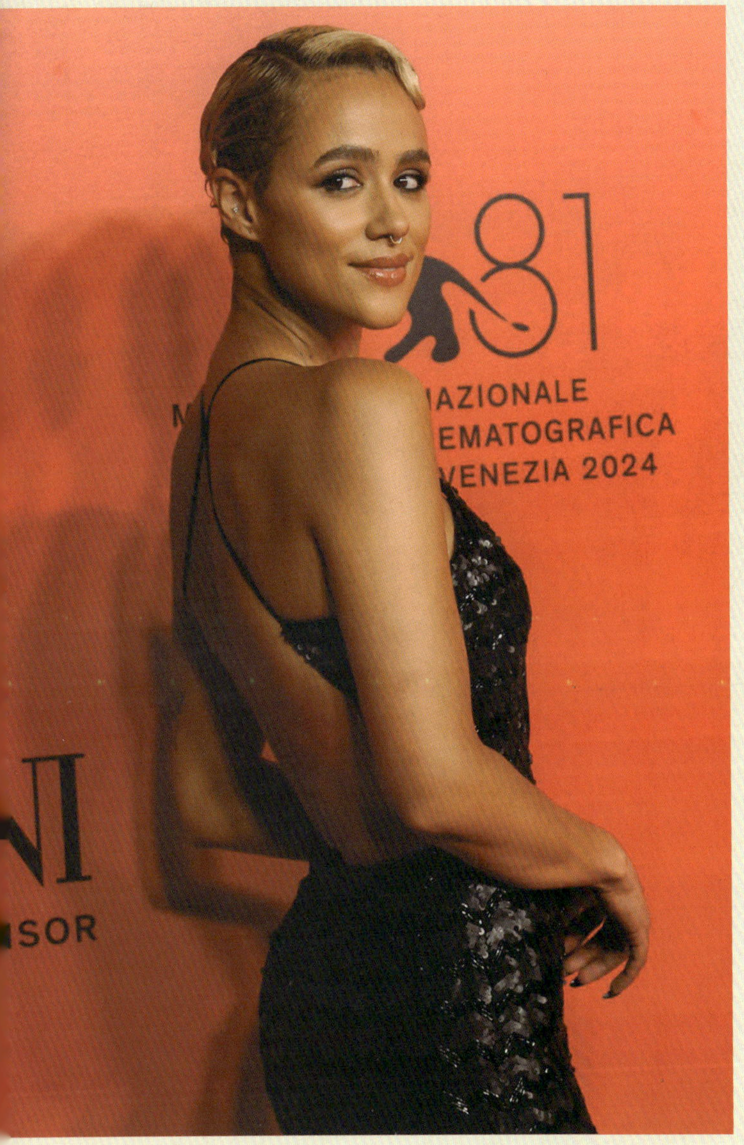

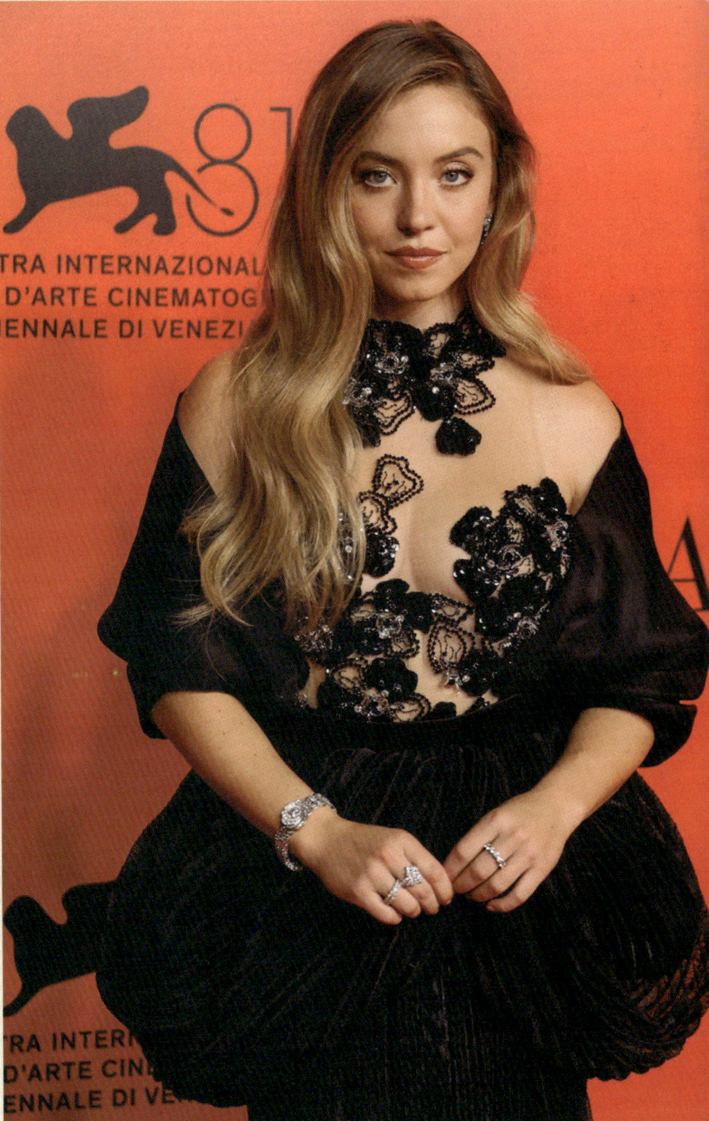

ABOVE: Nathalie Emmanuel (left) and Sydney Sweeney (right) pose for photographers at the Armani Beauty event during the 81st Venice Film Festival in Italy, 2024

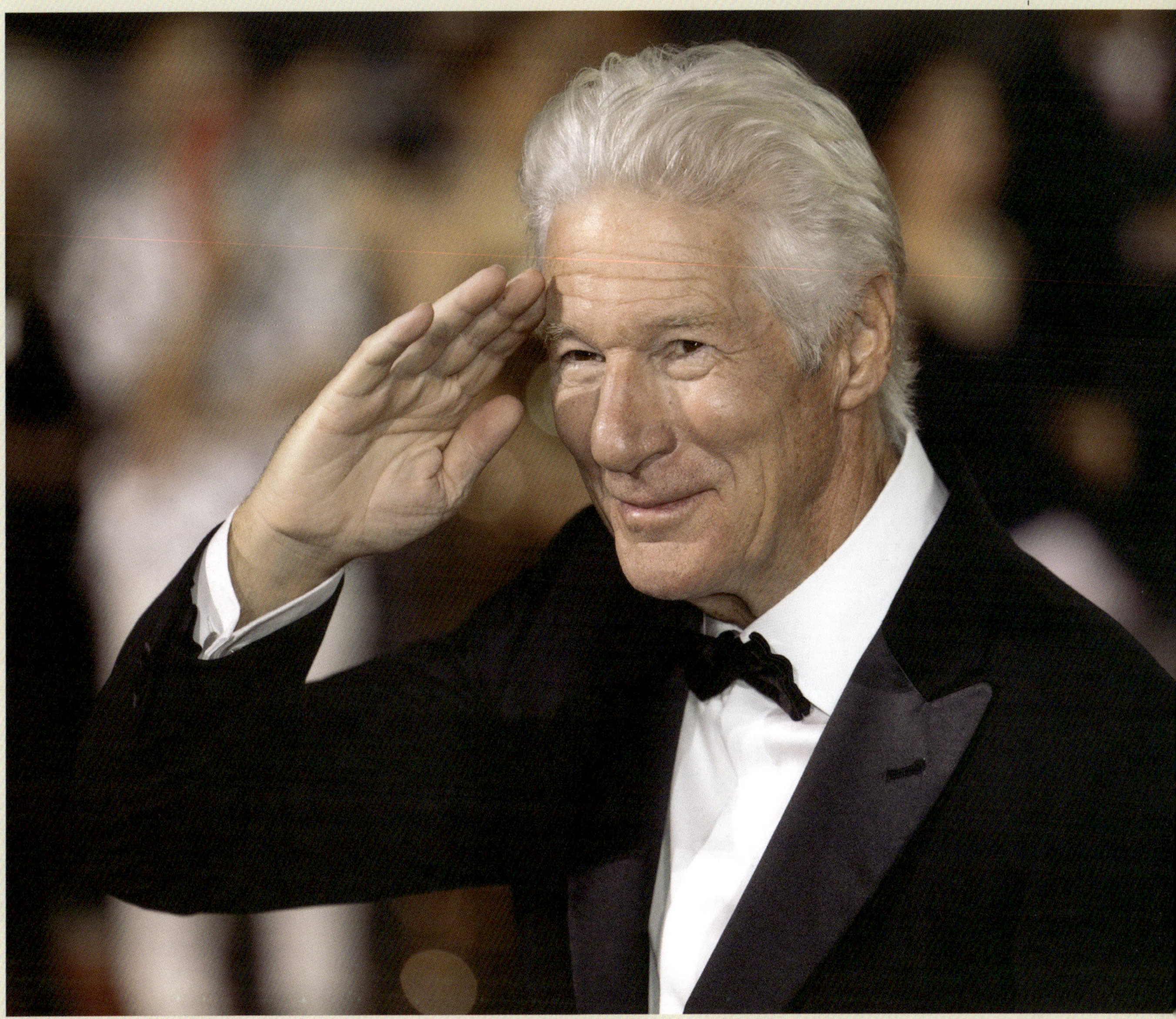

RICHARD GERE

Richard Gere's association with Giorgio Armani is most famously tied to the 1980 film *American Gigolo*. This collaboration became a milestone in both fashion and cinema, transforming Gere into a style icon and propelling Armani to global fame. Gere's character in the film, Julian Kaye, wore a series of sleek, perfectly tailored Giorgio Armani suits which were integral to portraying Julian's suave and sophisticated persona. Giorgio Armani himself reflected on this collaboration, noting that *American Gigolo* was pivotal in establishing the Armani aesthetic globally. Gere has remained a supporter of the brand, frequently appearing in Armani attire at red-carpet events.

ABOVE: Actor Richard Gere wearing an Armani suit at the 81st Venice International Film Festival, Italy, 2024

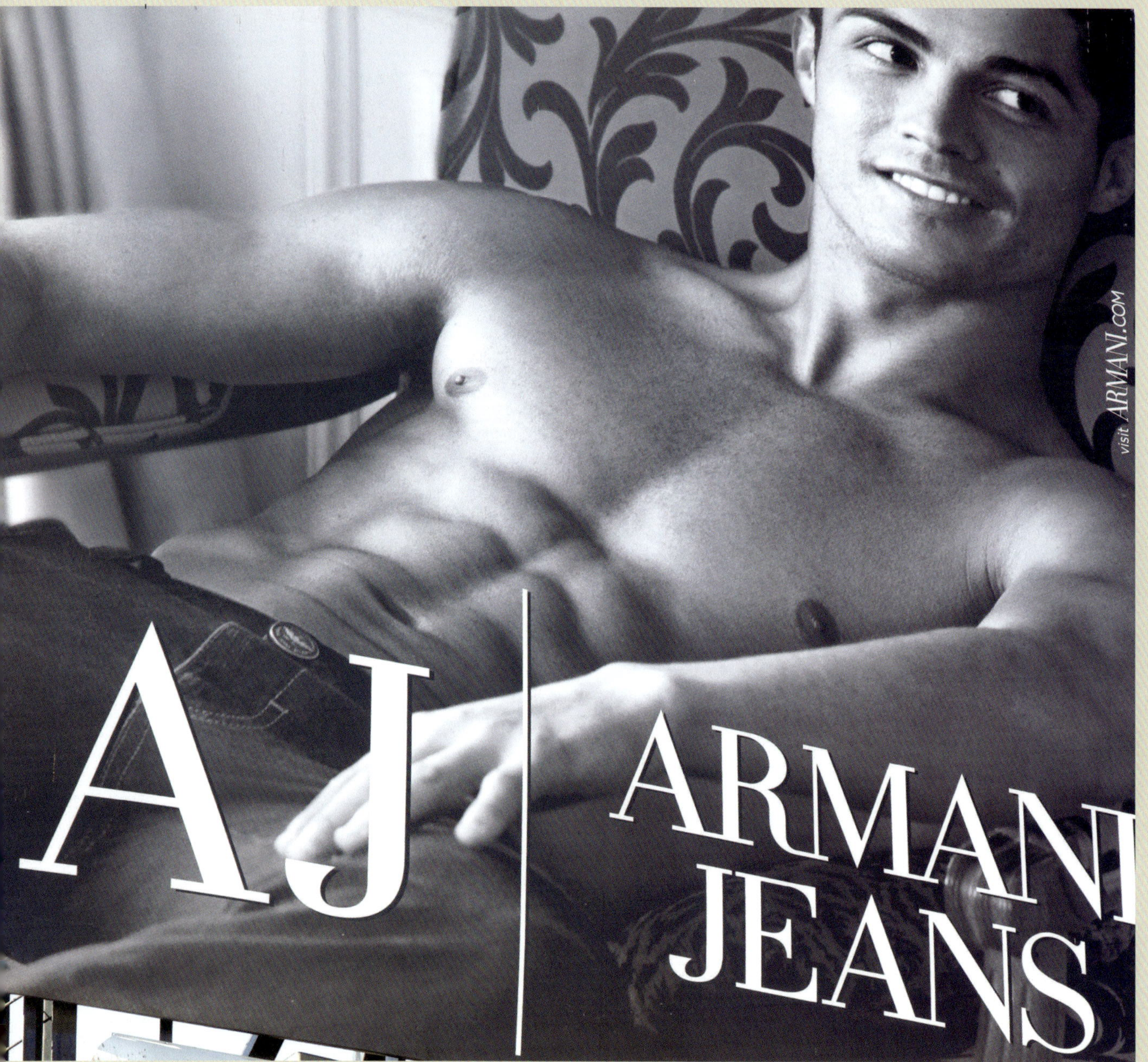

CRISTIANO RONALDO

As one of the world's most famous athletes, Ronaldo embodied athleticism and style in Emporio Armani campaigns for underwear and jeans in the 2010s. Giorgio Armani expressed his admiration for Ronaldo, stating, *'Cristiano is a great looking man with the perfect physique of an athlete. For me, he is the essence of youth—spontaneous, exciting, a real maverick.'* This partnership highlighted Armani's crossover appeal to both sports and fashion enthusiasts.

ABOVE: Cristano Ronaldo AX Armani Jeans Promotional Billboard in New York City

DAVID BECKHAM

In November 2007, Beckham signed a £20 million deal to become the global ambassador for Giorgio Armani's Emporio Armani Underwear line. His iconic status as a footballer and fashion figure coupled with his heartthrob status and athletic physique made him an ideal fit for Armani. In June 2008, a massive billboard featuring Beckham's image was unveiled in San Francisco's Union Square, attracting significant public attention. Later, in June 2009, Beckham appeared at Selfridges on Oxford Street in London to launch the Emporio Armani Underwear Fall/Winter collection, further cementing his association with the brand. Beckham's partnership with Armani not only boosted the brand's visibility but also set a precedent for athletes engaging in high-fashion endorsements.

The campaign's success led to subsequent collaborations, including joint advertisements with his wife, Victoria Beckham, for Emporio Armani Underwear's Autumn/Winter 2009–2010 line.

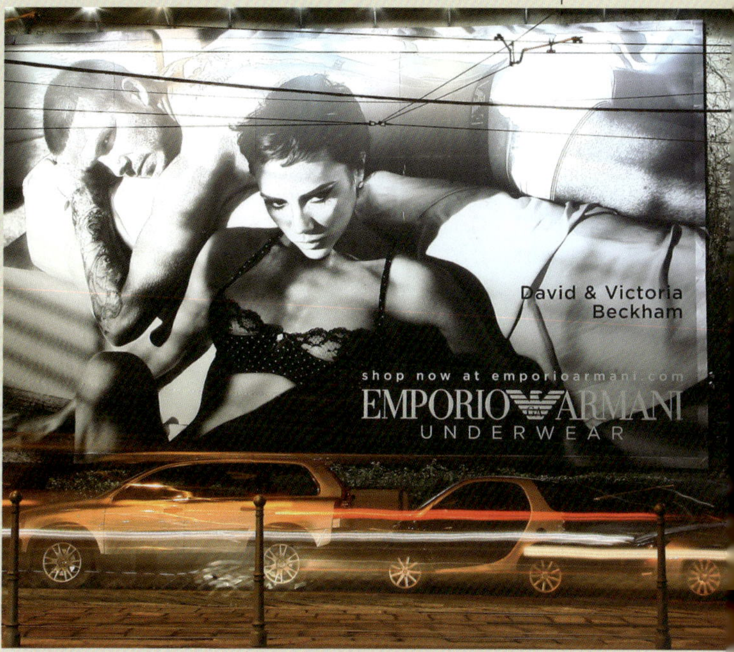

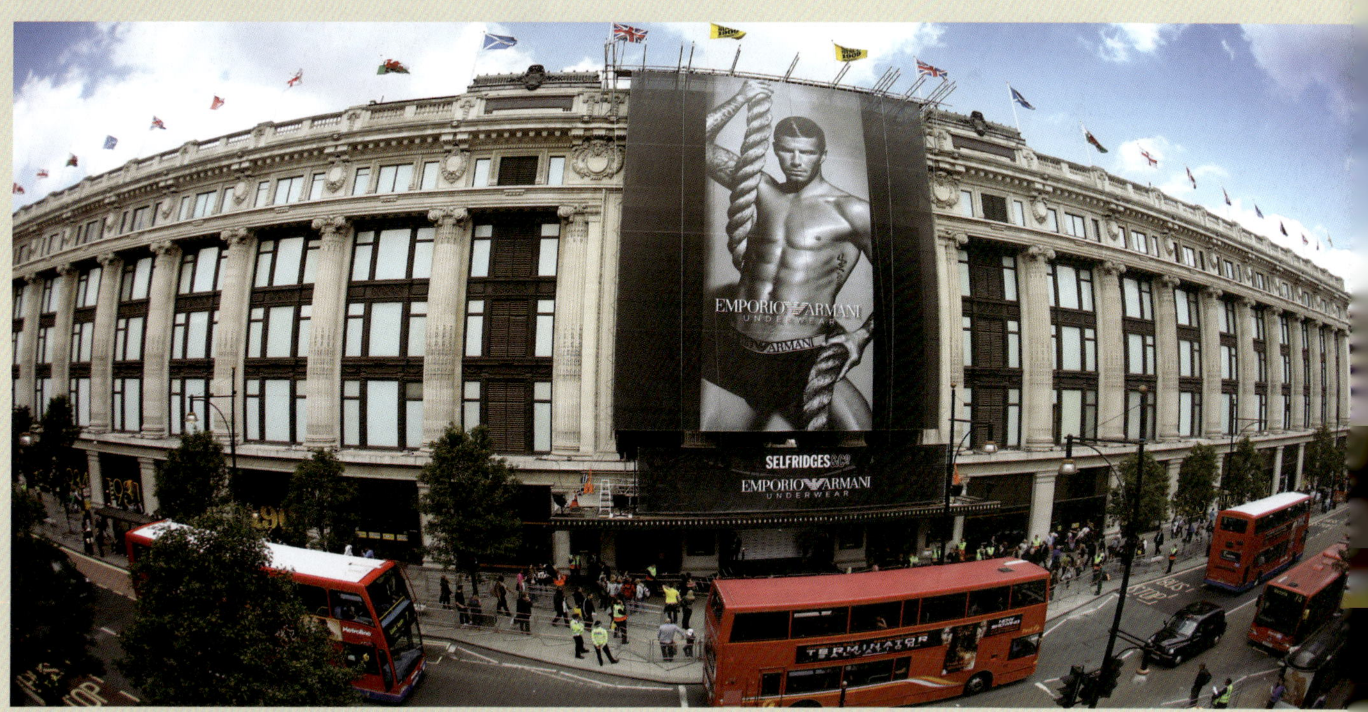

TOP: A giant advertising poster featuring David and Victoria Beckham posing for Emporio Armani underwear displayed in central Milan, Italy, 2009
ABOVE: David Beckham advertising Armani underwear on the side of the Selfridges store in London, England, 2009

ARMANI THE FUTURE

"I have built an empire. I want to make sure that it endures, but it has to endure my way"
Giorgio Armani

For over five decades, Giorgio Armani has shaped the world of fashion with his timeless designs, minimalist elegance and unparalleled craftsmanship. His brand has expanded from high-end couture to casual streetwear, fragrances, home décor and luxury hotels, making Armani more than just a name—it's a global lifestyle empire.

But as the fashion industry evolves, new challenges arise. The rise of sustainability, digital innovation and shifting consumer preferences means that Armani must adapt to a changing world while preserving the legacy that has made the brand a symbol of Italian luxury.

One of the biggest questions surrounding the future of Armani is who will lead the house after

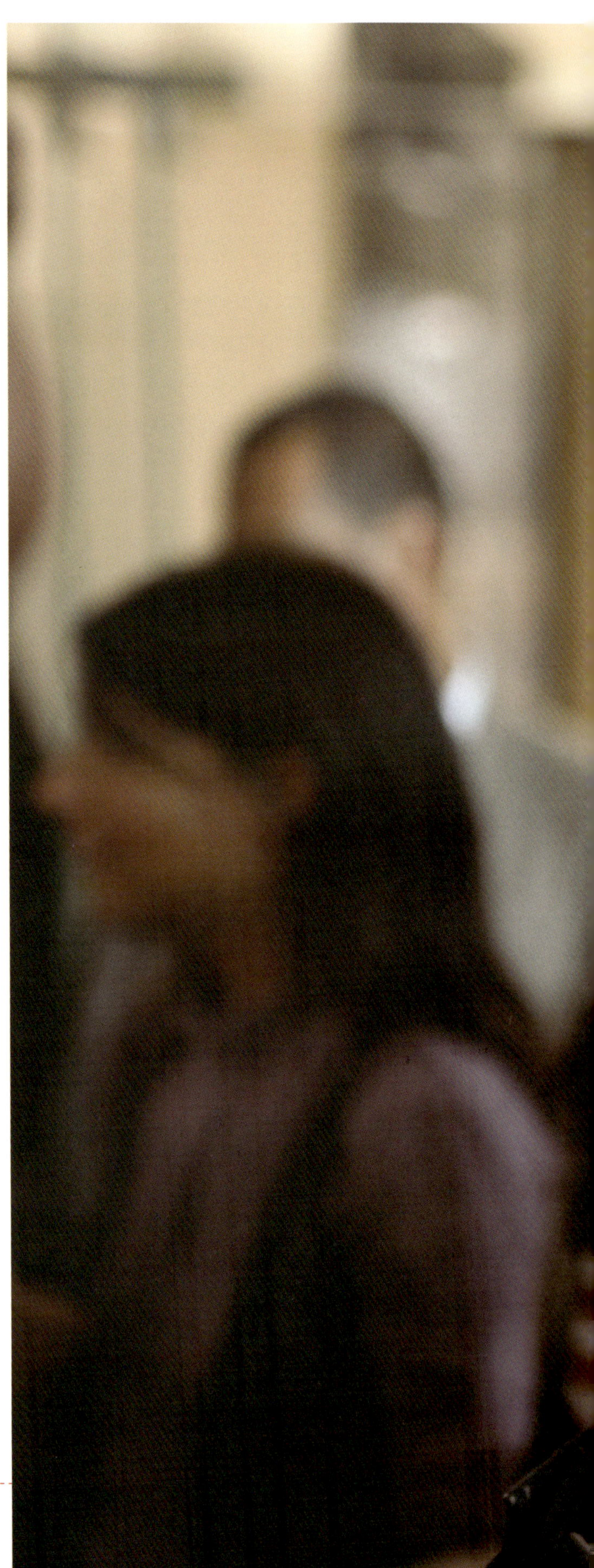

RIGHT: Giorgio Armani deep in thought during *Vogue Fashion*'s Night Out in September, 2009

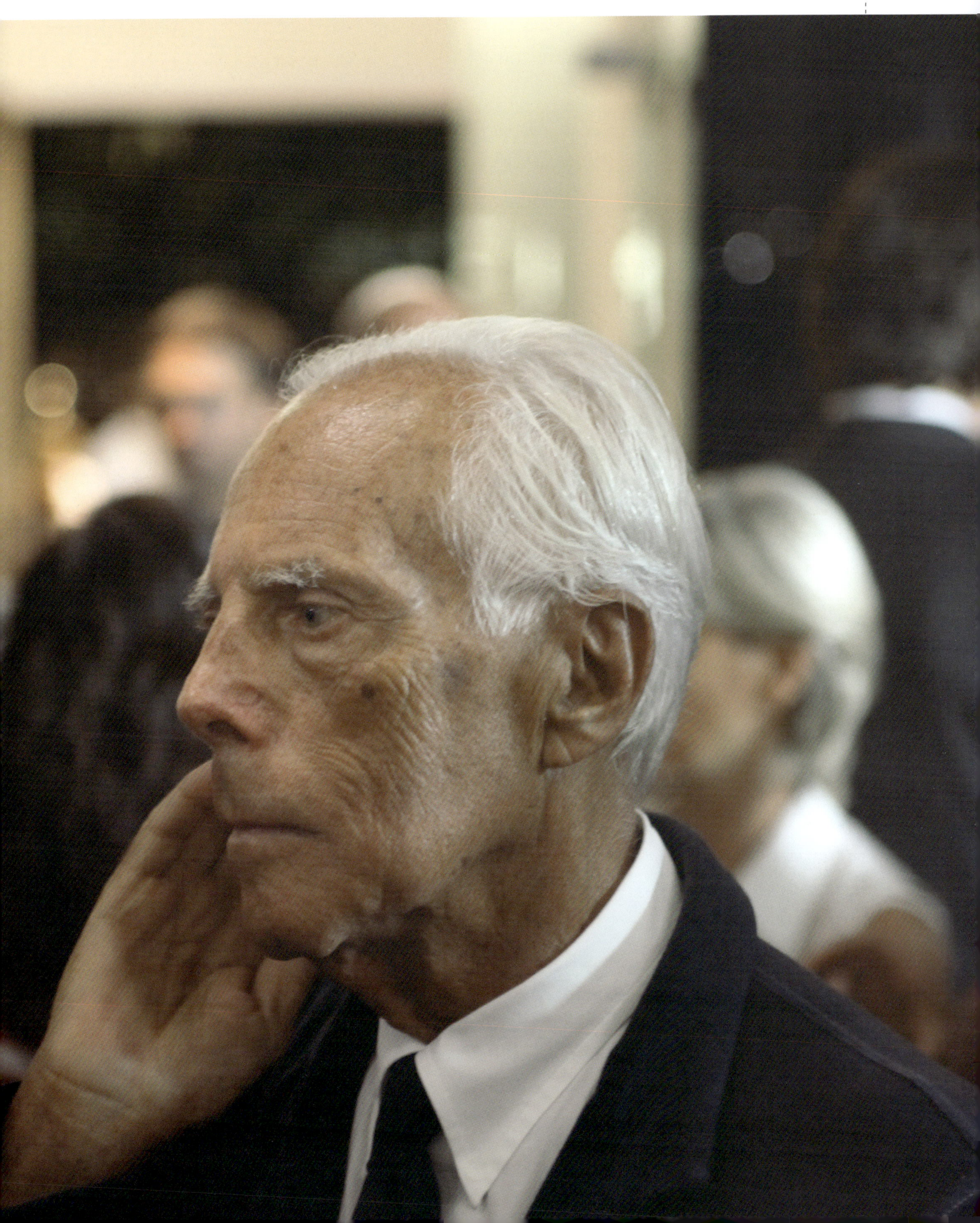

Giorgio Armani? Unlike many other fashion houses that have been acquired by luxury conglomerates like LVMH or Kering, Armani remains independent with Giorgio Armani himself maintaining full control of the company. He has no direct heirs so his plan may include passing control to a foundation that will preserve his vision and heritage. This suggests that Armani's future will prioritise heritage over profit, ensuring that his name remains synonymous with quality and elegance. Future leaders may be made up of his inner circle—the trusted executives and designers who have worked alongside him for decades. Or like Chanel and Valentino, Armani may choose a creative director to continue his design legacy.

Sustainability is another concern as Armani moves into the future with the brand already making eco-conscious changes.

'We must work toward a system that puts sustainability at the centre, without compromising beauty and quality,' he has himself said.

The brand has increased the use of organic cotton, recycled wool and sustainable leather. It has committed to reducing CO_2 emissions across its supply chain while also investing in water-efficient dyeing and fabric treatment processes. In 2021, the Giorgio Armani 'Sustainable Collection' was introduced, using ethically sourced materials. The Emporio Armani "R-EA" (Responsible Emporio Armani) is a line dedicated to recycled fabrics and eco-friendly production. Armani will continue pushing sustainability while maintaining the high standards of luxury that define the brand.

The fashion industry is rapidly evolving online, and Armani is ensuring that it remains at the forefront of digital fashion and e-commerce. It has expanded its online stores, making high-end fashion more accessible, and has hosted digitally-streamed runway shows.

The brand has started exploring NFTs (non-fungible tokens that are stored on a blockchain) and digital fashion, aiming to engage the next generation of consumers. Emporio Armani Watches & Accessories already incorporate smartwatch technology while Armani Beauty are investing in augmented reality (AR) makeup try-ons. With younger generations demanding more digital experiences, Armani is expected to continue blending luxury with technology, ensuring the brand stays relevant in the digital age.

Armani is no longer just about fashion and clothing—it's about creating a full luxury experience. A lifestyle, if you will. Armani Casa is expanding as demand for designer furniture and interiors rapidly grows. Armani hotels and resorts are looking to source new locations beyond Milan and Dubai. Potential sites include Paris, New York and Shanghai. There is also speculation about possible Armani Yacht & Aviation Collaborations—Armani-designed private jets & luxury yachts. With this in mind, Armani is expected

OPP PAGE: Leslie Bibb attends the Armani Beauty celebration of Luminous Silk in West Hollywood, California, 2025

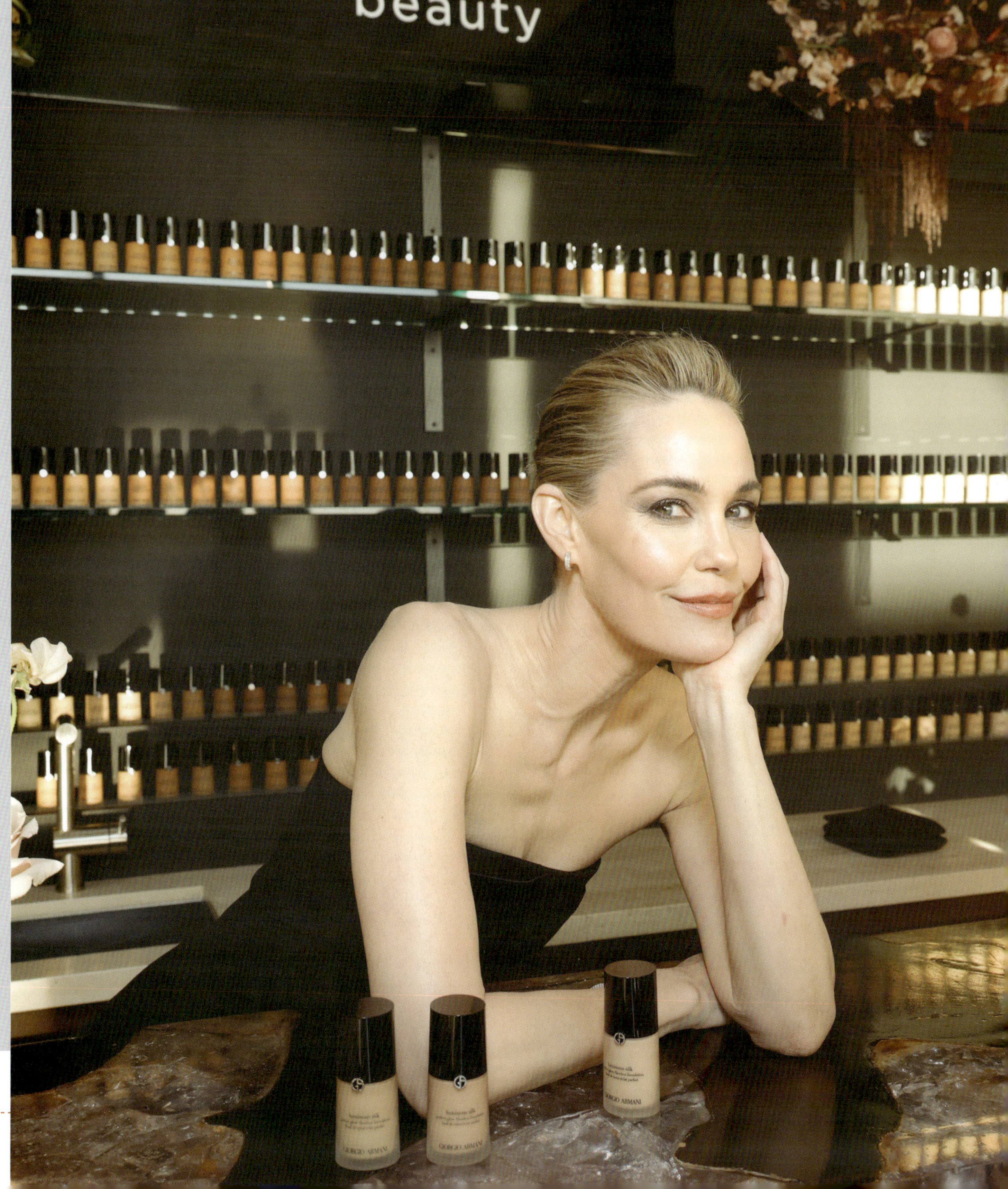
ARMANI
beauty

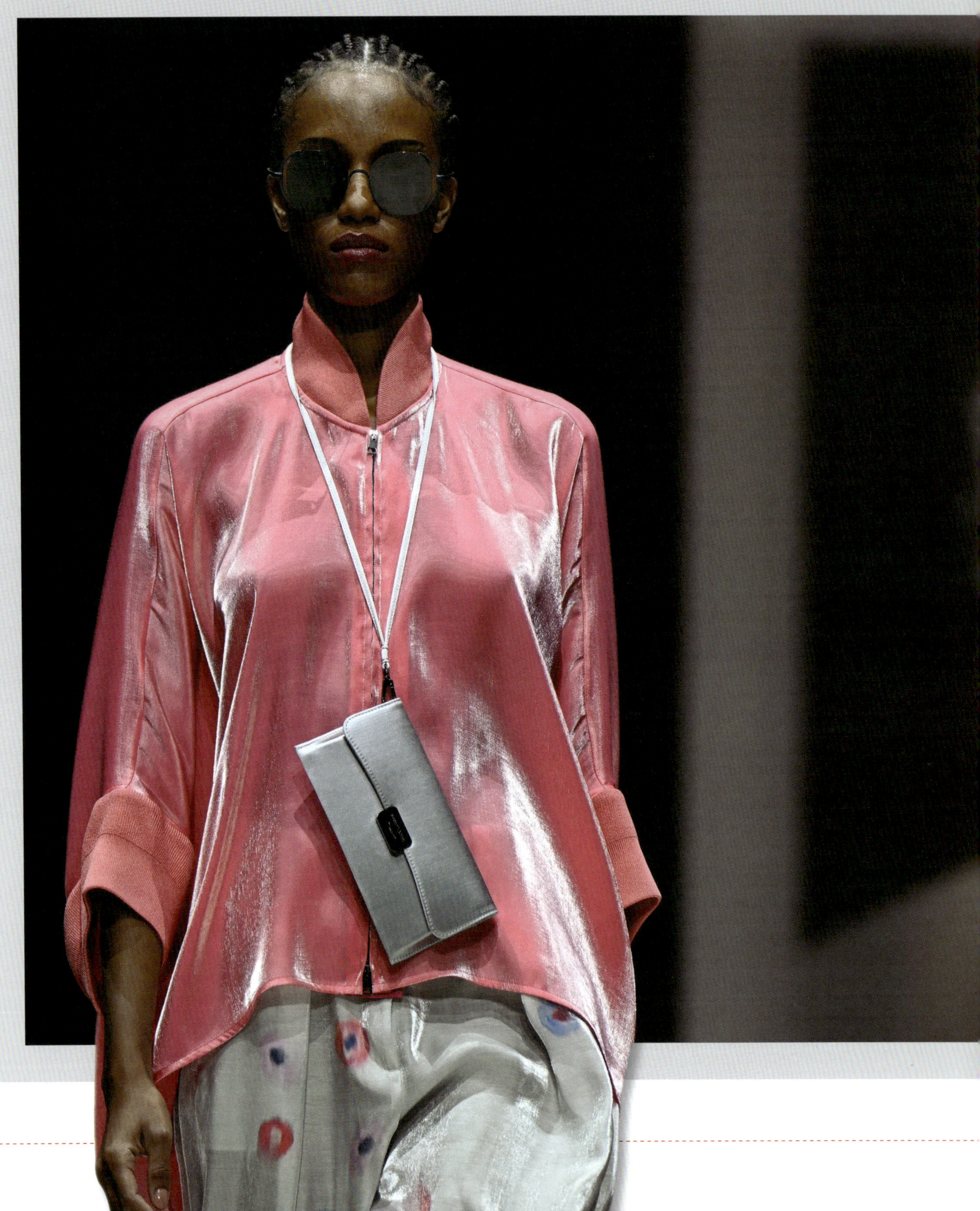

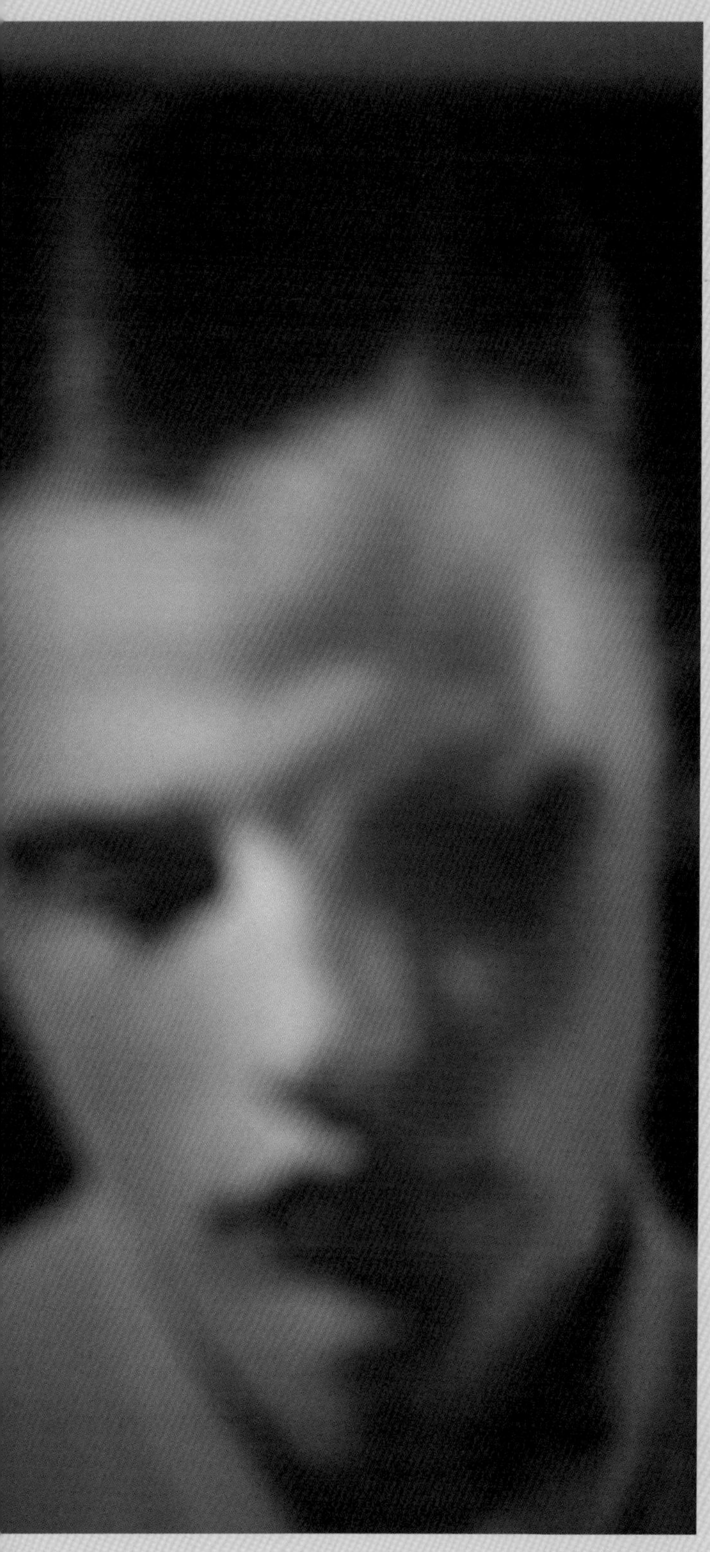

to continue expanding beyond fashion, creating an immersive luxury lifestyle that includes fashion, home, travel and beauty.

While fashion trends are forever changing, Armani's core aesthetic has remained timeless. As Armani has said on more than one occasion, '*Fashion fades but style is eternal.*' The future will likely see a return to classic minimalism with more tailored, elegant designs in response to the fast-fashion era; more sustainability in the world of couture with Armani Privé leading the way in eco-friendly haute couture; and Armani continuing to embrace gender-neutral designs & diverse models. However, unlike brands that constantly chase trends, Armani is known for its timelessness, thus the fashion house and lifestyle ethos as a whole is likely to evolve in a subtle sense rather than making drastic shifts.

'*I have created a style,*' Armani has said, '*not just clothes. My goal has always been to make people feel confident, elegant, and timeless.*'

Looking ahead, Armani will preserve its essence while embracing modern luxury and innovation. With its timeless elegance, strong brand identity and continued ability to move into the future and remain relevant, Armani is expected to remain a premier luxury brand for decades to come. Whether through fashion, home, travel or technology, the Armani name will continue to define modern sophistication and style.

OPP PAGE: A look from the runway during the Emporio Armani Womenswear Spring/Summer 2025 collection show at Milan Fashion Week, September, 2024

WE LOVE YOU, GIORGIO!

Words of love and admiration from Armani's celebrated friends.

Giorgio Armani is a true friend. His kindness has come into my life in many shapes and sizes (and, yes, ladies, loads of gorgeous clothes!), whether it's sharing his vacation home in Italy with me and Danny for our first anniversary or spending the afternoon playing with my daughter and her favourite rag doll. He has never forgotten my birthday. Every year, it is the note that accompanies the gift that is the treasure. I've saved them all. My love for Giorgio is endless and my admiration ever expanding, as he never stops challenging himself in new and beautiful ways

Actress Julia Roberts

Mr. Armani can walk into a room and turn everything upside down in this very quiet, authoritative way. Once we had decided on a dress for the Oscars. It was all fitted and ready to go. He arrived, shook his head, and then sent everyone scrambling for different fabrics and dresses. It was like an episode of I Love Lucy. Mr. Armani started pinning things and taping my boobs down while speaking to me in French with that adorable Italian accent, "C'est mieux comme ça, non?" And, yes, it was much, much

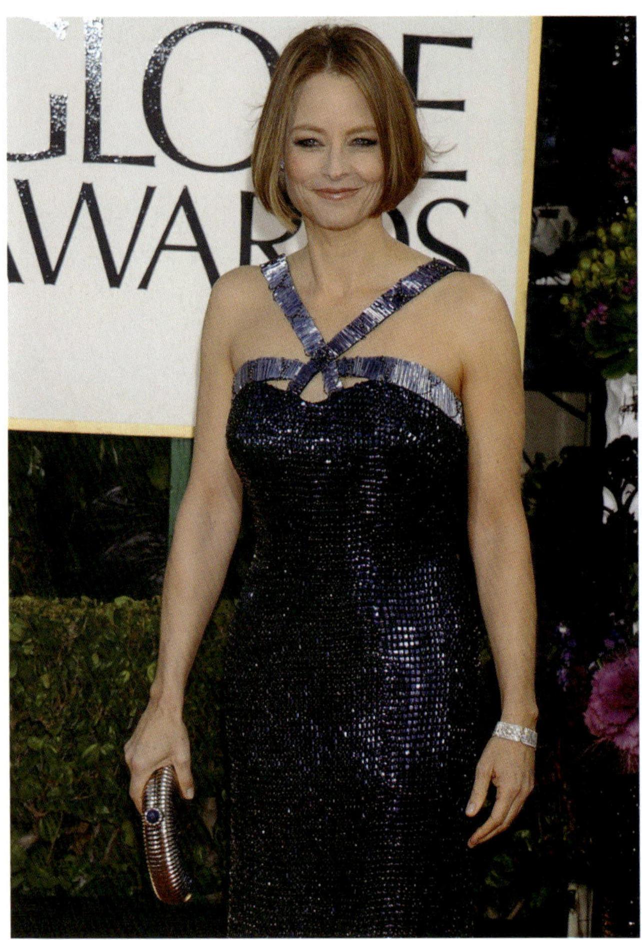

better. I have been wearing Armani for years. His clothes make me feel confident and comfortable

Actor and director Jodie Foster

ABOVE RIGHT: Jodie Foster in a custom Giorgio Armani navy blue sequin gown at the 2013 Golden Globe Awards
OPP PAGE: Julia Roberts in a men's Armani suit at the 47th Annual Golden Globe Awards in 1990

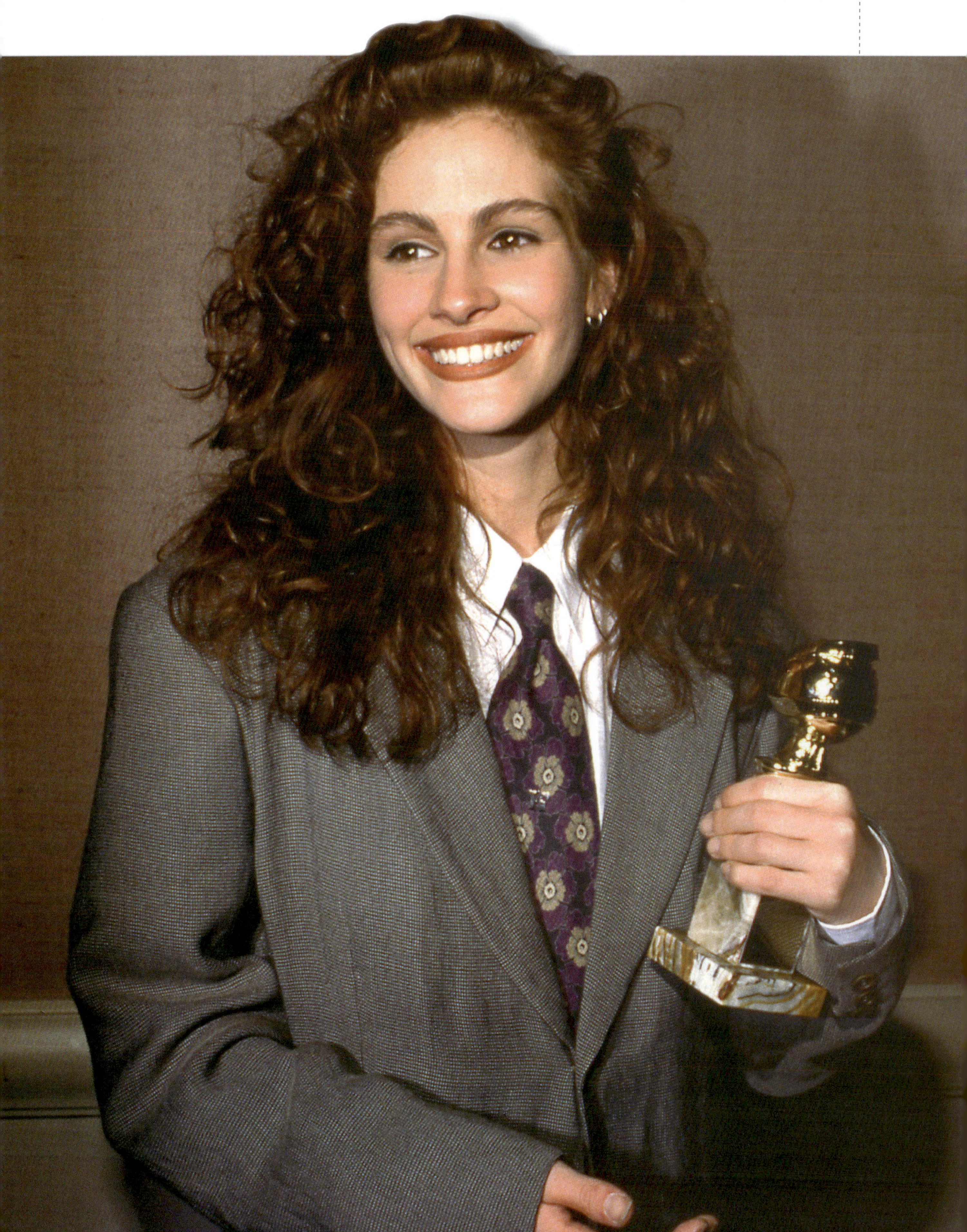

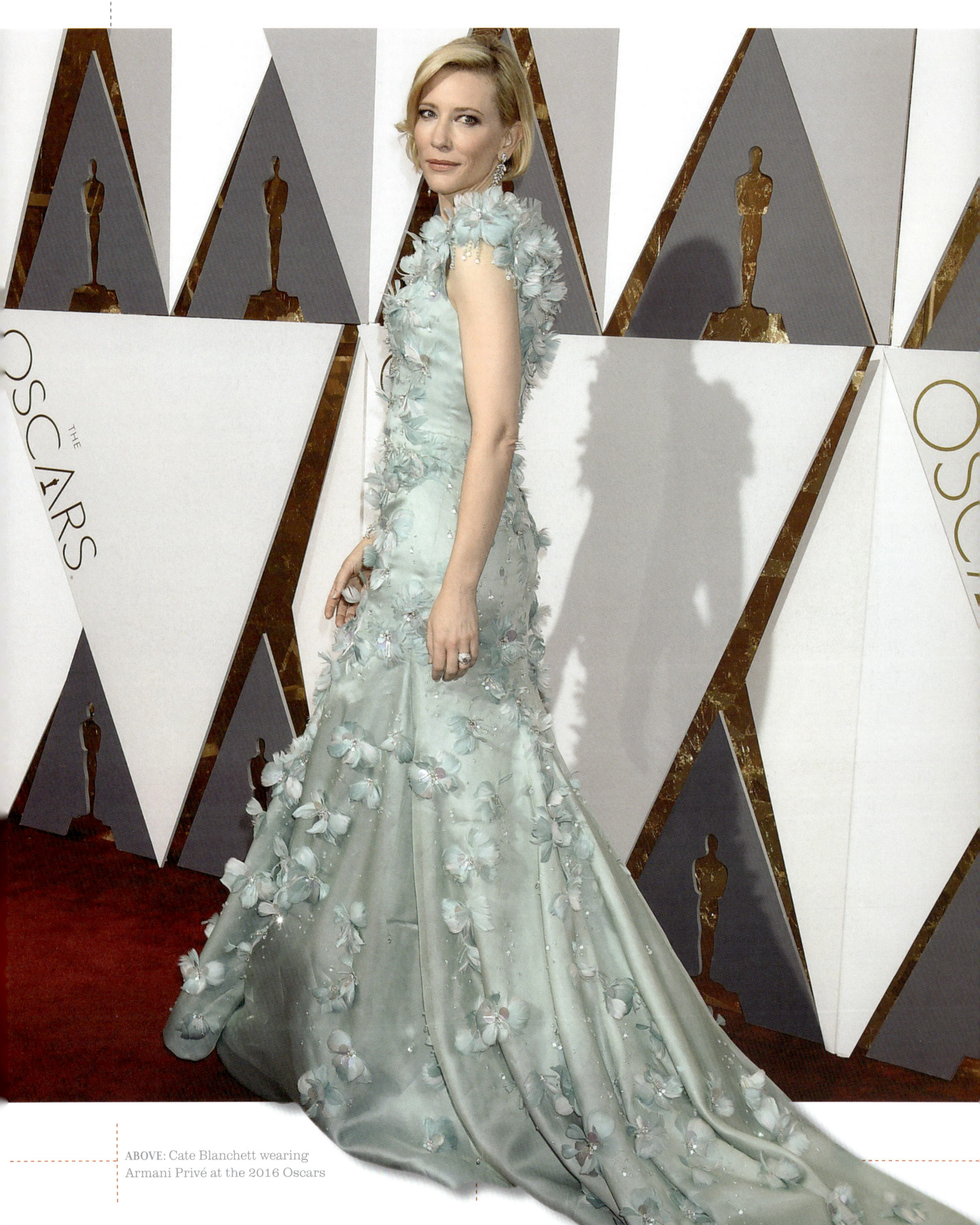

ABOVE: Cate Blanchett wearing
Armani Privé at the 2016 Oscars

' *Sitting with Mr. Armani, a deeply private man, for the first time was an intimidating experience. It was as if he was looking right inside me, beyond the surface, taking in the full measure of me as a person. Was I someone he could respect, let alone dress? Since then, I have witnessed his supreme generosity—personally greeting every dressmaker at the Sydney Theatre Company when he visited—his effervescence, his incredible wit and loyalty, but perhaps, above all, his God-given talent* '

Actress Cate Blanchett

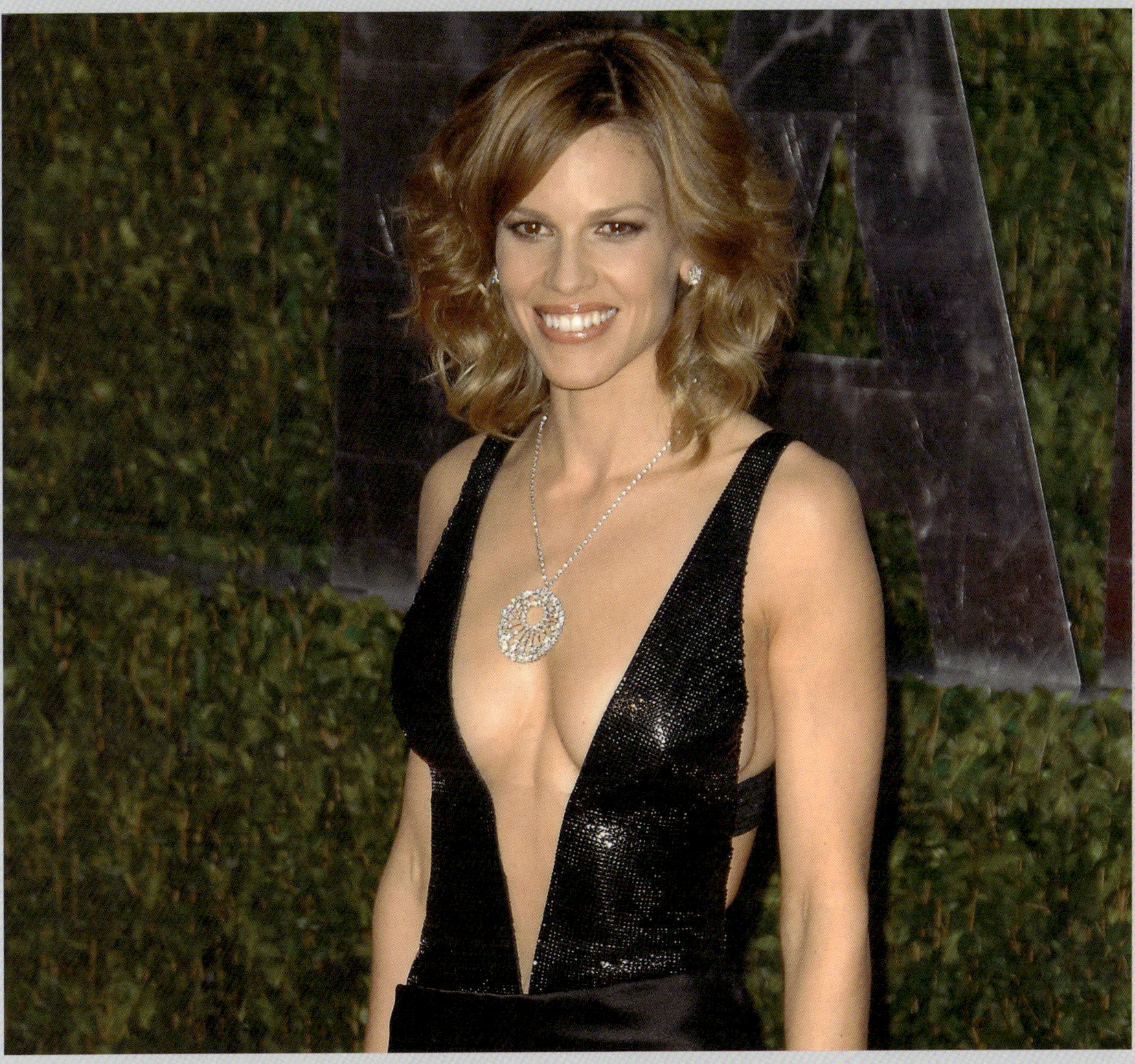

' *I was the lucky girl who was an honoured guest at one of Armani's first couture shows in Paris. It was such a celebration. Somehow, I ended up under the Eiffel Tower with half his design team and family, dancing to the light show. That's where genius leads you—to a place of light* '

Actress Hilary Swank

ABOVE: Hilary Swank wearing an Armani Privé gown at the Vanity Fair Oscar Party, California, 2010

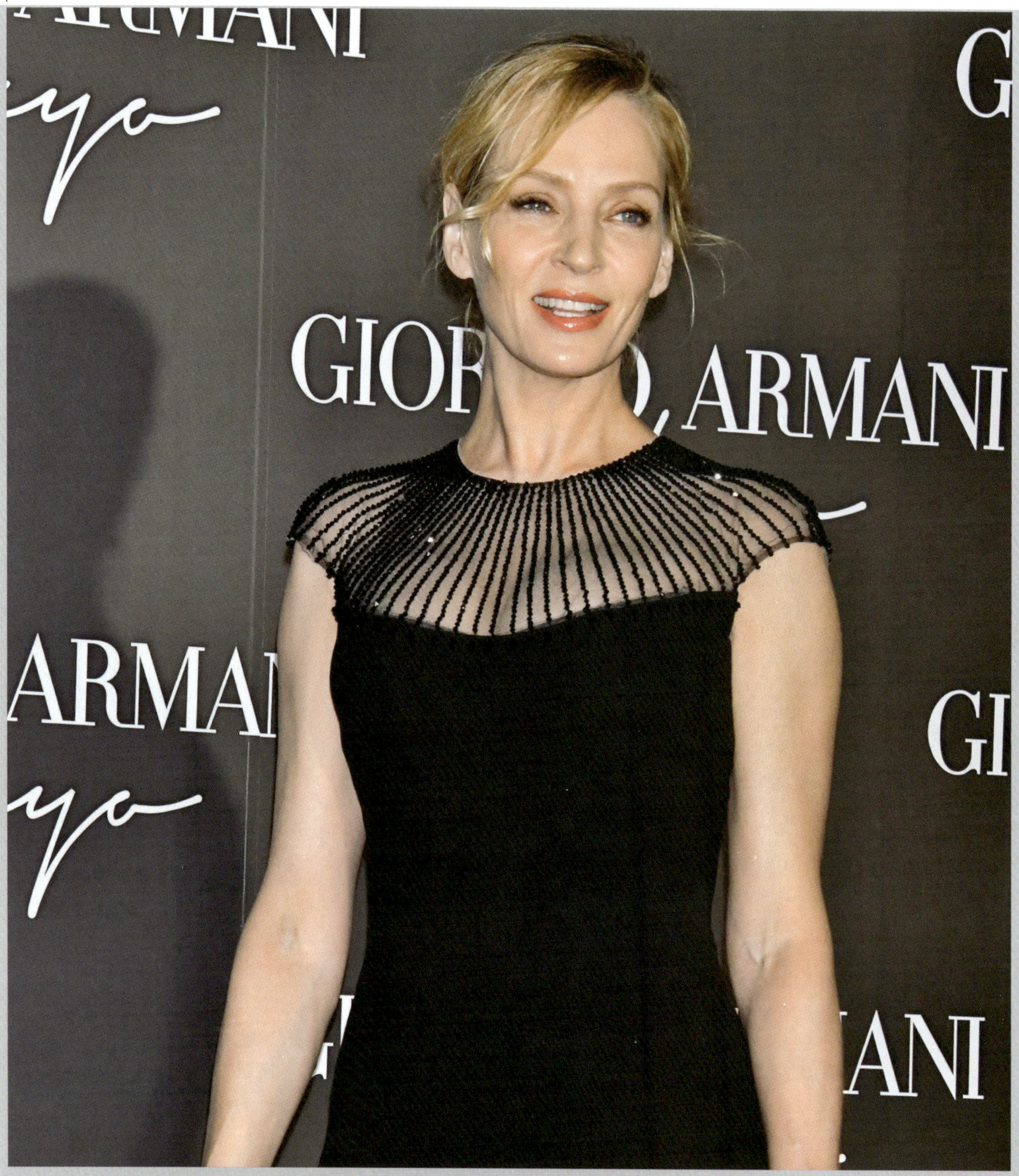

> Once I was with Mr. Armani on a red carpet at the Venice Film Festival for Martin Scorsese's documentary about him, *Made in Milan*. We were all so overwhelmed by the press that we grabbed hands. Mr. Armani, Michelle Pfeiffer, and I charged forward at them. Mr. Armani and his designs give you the confidence to do things like that. Who could ask for more? **9**
>
> **Actress Uma Thurman**

ABOVE: Uma Thurman attends the Giorgio Armani Cruise Collection in Tokyo, Japan, 2019

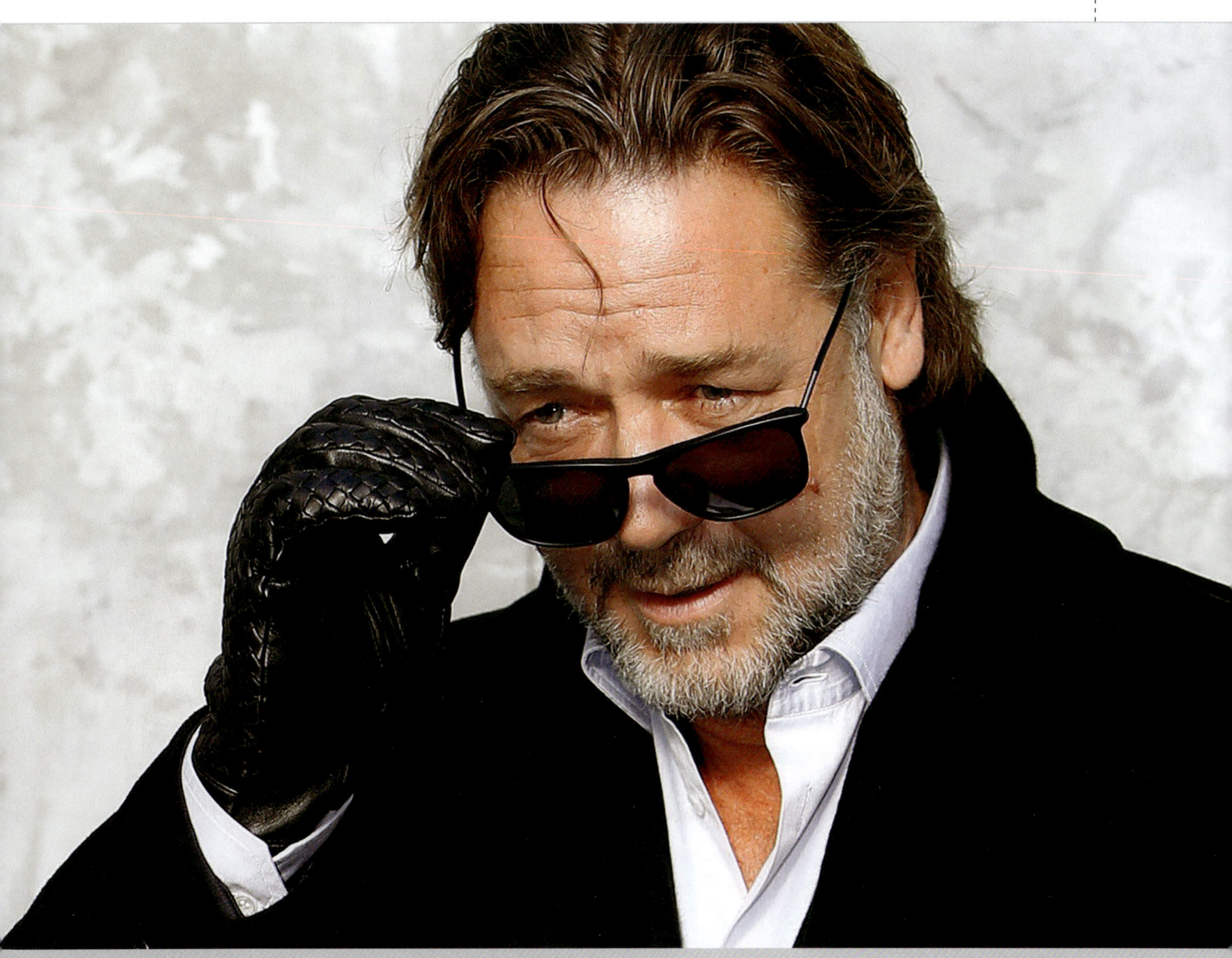

One magical night in Rome, we sat together with a group of his assistants in the Hassler Hotel. Giorgio produced a sketch of something he thought I might like to wear to the Academy Awards. Without really thinking, I took the pad and a pen and made adjustments. When I looked up, everyone else had a kind of blood-drained look, but Mr. Armani, ever gracious, took the pad back, studied it, scratched in some notes, and showed it to me again. I said, "Perfecto," and we laughed and celebrated. A few years later, I was in Milan with my then wife-to-be, Danielle, to see what Mr. Armani had designed for her wedding dress. When he brought out the sketch pad, he tied a blindfold around my eyes and said, "This time you don't get to see it first." I have a great respect for Mr. Armani. He has been a leader in his field for a long time.

Actor Russell Crowe

ABOVE: Russell Crowe poses for photographers at the Giorgio Armani Men's Fall/Winter 2016–17 collection at Milan Fashion Week, 2016

> *Giorgio's designs are timeless. They have a classic elegance that never goes out of style*

Actress Demi Moore

> *Attending Giorgio Armani's show was a wonderful experience. His creations are always so chic and sophisticated*

Actress Jessica Biel

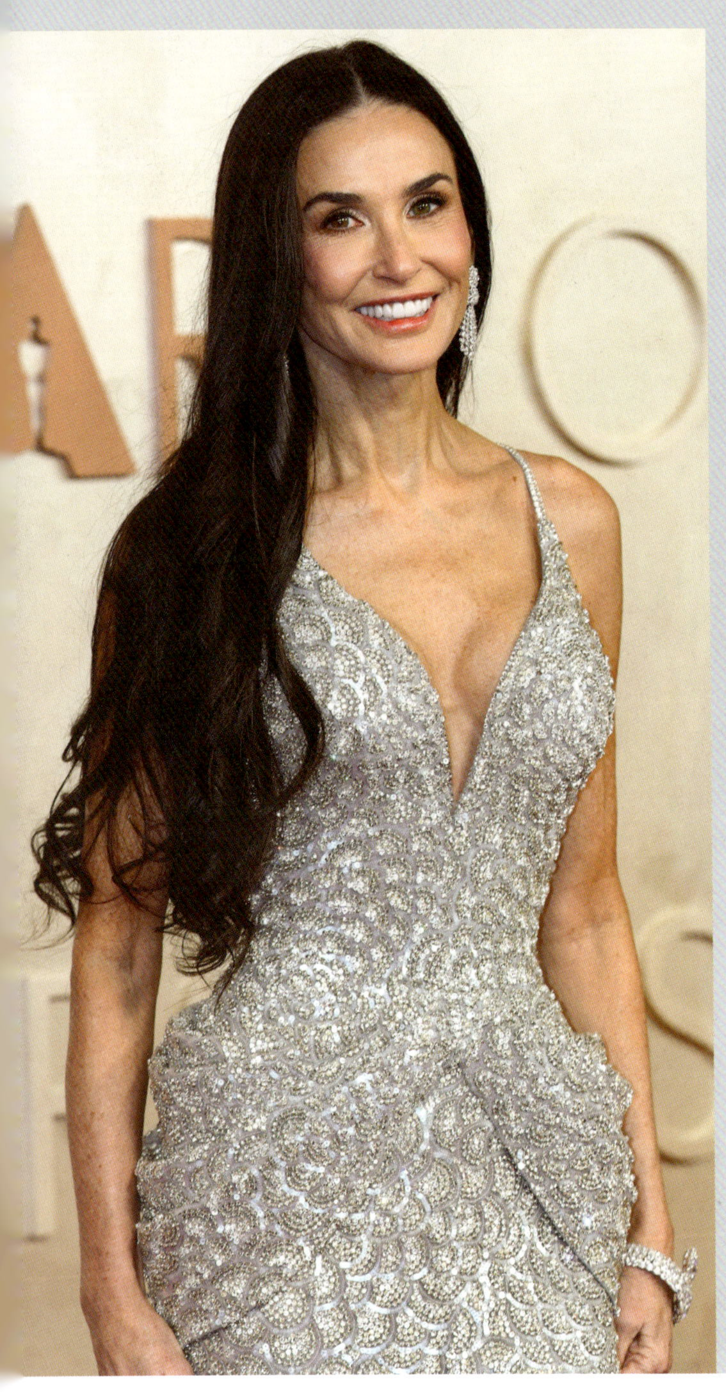

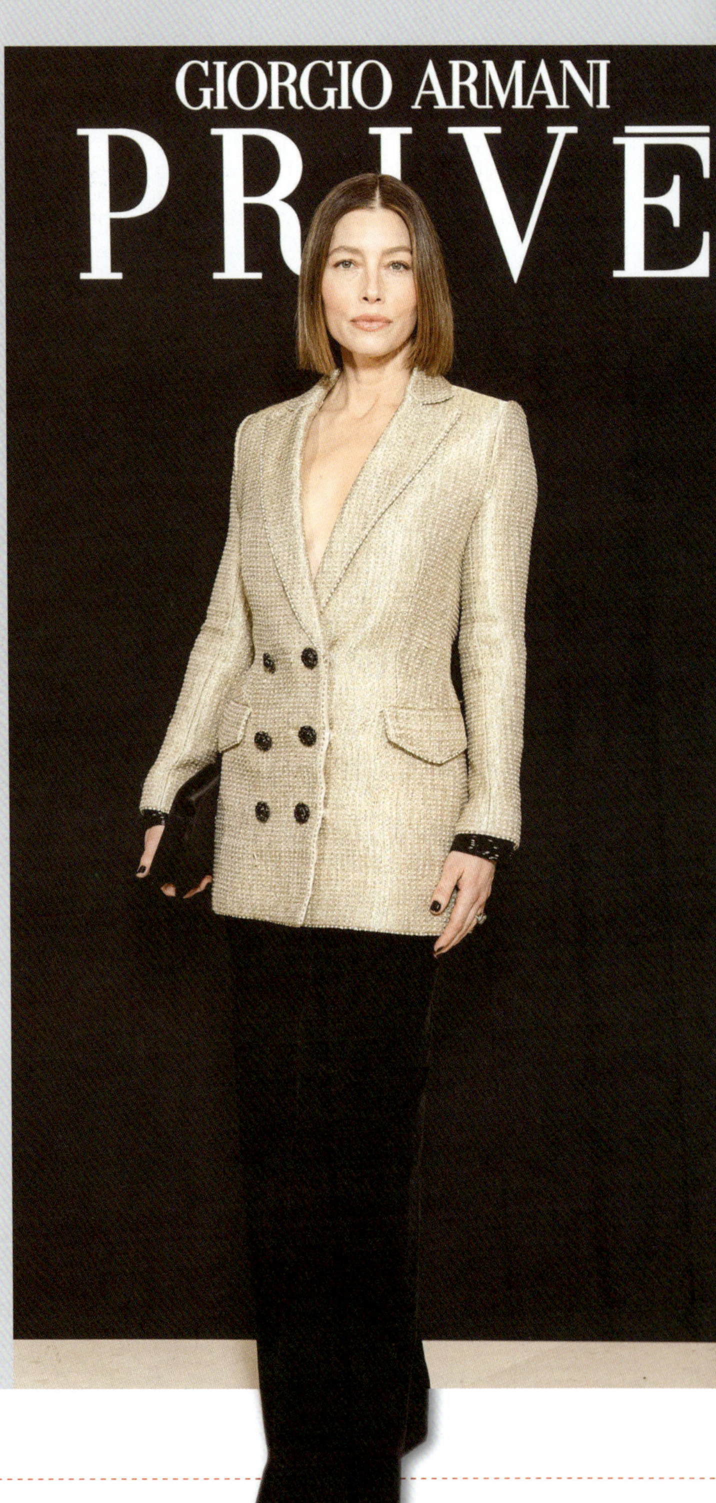

ABOVE LEFT: Demi Moore in a Giorgio Armani crystal-embroidered gown dress at the 2025 Oscars

ABOVE RIGHT: Jessica Biel in a plunging beaded blazer at the Giorgio Armani Privé Spring 2025 fashion show

> *Armani is unique. He's the only designer in the world who has been able to combine real creative genius with a tremendously astute business sense*

Fashion critic Sara Forden

> *There's never anything hip or chic or tied to the moment in Giorgio's work—it's truly timeless. His designs aren't meant to be gazed at on a runway— they're for people to wear, and to enhance their own sense of natural elegance*

Martin Scorsese

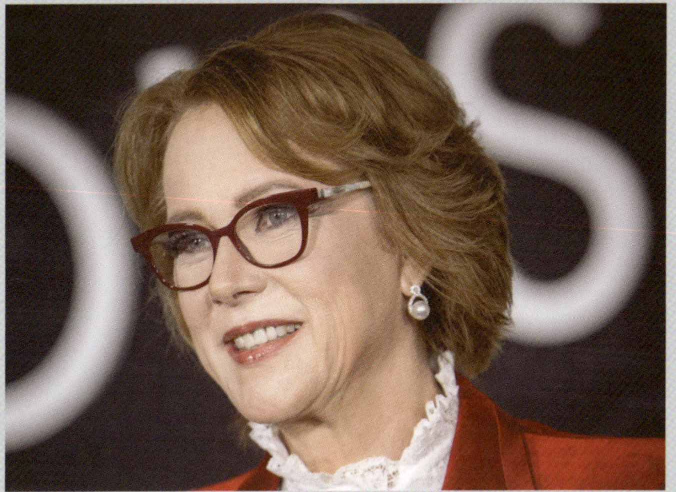

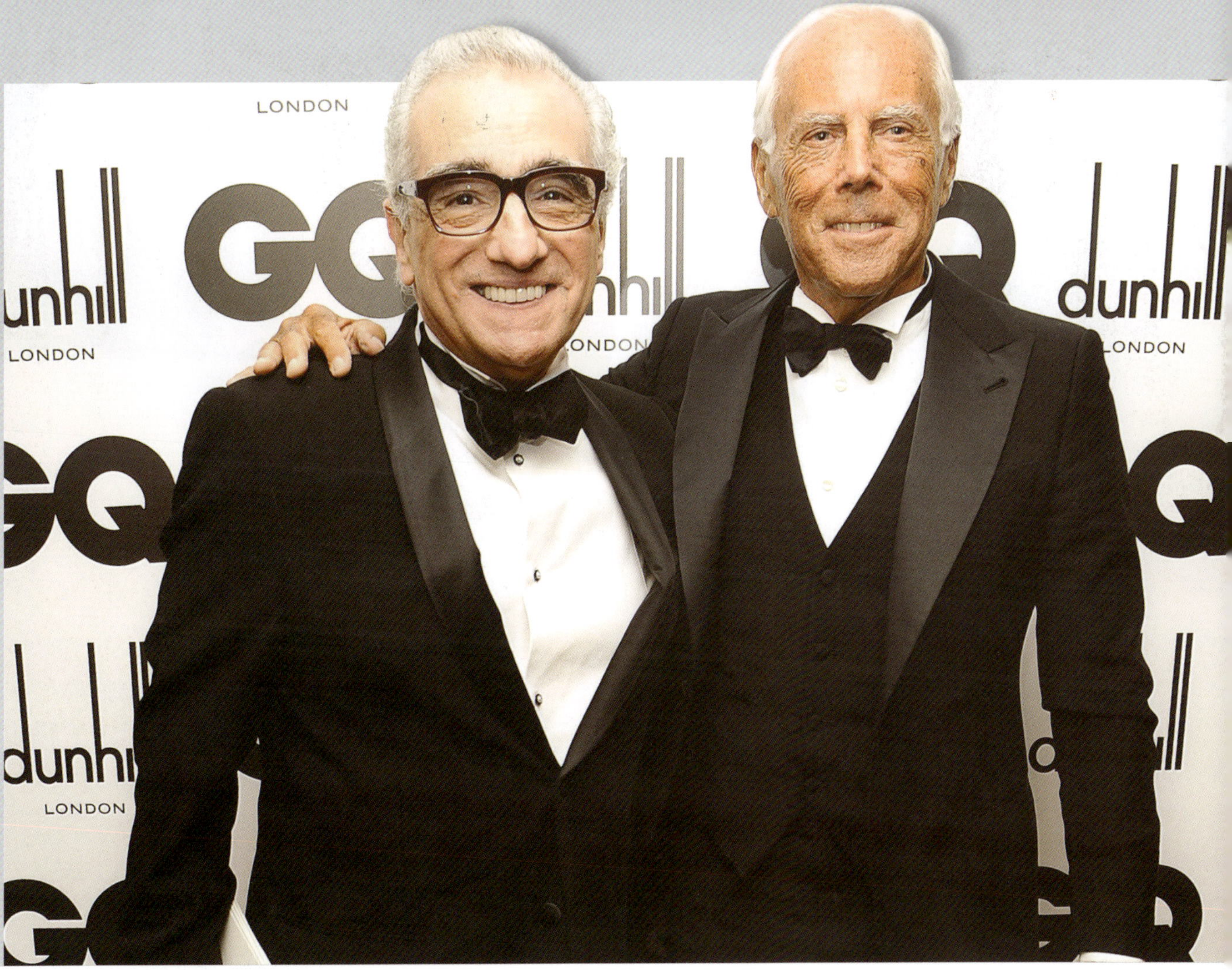

TOP: Fashion critic Sara Forden
ABOVE: Martin Scorses presents Giorgio Armani with his Designer of The Year Award, at the 2010 GQ Men of the Year Awards, Covent Garden, London

EPILOGUE:
GIORGIO ARMANI
R.I.P

"Life is a movie. And my clothes are the costumes"
Giorgio Armani

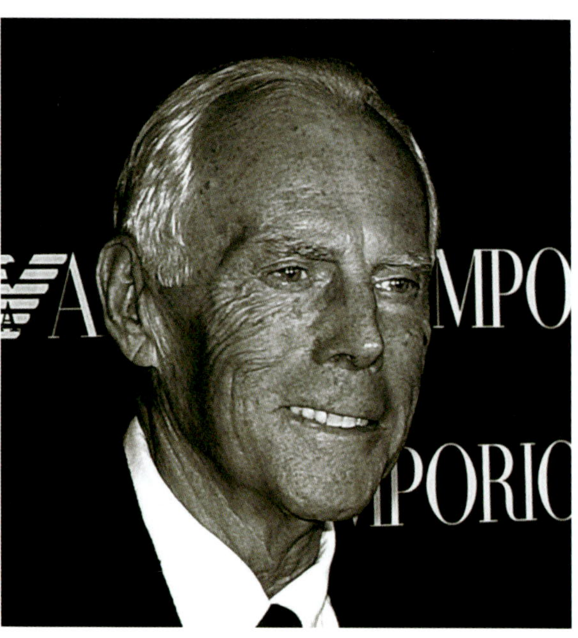

On September 4 2025 at his home in Milan, Giorgio Armani passed away peacefully at the age of 91 surrounded by his loved ones.

Almost immediately tributes poured in from friends, collaborators, rivals and admirers – many of whom knew him as *'Re Giorgio'* (King Giorgio).

Donatella Versace, a fellow fashion icon and friend, captured the magnitude with quiet grace. *'The world lost a giant today,'* she announced. *'He made history and will be remembered forever.'*

Anna Wintour, the former editor of American Vogue said*, 'Giorgio Armani had such a clear force of personality and vision that you knew his work instantly, wherever you found it.'*

Victoria Beckham, who counted Armani among her close confidants, offered a personal reflection. *'The fashion world has lost a true legend in Giorgio Armani - a visionary designer whose legacy will live on forever. I feel honoured to have called him a friend.'*

Her husband, David Beckham, echoed her sentiments. *'A very sad day as we say goodbye to a very special man... Kind, generous, humble & a true gentleman. Giorgio Armani—one of a kind.'*

Actress Julia Roberts, whose early Red Carpet ascendancy included a now-legendary Armani-

ABOVE RIGHT: Giorgio Armani in 2009

designed suit, simply wrote, *'A true friend. A Legend.'*

While Australian actor Russell Crowe recalled how one chance moment defined their lifelong connection. *'1997 at the Cannes film festival... that began a love affair with Armani suits that continues to this day. He made a deep contribution to fashion, to design, to popular culture. His energy, vision and finesse have made a mark acknowledged around the globe. I adored him. What a life he had. You will always live in my heart.'*

Morgan Freeman, whose collaborations with Armani spanned decades, shared a sentiment of gratitude and admiration. *'On screen and off, in quiet moments and on the grandest stages, I have had the honour of wearing Armani. Today, we remember a man whose genius touched many lives and whose legacy of grace and timeless style will endure.'*

These voices underline the quiet yet sweeping impact Armani had. Not just a designer, he was a confidant, muse, mentor and total master of his craft. He remained true to one principle throughout his life - that elegance is felt not shouted. His approach remained consistent, refusing to bend to fleeting trends. Instead, he pursued class, clarity, proportion and wearability. Even as the world raced toward the loud, the ephemeral, the novel for novelty's sake, Armani remained steadfast until the end. There was never any retirement for him. No standing down. Collections continued to debut under his eye, projects continued to unfold - all proof of a lifelong devotion to his craft.

Indeed, his House confirmed that he *'worked until his final days, dedicating himself to the company, and the many on-going and future projects'.* He built more than a brand - he created entire worlds. From the design of homes and hotels to the sensory layers of fragrance and ambiance, he offered total environments - spaces shaped by collaboration, context and an unwavering sense of who he was.

What physically survives after his death – the hotels, the stores, the heritage garments - is meaningful but the truer legacy lies in the way he lived his life. Through the tributes of peers and partners, clear lessons emerge. Elegance without excess. Craft without compromise. Influence without ego. In each tribute we find hints of Armani's humanity. Crowe's recognition of kindness. Beckham's reverence for humility. Versace's respect for innovation... These words remind us that Armani's greatest success was nurturing trust as much as design and tailoring. Armani's influence remains tangible not only in the fashion world but also in the everyday - a return to thoughtful dressing, to exquisitely decorated and furnished spaces, and to an unstated beauty that doesn't scream for attention. His passing encourages us to consider elegance in our own lives - in the objects we choose, the spaces we occupy, the way we carry ourselves. Armani's legacy lives in these quiet acts of refinement. In acknowledging his loss, we also acknowledge his inheritance - the legacy of a man who taught us that elegance is not about being noticed but about being remembered.

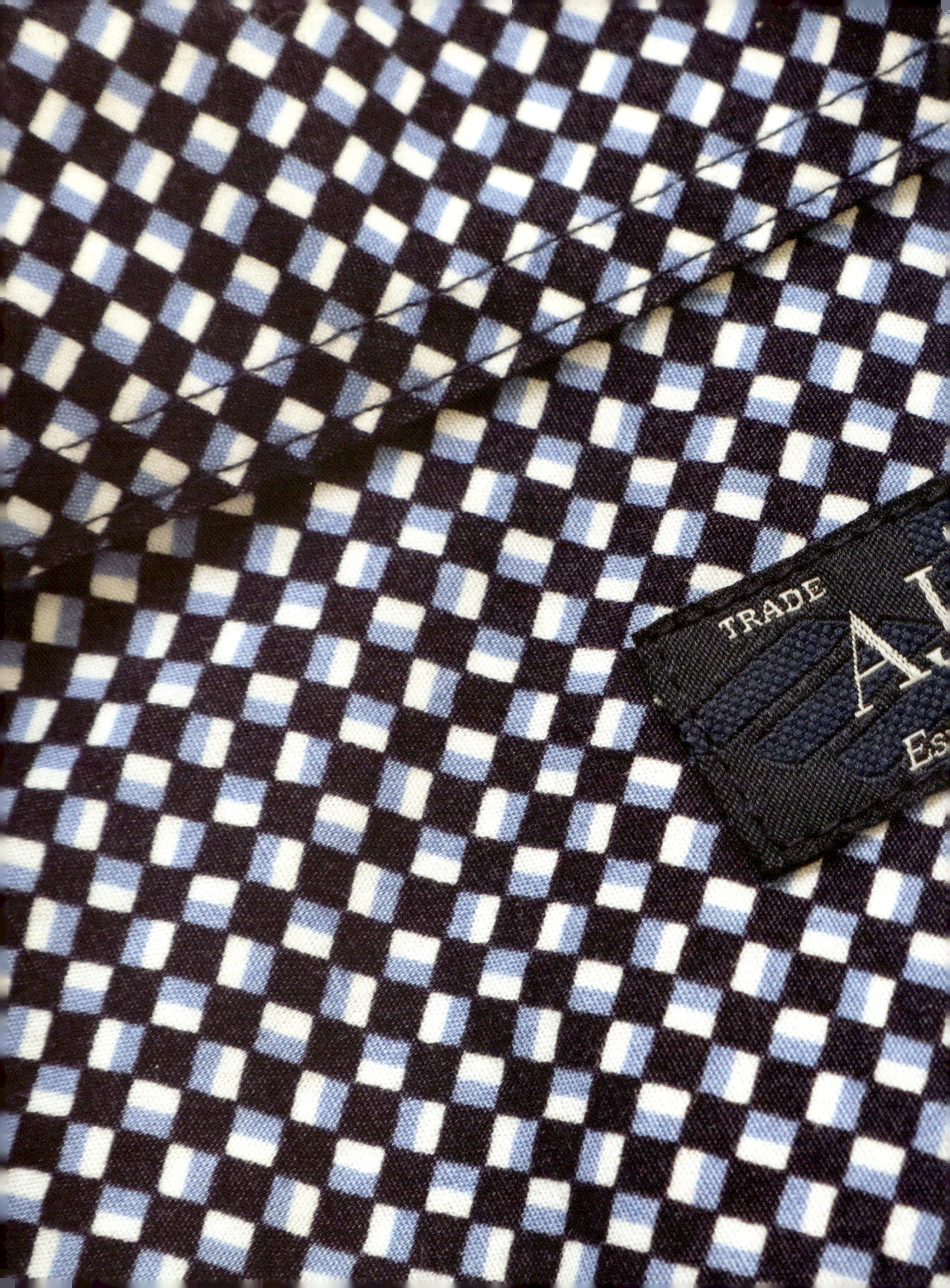
TRADE
A
Est